# Copycrafting

## Editing for Journalism Today

Kenneth L. Rosenauer

MISSOURI WESTERN STATE UNIVERSITY

New York     Oxford
OXFORD UNIVERSITY PRESS

Oxford University Press is a department of the University of Oxford. It furthers the University's objective of excellence in research, scholarship, and education by publishing worldwide.

Oxford   New York
Auckland   Cape Town   Dar es Salaam   Hong Kong   Karachi
Kuala Lumpur   Madrid   Melbourne   Mexico City   Nairobi
New Delhi   Shanghai   Taipei   Toronto

With offices in
Argentina   Austria   Brazil   Chile   Czech Republic   France   Greece
Guatemala   Hungary   Italy   Japan   Poland   Portugal   Singapore
South Korea   Switzerland   Thailand   Turkey   Ukraine   Vietnam

Published by Oxford University Press.
198 Madison Avenue, New York, NY 10016
www.oup.com

Oxford is a registered trademark of Oxford University Press

**Library of Congress Cataloging-in-Publication Data**
Rosenauer, Kenneth L. (Kenneth Lee), 1949-
   Copycrafting : editing for the 21st century / Kenneth Rosenauer.
      p. cm.
   ISBN 978-0-19-976365-8 (pbk. : alk. paper)—ISBN 978-0-19-976366-5 (instructor's ed. pbk. : alk. paper)   1. Journalism—Editing.   2. Copy editing.   I. Title.
   PN4778.R625 2012
   070.4'1—dc22                                                              2010053118

9 8 7 6 5 4 3 2 1

Printed in the United States of America
on acid-free paper

# Dedication

Writing a textbook or workbook is a considerable task, one that requires hours too many to count and effort too great to measure. Beyond the hours and effort is the sacrifice it takes to complete the project — sacrifice not only for the author but also for his family. Therefore, this text is dedicated to them: my daughters, Courtney and Mary Beth; my son, Brent; and my wife, Janet. Thanks for being there for me. I love you all.

# Brief Contents

# Contents

# Preface

Welcome to Copycrafting: Editing for Journalism Today, designed to meet the needs of copy editing courses.

Today, journalism continues to change rapidly. Fewer daily newspapers serve their communities — especially in major markets — from a high of 1,878 in 1940 to 1,437 in 2010. Even for those daily newspapers still operating, newsroom jobs have dropped 30 percent in the last decade. Interestingly, the number of weekly newspapers has increased during the past 30 years, now totaling 6,700.

Magazines are enjoying growth and now number 20,600, mostly the result of additional special-interest titles. Likewise, TV and radio stations continue to prosper.

Increasingly, traditional media use online sites to deliver content already published or broadcast, with many posting Web-first and Web-only material. At last count, newspaper-related websites totaled more than 1,500, with online-only news sites numbering about 200.

Social media have become powerful, often supplanting traditional media in their ability to deliver news and information and to interact with audiences in ways that traditional media never could. Think curation, trending topics, crowdsourcing, citizen journalism and hyperlocal media.

Yet, one thing remains constant for all news media: They continue to need well-trained editors who can help to deliver their content effectively — and *correctly* — regardless of the platform used.

Copycrafting was written to answer that demand and covers all aspects of editing, including the following:

- Basic copy editing background, including copy editors' roles, editing practices and ethics and diversity issues.
- Rules, explanations, and examples for punctuation, grammar, spelling and usage.
- Coverage of AP style in logical categories — including explanations and examples, not just presentation — as opposed to the alphabetical approach followed in the stylebook, a challenge to use at times even for professional journalists. The goal is not to replace the stylebook but rather to help students learn its content more easily.
- Instruction in editing leads, especially common problem leads.
- Guidance for writing headlines, editing images and designing pages, including effective examples of these.

Importantly, each chapter in Part 2, Part 3 and Part 4 offers exercises to give students practice applying specific rules and to let instructors know how well their students are learning the material. Chapter 28, "The Full Story," brings everything together with errors across the spectrum and provides ample stories for students to edit, 20 in all. They also will have opportunities to write headlines for each. Additional exercises are available online at www.oup.com/us/rosenauer.

An appendix includes a directory for students to consult as they complete the exercises, which are set in Heartland, Mo., a fictional town located in the center of the state and near the center of the nation. The Appendix also includes a listing of online resources for most of the chapters as well as additional supporting materials.

Copycrafting is a concise package that meets the needs of college and university editing courses and makes the demanding task of teaching those courses more manageable and learning that content more effective.

Let me know what I can do to make it even more effective for both students and instructors by contacting me at rosenauer@missouriwestern.edu.

# Acknowledgments

No one ever writes a textbook or a workbook in a vacuum, nor is it ever truly the sole product of the author. It results from the influence of a long list of people who contributed in small ways and large to the education, the experience and the growth of that author. That certainly is true in my case.

Teachers have influenced me over the years; many are gone now, but their memories and the legacy of their teaching live on in these pages. They include Richard Taylor, my first college journalism instructor; Paula Vehlow, my advanced composition instructor; and Mary Drummond, adviser to The Griffon News, the college newspaper that forged my love of journalism and taught me its power.

Newspaper editors with whom I worked did their parts in shaping me as a journalist: Ed Lee, publisher and editor of The Savannah (Mo.) Reporter, a little country weekly where I honed my reporting and writing skills; Lee Schott, a great wire editor at the St. Joseph (Mo.) Gazette; and two other Gazette editors, Steve Huff and Jim Sherman.

Certainly I appreciate the input from reviewers of this text, who helped me to shape it into its final form. Those include the following:

Timothy G. Anderson — University of Nebraska–Lincoln

Robert Bohle — University of North Florida

Michael Buchholz — Indiana State University

Susan Burzynski Bullard — University of Nebraska–Lincoln

Bridgette Colaco — Troy University

Mary Carmen Cupito — Northern Kentucky University

Michael A. Deas — Northwestern University

Coke Ellington — Alabama State University

Peter Friederici — Northern Arizona University

Robert O. Grover — University of Maryland College Park

Nicole Kraft — The Ohio State University

Carolyn Lepre — Marist College

Ron Marmarelli — Central Michigan University

David Merves — Miami Dade College

Perry Metz — Indiana University

Burnis R. Morris — Marshall University

Hank Nuwer — Franklin College

Stephen E. Stewart — Troy University

Bruce Swain — University of West Florida

I acknowledge, too, the generous support of David Bradley and Dennis Ellsworth, of NPG Co., without which this book would have been much tougher to write. I would also like to thank everyone involved at Oxford University Press who made this happen.

Finally, I am indebted to my students of the past 35 years. I've always said that they have taught me more than I could learn from any book.

Thanks to one and all.

July 1, 2012
At Country Club, Mo.

# PART 1

# The Basics

**CHAPTER 1**

# The Role of the Copy Editor

*"The best editors have the eye of an eagle, the touch of a butterfly, and are completely without ego. There aren't many of them around."*

~Anonymous

This is an exciting time to be a journalist and, more specifically, to work as a copy editor. While technology continues to remake how journalists deliver their products and how these are delivered to audiences, one thing remains consistent: Copy editors are critical to the process.

What they do is not only the focus of this chapter in particular but also of this entire book.

## What Copy Editors Do

Google the term copy editor, and the following are typical of the kinds of hits you will get:

- [A] "person whose work is editing and correcting the grammar, punctuation, etc. of articles or manuscripts, as in a newspaper office or publishing house."[1]
- [A] "person responsible for correcting errors within a manuscript, such as grammar, spelling, and consistency, querying the editor and author with problems to solve, and preparing a style sheet of names, places, etc."[2]
- "A copy editor looks for grammar, spelling, and style mistakes in a story (or any other text for that matter) after it is written and edited for content and clarity."[3]

3

Consistent among these definitions are several terms: errors, mistakes and correcting. Reading stories line by line — hence the title line editor that sometimes is used instead of copy editor — to find and fix errors in spelling, punctuation, grammar and usage are chief among the tasks copy editors complete. However, they do much more than proofread, which is a mostly technical activity checking for mechanical mistakes.

Part 3 of this book, including Chapters 13 through 23, covers basics of punctuation and usage. However, many copy editors today also will do the following:

## Check Facts and Figures for Accuracy

Copy editors must check the spelling of each name using directories and other resources. Misspelled names suggest sloppiness and may lead readers to question the credibility of a story or even an entire publication or website. Moreover, copy editors should see that historical and local facts are correct. In what year *was* Missouri admitted to the Union? (By the way, that's 1821.)

When reporters include numbers in stories, copy editors should check the math to see that everything adds up correctly. Even with simple usages, such as a lead that says a school board discussed four proposals, editors should check that numbers match, that the story covers four — not three or five.

Chapter 7, "Numerals," offers a quick review of basic mathematical formulas that copy editors likely will need to know.

## Check Style for Consistency With Associated Press and House Guidelines

Style involves how to present material. Whereas the style guide for journalists is The Associated Press Stylebook, many publications and websites have in-house style guides that deal with local issues and may even disagree with the AP guidelines.

Part 2 of this book, comprising chapters five through 12, covers all aspects of AP style.

## Review Stories for Potential Legal and Ethical Problems and Resolve Them

As you will see in Chapter 4, "Legal, and Ethical and Inclusive-Language Concerns for Copy Editors," all journalists must check that stories do not overstep legal and ethical boundaries. Such missteps can cost publications significantly, including paying both attorney fees and court-ordered penalties. Ethical errors won't cost money, at least not directly. Instead, unethical practices damage the professionalism and credibility of reporters and the media for whom they work.

## Cut, Add, Replace or Rearrange Words, Sentences and Paragraphs

Copy editors should make whatever minor revisions are needed to correct and improve story content. The editor usually does these without consulting the reporter. However, it is not the job of copy editors to rewrite stories, even if the result is an improvement. Reporters should take care of significant revision or rewriting.

## Check for Focus, Readability and Organization

This involves making sure that story leads target the right news elements in interesting ways and that stories flow well and speak to their audience. Readability may be a grand goal for all writing, but it is especially vital for journalistic products.

Today, readers want stories they don't have to work to understand, that don't take time to figure out. Rather than a "dumbing down" of writing, it's much more demanding to write even complex stories that read easily and clearly. Copy editors must identify their audience, what it already knows and what it needs to know to ensure that stories communicate intended messages.

We will cover leads further in Chapter 24, "Leads."

## Work Closely and Creatively With Reporters

Fixing mistakes and improving stories are among the immediate goals for copy editors. However, in the process they would be wise to help reporters avoid problems in the future. Thus, their role also includes working with reporters, who should learn from their mistakes and capitalize on their successes.

## Write Effective and Appropriate Headlines

Once copy editors have made sure that a story is clean, correct and polished, they usually finish by writing a headline. This element is among the first readers will see, so success here may determine whether a story will be read.

In Chapter 25, "Headlines," we will cover various aspects of effective headline writing.

On some publications, particularly those with smaller audiences and fewer staff, copy editors also may design pages. Even though Copycrafting does not cover page design, you may wish to check online resources for design or enroll in a publication design course.

In addition, copy editors of online publications often complete the following tasks:

- Ensure that text formatting and use of color are consistent.
- Confirm that visual elements are strong and that design follows the site's signature look and is appropriate.
- Check that hyperlinks are working and are correct.
- See that text is optimized for search engine ranking.

These also extend beyond the scope of Copycrafting. However, as noted previously, you can consult online resources or consider enrolling in a course dedicated to online design and development.

# Traits of Good Copy Editors

Not everyone is cut out to be a strong copy editor. Some journalists prefer to work as reporters, covering beats and writing stories or columns. Others enjoy the visual aspects of journalism as photographers, graphic artists or designers. If you're considering the job of copy editor, though, the following traits are those that may help you to be a good one.

## Strong Grounding in Basic Skills

Copy editors must be the staff experts in spelling, punctuation, grammar, usage and style. It's not necessary that you *know* everything involved with all of those skills, but you must have a good working knowledge of each. You must be able to spot potential errors, check for answers and correct them.

## Attention to Detail

There's little doubt that at least some attributes of the Type A personality may be useful here — perfectionist, time conscious, deadline oriented, competitive and assertive. Good copy editors, ignoring the popular wisdom, *need* to sweat the small stuff. They should care about errors, both those they miss and those they make. They must be concerned with meeting deadlines.

## Love of the Written — or Spoken — Word

Lots of evidence supports that frequent readers are better writers. It's hard to be a strong writer and to grow in the craft if you don't read much. Likewise, it's hard to edit effectively if you're not an effective writer. This continuum suggests that you will enjoy editing and do a better job with it if you love working with words.

## Curiosity

Curiosity is a must for copy editors. You have to wonder about things, enough to push you to find the answers.

## Creativity

Being able to see things in new ways or from different perspectives is what creativity is about. Although it may be easier to be creative when dealing with something that is new and exciting, it's tougher to do so when presenting the routine. This trait is one that all journalists need, regardless of their particular roles. Thus, creative copy editors — working with creative reporters, photographers, artists and designers — have potential for producing great content, in print or online.

## Familiarity With and Knowledge of Particular Media

If you rarely read newspapers, magazines or online media sites, you're going to be hard pressed to work effectively editing the content of those media. Each platform offers unique material, often presented in unique ways to particular audiences. Understanding their uniqueness better prepares you to work within their confines. Bottom line, it's hard to hit a target you've never seen.

Since copy editors for many media are the last ones to read stories before they are published or posted, their job is critical. They are the final defense against poor journalism. Copycrafting will give you the tools you will need to do that job and do it well.

# Newsroom Organization and Copy Flow

So, how do copy editors and what they do fit in the operation of a newsroom? Although each medium has its own particular organization, we can examine a generic, traditional newsroom structure to get an idea of what happens in most newsrooms.

The traditional newspaper newsroom is a well-oiled machine that moves the news product along an assembly line to create each edition. At the top of this hierarchy is the editor, who sets policy and direction for the newspaper and controls the spending on the editorial side of the paper.

Under the editor is the managing editor, charged with overseeing the daily operations of the newsroom. He or she coordinates assembly of the newspaper, assigning space to each section, making sure each meets its deadlines and — consulting with the editor and other members of the editorial board — deciding what stories to play on the front page.

Under the managing editor are the middle-management departments, or desks, including city, features, sports, business, copy, design and photography. Chiefs are in charge on copy and design desks, with editors managing the others. The remaining

**FIGURES 1-2 & 1-3** Much has changed in newsrooms over the past 50 years, as is evidenced by these two shots at the New York Times. The one at top shows the newsroom in 1942 while the other is a more recent shot.

positions in the newsroom — copy editors, designers, reporters and photographers — answer to each of these desks.

The stories reporters complete each day go to their respective desks for initial review and editing. From there stories go to the copy desk, where the copy chief, or slot, distributes them to copy editors, also called rim editors. Here's where final editing takes place. Here, too, is often where editors assign stories and write headlines.

**FIGURE 1-4** This depiction of an interactive, multimedia newsroom was designed by Innovation Media Consulting. Note the open spaces and lack of walls in this hub with the Superdesk in the center.

As convergence continues to influence newspaper operations, many newspapers have become media outlets, developing new organizational structures that make more efficient use of resources, both the people involved and the work they do. In addition to new physical layouts, these operations demand a different mindset. News and information are their common product, but how they're delivered — print, online or broadcast, or mobile, platforms — is based on the best, most suitable method for each story and its audience. Rolling deadlines often replace the fixed deadlines of traditional media.

In newsrooms such as those designed by Innovation International Media Consulting Group, the hub, or superdesk, is where all the chiefs sit. The assignment desk coordinates the efforts of all reporters. A graphics desk coordinates visual content to support coverage that shows rather than tells — the new mantra of the converged media operation. A variety of other desks comprise the rest of the operation, all dedicated to delivering content that is more accessible and relevant to a contemporary audience.

Regardless of actual organization, the copy editor continues to be essential in that delivery.

For additional information, consult online editing resources in the Appendix.

## CHAPTER 2

# Editing Content

*"Copy editors are the secret scourge and saviors of the publishing world, insane sticklers who make your life miserable and your prose sing. Good ones are hard to find, and harder to love: punctilious, detail-oriented people, they think commas have consequence, facts can never be fiction, and every sentence is capable of improvement."*

~Ruth Reichl

Content involves many issues concerning what a story says and how it says it. While entire textbooks are devoted to what comprises good journalistic writing, Copycrafting assumes that students have completed previous courses in reporting or news writing and the like. Just to make sure we're all on the same page, we will quickly review some basic principles and cover key story components to refresh your understanding.

In this chapter, we will begin by focusing our discussion on the Three C's and how they apply to all aspects of journalistic stories. We will follow that with a review of leads and the body and organization of a story.

# Three C's: Clarity, Conciseness and Correctness

It's straightforward to say that you should edit copy to make it clear, concise and correct. Were it simple enough just to *cite* the need for these three, of course we wouldn't need journalism classes and books to teach you effective editing. The Three C's should be key concerns regardless of exactly what you're editing. Although each carries a different meaning, all relate to and support one another.

## Clarity

Reporters achieve clarity in writing when what they intend to say is what the stories end up saying — and what readers end up understanding. This consistency between what reporters intended and what readers understood, what was sent and what was received, is critical. You will be more successful editing copy if you read as your readers will read. You will more likely catch gaps in content that leave readers scratching their heads and imprecise or confusing words that not only slow understanding but also may make it altogether impossible.

As you edit for clarity, read carefully, paying attention to exactly what is there. Don't do the reporter a favor by mentally filling in any holes, a common practice when many of us read our own writing or when we read others' writing too quickly. A few tricks to help you read carefully include the following:

- Give the story a quick read before you edit so you have a better sense of how a reporter has handled the story. That should equip you to do a better job editing.
- Read a story aloud. While this seems juvenile, it's a great method for slowing your reading and using your ears to help catch problems. If you're using Microsoft Word to edit copy, use the speech function to have the computer read the text aloud. If something you're hearing doesn't *sound* right, it likely isn't right. Change it so it is. Of course, this is a practice that you won't necessarily take into the newsroom as a professional.
- Read from the bottom up. Start with the last paragraph in a story, and read from the last sentence to the first as you move up the screen or the page. This forces you to consider sentences — and the words that comprise them — more individually.

**FIGURE 2-1** Clarity, conciseness and correctness are key to effective editing.

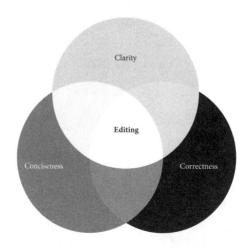

- Increase the font size. If your computer or terminal allows it, increasing font size makes it easier to read what's there.
- Look for repeated errors. For example, if a name is misspelled, use the search function to see if all occurrences are misspelled. If the reporter is dropping commas following introductory clauses, check all introductory clauses for commas.
- Read copy more than once. On each pass focus your attention on something different. The first may involve style, the second punctuation, the third grammar and usage and the fourth content, including continuity and relationships between sentences and paragraphs.
- Double-check names, phone numbers, addresses and other identifying information.
- Check numbers. If a lead says that the City Council approved $150,000 for three public works jobs, make sure that the story lists three and that the amount totals $150,000.
- Check other facts that are critical to the story, especially those that don't seem to ring true. It's your job to be skeptical and make sure reporters have provided accurate details.
- After making a correction, *reread* the passage to make sure it works. Be especially cautious that you haven't introduced new errors.
- If you're editing on a computer with Microsoft Word, consider using the spelling and grammar tool. However, do not follow every suggestion, especially for grammar. Word is not infallible in its spell- and grammar-checking functions, but it may alert you to passages to check more carefully.

Making sure that the words in the story fit the context within which they're used aids clarity. Words carry specific meaning. Whereas some may come close to fitting the idea being developed in the sentence, it's up to you as editor see that each is on the mark. For example, Chapter 9, "Commonly Misspelled and Misused Words," presents two words, *anxious* and *eager*. Although they are similar, they are not interchangeable. *Anxious* is an

**FIGURE 2-2** This newsroom is in Berlin at the Axel Springer Haus, the largest and most influential German newspaper house.

adjective meaning to be nervous or fearful, as in the following: *Eddie was anxious about his dental appointment.* *Eager*, on the other hand, is an adjective meaning to be excited, as in the following: *Julie is eager to go to the game arcade Saturday.*

## Conciseness

The second C, conciseness, involves paragraphs, sentences and words. Paragraphing in journalism is a visual device that aids readability and moves readers along comfortably. Shorter paragraphs, often only single sentences, are common. This follows the principle of one idea to a paragraph. Conciseness also is a problem in sentences that try to say too much, that use too many words or that use too-long words. Some reporters assume that longer sentences with longer words *seem* more important. Both go against a primary directive in journalistic writing: Shorter and simpler are better.

If a phrase can replace a clause, use it. If a word can replace a phrase, use it. Consider these examples:

- *The dog that was in the cage is mine. — > The dog in the cage is mine.*
- *The paper makes an argument against abortion. — > The paper argues against abortion.*
- *He gave an explanation to his students. — > He explained to his students.*
- *The bleachers were filled to capacity. — > The bleachers were filled.*

Ensure every word is necessary and carries meaning that contributes to the message. If not, cut the fat. We will cover this more thoroughly in Chapter 20, "Prepositions," which covers both wordy and problem prepositions, and Chapter 22, "Wordiness."

Of course, varying paragraph and sentence length is necessary to avoid the tedium of sameness. In addition, occasional paragraphs and sentences that are extra-short lend emphasis.

Finally, most of the time reporters can pick the words they use. For example, in the last sentence, either *pick* or *select* and *use* or *utilize* would have worked. Go with *pick* and *use* because each is shorter than its synonym. Follow the same practices in editing your reporters' stories.

## Correctness

Correctness, the third C, is a matter that a good deal of this book covers. The lack of clarity and conciseness is a problem that weakens effectiveness, interferes with understanding and diminishes the professional quality of stories. The lack of correctness, though, is sloppy and unforgiveable. As editor, yours probably are the last pair of eyeballs to read stories and catch mistakes. These can run the gamut, from errors in abbreviations or word choices that violate AP style to misspelled names or misused commas. You must be meticulous to make sure copy is correct.

# Leads

Of all the work that reporters do, crafting strong leads is among the most important, and it's up to you as editor to make sure they've done their jobs well. Regardless of the particular type of lead used with a story, we can establish some basic criteria that all should meet.

First, remember that leads serve the following purposes:

- They tell the reader what the story is about.
- They help to organize the story.
- They capture readers' attention and lure them into the rest of the story.

Examine the lead carefully. Does it tell readers what happened? Does it capture what you want readers to take away from a story? The best storytelling journalists suggest that a lead should sound like what you'd tell a friend or family member who asks what you're writing about. Comfortable and conversational are much more effective than forced and formal.

Remember, too, that most lead paragraphs are short, typically a single sentence of fewer than 25 words. Rarely do effective leads run longer.

Regardless of the approach reporters take to begin a story, a lead should be interesting, provocative, telling and inviting. If it is not, then all the effort reporters put into the rest of the story may be for naught: It won't be read. It's your job to see that doesn't happen.

We will examine lead editing and revision in Chapter 24.

# The Body and Organization

The body of a story expands on and develops the promise of the lead. It is where readers' expectations must be fulfilled if the story is to be successful.

## Questions to Consider

As you edit a story, answer the following questions:

- What is this story about? What's the point?

    If you don't know the answers, your readers certainly won't. If the problem is in the lead, fix it if you don't have to make too many changes. Otherwise, send it back to the reporter. If the problem is in the body of the story, is it missing content or does it have confusing organization? As with a problem lead, if you can correct the problem with moderate changes, do so. If not, shoot it back to the reporter to fix.

- What should this story mean to its readers?

    Most stories you edit benefit from identifying and explaining their context; that is, how does this coverage fit into the larger scheme of things? Such background and connections aid readers in understanding — as opposed to just getting the details of a story — and in situating the story within their lives.

- Who will this story affect? How? Why?

    Readers need to know if a story on new taxes, for example, involves *their* taxes. Whereas all readers may be concerned about all taxes that governments levy, they're much more interested if those taxes affect them personally.

- Who or what is responsible?

    Although this seems a given for most stories, it is a point that reporters and editors can overlook.

- How and why did this happen?

    Again, in the process of focusing on the "what" of a story, some reporters may forget to cover its causes.

- Is the story fair?

  Whereas the previous yardstick for measuring this suggested the notion that all stories have two sides, each of which should be represented to be fair, journalists today recognize that many of their stories have more than two sides. Therefore, fairness expects that the story gives voice to all sides.

- What are the consequences of this story? Where will this lead?

  Both of these get at impact. As you edit, make sure the reporter has covered this concern.

- Who serves to gain from this coverage?

  This point bears consideration, particularly when a reporter's source may have an ax to grind or benefits from the story's publication.

## Inverted Pyramid

Issues of body content also involve how reporters present a story. The common pattern for organizing straight news stories is the inverted pyramid, wherein material is presented most to least important. This pattern, you may recall, has no conclusion; it just ends with the least-important detail. The inverted pyramid — among the oldest and most reliable of journalistic practices — still has two benefits today.

First, many readers don't stay with a story to its end, so this pattern ensures that they don't leave a story that has more important material below their stopping point.

Second, even though editions digitally place text onto a page in the vast majority of publications and online — as opposed to cutting and pasting printed text onto a paper galley — the inverted pyramid makes editing a story to fit available space quicker and easier.

One way to check correct use of the inverted pyramid is to examine the story from the bottom up. If anything you read is more important than material that precedes it, move it toward the beginning.

**FIGURE 2-3** The inverted pyramid.

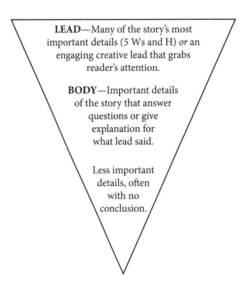

LEAD—Many of the story's most important details (5 Ws and H) *or* an engaging creative lead that grabs reader's attention.

BODY—Important details of the story that answer questions or give explanation for what lead said.

Less important details, often with no conclusion.

## Other Story Formats

Of course, not all stories *should* follow the inverted pyramid in their organization. As we saw earlier in the discussion of leads, the organization of many features and some news stories often relies heavily on the chronology of good narrative or the sensory details of good description, and sometimes both. Understand, too, that this type of story may finish with a conclusion.

As you edit such a creative piece, check that the organization works. Reading as your readers will read, consider the following questions:

- Does the story unfold comfortably and logically? Is it easy to follow, or does it demand too much effort to read?
- Does some clear theme or thread subtly link parts of the story?
- Does the reporter introduce too many "characters" or sources, making it hard to track who is doing or saying what?
- If the story has a conclusion, is it perfunctory, or — like the soft candy center of a Tootsie Roll Pop — does it offer readers a reward for making their way to the end?

For any of these questions whose answers are "no," revision may be necessary. How much revision will determine whether you apply some simple, quick fixes or send it back to the reporter for more serious rewriting.

## Finishing Up

Frequent use of the AP Stylebook should become a habit you develop. Good editors have well-worn paper copies at their desks. Those with access to the online stylebook have found that checking style has never been faster and easier. This must be a regular part of your editing

Although you will find style guidance in Copycrafting that matches that in the AP Stylebook, this book shouldn't replace your stylebook. In fact, it should help you to better learn what's in the stylebook and how to locate it there. In addition, entries and guidance in the stylebook change. A check of the online AP Stylebook lists more than 100 new entries since the most recent publication of the print version. To keep abreast of the most current style guidance, you must constantly check the stylebook.

Certainly, the last step of any editing process should be running spell-check and grammar-check, if available. Although neither computer function is perfect, each gives you the opportunity to consider the hits they bring up and decide whether these are errors or are OK as is.

Finally, never guess at style, spelling or grammar. Look each up. That's your job.

For additional information, consult online editing resources in the Appendix.

# Copy Editing for Print and Online

*"Cybermedia will make every man his own editor, which in turn makes every writer a fool. The Internet will transmit misinformation very efficiently. We will miss the gatekeepers."*

~Neal B. Freeman

One point you should understand up front: Writing for print media is different than writing for online media. Therefore, your expectations as editor also should be different. Let's begin by reviewing the basic characteristics of each format, which should help define your expectations.

## Characteristics of Print Stories Versus Online Stories

Characteristics of stories in print media include the following:
- Stories open in a variety of ways, including summary leads or narrative/descriptive scene-setters.
- Writing is concise and tightly focused, although narrative approaches allow some license to pull the reader along through experiences, with some pieces running thousands of words.

**FIGURE 3-1** Some newspapers continue to maintain paper archives of their issues.

- Stories tend to be linear, using either inverted pyramid or narrative development.
- Most material in the body of stories is fully expressed and developed.
- Background for stories — particularly second-day coverage — is included, usually high in stories.
- Stories have a number of redundancies embedded in headlines, leads and story development.
- Stories may be supported by graphics — including photos, art and charts/graphs — but many are not.

Characteristics of stories in online media include the following:

- Stories launch with strong summary leads that give readers the essential information up front.
- Writing is concise — even more than with print media, and overall text tends to be shorter, often capping at 600 words. When coverage needs are greater, reporters write additional short pieces.
- Story contents tend to be chunked — broken down into modules that are nonlinear and can be accessed by readers at any point that interests them.
- Bulleted items are common for presenting material.
- Background and related content are hyperlinked — text links that readers click to bring up a window or another page with the material.
- Stories have less redundancy.
- Stories often include photographs, art and charts/graphs, but they also can include hyperlinks, audio, audio slideshows and video — all created to give readers a diverse, in-depth, rich experience that they can choose to examine or not.

# Being Aware of Search Engine Optimization

If you're editing online content — an increased possibility in today's mediascape, then you must be aware of search engine optimization. SEO involves ways of presenting Web content that makes it more accessible to search engines, and search engines like Google and Yahoo drive visitors to your site.

Fortunately, much of what you already do well in editing copy and writing headlines improves the SEO for your media site. Whereas many of the techniques for improving SEO are more the province of Web page designers, the following certainly relate to the basic tasks that editors complete:

- Content is the most important feature of websites. Emphasis is on keywords and keyword phrases. Thus, well-written headlines and well-written and well-edited stories should improve search engine rankings.
- If your media site updates regularly with new content, that's another SEO-related benefit. Fresh content improves rankings.
- Search engines prefer natural language content, not just text overloaded with keywords. Again, well-written stories and headlines will take advantage of this.

SEO may not be your main job as an editor, but doing your job well is essential to improved search engine rankings and increased traffic to your website.

## ONLINE INSIGHTS > SEARCH ENGINE OPTIMIZATION TIPS

Search engine optimization involves various specific activities that increase the visibility of websites to search engines.

How much increase? In a study by iSL Consulting, search engines accounted for 61 percent of all traffic while direct traffic — wherein users type in the URL manually — involved 20 percent of traffic, and referring sites claimed 17 percent.

These numbers make it clear how important it is to optimize your media website for search engines. You or your Web team can perform many of the optimization steps, or you might contract with one of hundreds of online services to do so.

Regardless of *how* you do it, you must optimize your website if you hope to compete successfully in the vast Web marketplace.

First, you must understand that a search engine completes four key tasks:

- It crawls the Web. A search engine sends out automated programs called "bots" or "spiders" to crawl the Web in search of documents, such as Web pages, images, movies, PDF files and so on.
- It indexes documents. The bot crawls the documents and then indexes the contents in a database.
- It processes queries. When users type keyword searches into the search engine, it finds those documents containing the words and retrieves them from the database.
- It ranks results. Once the search engine has determined which documents match the search request, it decides which results are most relevant to the request, using a complex algorithm that varies among the different search engines. Finally, it ranks them from most to least relevant and presents the results to the user.

The last task is the one the most important to you because it determines where your site will appear. Recent statistics show that about 80 percent of Web surfers won't go past the first page of search engine results. Thus, you must optimize to land in the top 10 spots that a search returns.

ONLINE INSIGHTS > **Continued**

**Steps Involved With SEO**

The specific advice and procedures may vary somewhat among online experts, but most agree with the following steps:

- Determine which keywords are best to use on your site.

  This involves research, and there are services such as Google Trends, which we will discuss later and which can help you make smart decisions about which keywords are essential. In addition, the use of sitemaps — an index to all the content on a website — may be helpful to a visitor, but they also make your site bot-friendly.

- Optimize content around keywords.

  An important part of this step involves adding or revising meta tags, title tags, H1 tags, H2 tags and alt tags for images using the essential keywords you have found. One goal is to establish an appropriate keyword density on your site, aiming for a 3 to 5 percent target, according to many SEO pros. Content in header tags as well as bold, italic, anchor text and other formatting options increases the weight this text carries. Many experts recommend greater emphasis on phrases versus single words, which should draw better search-engine response for users seeking more specific content. Finally, although Flash-based sites tend to be alluring to the visitor, their downside is that search engines cannot read Flash. Therefore, keep Flash content to a minimum. Also, because bots cannot read images either, that is why you should provide well-written alt tags.

- Complete link building.

  The first part of your link-building strategy is submitting your site to online directories, online data banks of various sites organized by subject. Second, build appropriate reciprocal links. This involves link exchanges with relevant related sites that make sense to visitors and search engines. They are reciprocal because you agree to link to their sites if they link to your site. Such inbound links help to raise your site's status among search engines.

Entire books take on the task of search engine optimization, and many companies offer this expertise. The goals here are to raise your awareness of the importance of optimization and to give you a basic understanding of what it involves.

# Editing Approaches to Print and Online

Regardless of whether you are editing a story for print or for online, some basic approaches are consistent. While we covered various aspects of editing in Chapter 2, "Editing Content," key information and advice bears repeating.

Follow the steps listed here as you work with both print and online stories:

- Read the entire story. First. Always.
- Find the lead and make sure it does its job of telling readers what the story is about.
- Check the flow of the story to see that it hangs together and makes sense.
- Check the grammar — including preference for active versus passive voice, spelling (especially of names), punctuation and other usage.
- Check the story for AP style.
- Reread the edited story to make sure you've caught errors and weaknesses and to see that you haven't introduced any problems or mistakes with your editing.

## ONLINE INSIGHTS > **USING GOOGLE TRENDS**

Because Google blows away all the other search-engine competition, optimizing your website for Google searches makes sense. Likewise, using Google services — many of which are free — enhances the likelihood of your site responding well to Google searches. Here, we discuss Google Trends. This and other Google services are relatively simple to use, and tutorials covering them are widely available if you want to negotiate some of their finer points.

Google Trends is a Web-traffic tracking tool, which allows you to compare the popularity of words and phrases across the Internet. This will aid you in picking the best keywords to drive traffic to your site because those words are the ones most users type into search engines.

The Google Trends site analyzes Google Web searches to figure how many searches have been done for the terms entered relative to the total number of searches done on Google over time, which can be configured between 30 days and 10 years.

The main data from a search of one or more keywords is the Search Volume Index Graph, which also displays the number of times the topics appeared in Google News stories. A spike in the volume of news stories for a particular search term generates a headline of an automatically selected Google News story written near the time of the spike.

Trends also shows the top regions, cities and languages in which people searched for the first search term entered.

Another useful feature of Trends is its listing of the top 100 hot trends — searches that have seen a significant increase in popularity recently. Using these can help you decide which topics will draw strong traffic in the short term.

- Write a headline that supports the story without merely repeating the lead or stealing the surprise of some stories written for that effect.

Jakob Nielsen writes in his "Alertbox" blog about distinctions between print and online:

> In linear media — such as print and TV — people expect you to construct their experience for them. Readers are willing to follow the author's lead. In non-linear hypertext, the rules reverse. Users want to construct their own experience by piecing together content from multiple sources, emphasizing their current desires in the current moment. People arrive at a website with a goal in mind, and they are ruthless in pursuing their own interest and in rejecting whatever the site is trying to push.[1]

As you edit online stories, these concerns deserve your attention:

- Online readers want to know *what* happened, but they also are more interested in *why* the story should matter to them. Make sure the story tells that.
- Online readers scan Web pages, noting particular words and sentences. Some research suggests that four out of five readers always scan new pages, with only one in six reading word by word. With this in mind, editors of online media typically do the following:
  - ▶ Add highlighted and hypertexted keywords.
  - ▶ Write informative subheads.
  - ▶ Revise some content as bulleted lists.
  - ▶ Strive for one idea per paragraph.
  - ▶ Make sure content is chunked into modular packages that make reading quick, easy and reader selectable.

> ► Avoid repeating keywords in headlines, blurbs or subheads.
> ► Tighten, tighten, tighten.
- Online readers prefer straightforward headlines to clever or cute.
- Most online stories include a tightly written summary in a blurb that bridges the headline and the lead.

# Editing Hard Copy Versus On-Screen

It's safe to say that nearly all copy editors do their work on computers. Therefore, if you haven't made the transition from reading and editing stories in hard copy to reading and editing on-screen, you should be prepared to do so.

That said, however, most studies suggest that people are more successful editing hard copy text. You may complete the exercises in this book in hard copy form. Over time you should be able to wean yourself from hard copy and begin editing on-screen.

Here are some tips to consider as you edit hard copy stories, a few of which we saw earlier:

- Read the entire story without editing.
- Read the story aloud, which has two benefits:
  > ► It forces you to slow your reading.
  > ► It lets you use your ear to help catch problems in what you read.
- Put a ruler or piece of blank paper under each line as you read, helping to guide your eyes down the story.

**FIGURE 3-2** At times an editor may have a reporter review a story with him, especially if the reporter is less experienced or the story was complex.

- Use several passes through the story, reserving each for a different concern, such as word choice, punctuation, grammar and usage and content, including the flow and relationships between sentences and paragraphs.
- Double-check names, phone numbers, addresses and other identifying information.
- Double-check numbers to make sure they match and total correctly.

When you edit on-screen, use the preceding tips — as appropriate — as well as the following to improve your success:

- Use the computer's spell-checker and grammar-checker, if available, but don't take every suggestion on its face. As helpful as they may be, these tools are not always correct. Use them as guides for what to check more closely.
- If you find a name misspelled, use the computer's search and replace function to locate other misspellings of the name and correct those.
- If your software has a text-recognition and/or speech feature, run that instead of reading the story aloud.

**FIGURE 3-3** Copy editing marks.

| | |
|---|---|
| New paragraph indent | Heartland residents will have the chance to vote on |
| No new paragraph or join together paragraphs | arrested following the crash. Smith was taken to the Cooper County Law |
| Transpose words or letters | to Heartland Hospital Memorial from her home |
| Use figures or write figures out | The seven-year-old asked for 2 birthday gifts |
| Abbreviate or don't abbreviate | Jefferson City, Missouri, is in southern Mo. |
| Uppercase or lowercase letters | Heartland city council asked the Mayor to report |
| Close up space or add space | Religion in fluenced him from an early age |
| Remove word or insert word | His very unique talents included juggling |
| Insert comma | his home in Independence Mo. was |
| Insert period | The end was near However, she was not ready for |
| Insert apostrophe | Janets brother |
| Insert question mark | Are you kidding |
| Insert exclamation point | No A thousand times no |
| Insert quotation marks | Andy asked, Are we there yet? |
| Insert hyphen or insert dash | The 2 year old girl actually my wife's niece is here |
| Retain original | Jen was unwilling and unable to finish the task that |

# Copy Editing Marks

The use of copy editing marks is rare today. Few editors of any kind of publication use them, preferring instead to edit digital copy on screen. However, the marks are useful for such tasks as editing the printed text in this book.

The AP Stylebook recommends the marks shown in Figure 3–3. Like so much in journalism, these standard marks provide consistency and make clear the revisions and corrections that editors make. Prefer pencil to pen for your work, and when you cross out material, use a simple clean line rather than blacking out the original with pencil lead.

Of course, using copy editing marks is not critical to good editing, even of the exercises in Copycrafting. Your instructor may offer alternative instructions to complete exercises. What is important is that whatever corrections and changes you recommend are clear.

For additional information, consult online editing resources in the Appendix.

## CHAPTER 4

# Legal, Ethical and Inclusive-Language Concerns for Copy Editors

*"Journalism without a moral position is impossible. Every journalist is a moralist. It's absolutely unavoidable."*

~Marguerite Duras

This chapter focuses on fundamental legal and ethical issues, as well as the need for inclusive language, all of which are essential for editors to understand and follow. Whether required or not, you'd be wise to delve further into these subjects in courses focused on media law and ethics.

**FIGURE 4-1** The gavel is the traditional symbol of rendering judgment.

# Distinguishing Between Law, Morals and Ethics

Editors and reporters have three well-established codes of conduct for their professional work: law, morals and ethics. Law tends to be the most fixed of the three: federal and state governments design the law to guide how people should act. Religious groups may establish morals, yet culture and society also play a significant role in defining appropriate moral behavior. Finally, ethics tend to be closely related to professional groups, most of which have organized their own codes of ethical behavior.

All of these codes tend to change over time, and it is up to you as an editor to remain current, particularly with legal and ethical concerns.

The Project for Excellence in Journalism cites the role of journalism as "helping define community, creating common language and common knowledge, identifying a community's goals, heroes and villains, and pushing people beyond complacency."[1] Editors and reporters support this role by following what PEJ terms the nine core principles:

1. Journalism's first obligation is to the truth.
2. Its first loyalty is to citizens.
3. Its essence is a discipline of verification.
4. Its practitioners must maintain an independence from those they cover.
5. It must serve as an independent monitor of power.
6. It must provide a forum for public criticism and compromise.
7. It must strive to make the significant interesting and relevant.
8. It must keep the news comprehensive and proportional.
9. Its practitioners must be allowed to exercise their personal conscience.

With this as background, let us examine basic legal and ethical matters.

# Legal Concerns — Libel

Two aspects of law that copy editors must understand and follow are libel and privacy.

According to the online First Amendment Handbook, libel "occurs when a false and defamatory statement about an identifiable person is published to a third party, causing injury to the subject's reputation."[2] While you may understand what a false statement is, you may be less familiar with defamation. The standard definition is communication that "exposes a person to hatred, ridicule or contempt, lowers him in the esteem of his fellows, causes him to be shunned, or injures him in his business or calling."[3]

State statutes set most libel guidelines, meaning that the specifications for libel and punishment for violations can vary from one state to another. Also, most libel suits are civil, as opposed to criminal, so if you're found guilty of libel, you're not likely to be jailed. Before you breathe a sigh of relief, understand that the media company for which you work may face considerable financial penalties if a court finds you guilty of libel.

Bottom line, most media law textbooks suggest that the best protection against being found guilty of libel is *provable* truth.

In libel suits the burden of proof is on the plaintiff, the one who claims to have been defamed. Most states require plaintiffs to prove all of the following:

- The material is false.
- The material is defamatory, either on its face (*per se*) or indirectly (*per quod*).
- The material is about one or more identifiable persons.
- The material is distributed to someone beyond the offended person.
- The material is made with fault.

Libel *per se* is more serious than libel *per quod* because plaintiffs don't have to prove they have suffered damages or loss. They only must show that a reasonable person would recognize the libel because it is obvious or evident due to the language used. Because thousands of words and phrases in English meet this requirement, you must examine carefully the word choices in stories you edit.

Libel *per quod* doesn't deal with words, phrases or statements, which typically may be harmless in themselves. However, attached circumstances may make them libelous. Defamation by circumstance is more common and a result of errors or negligence.

Most libel laws distinguish between public and private individuals. The law tends to provide less protection for public individuals, who because of election or occupation have put themselves into the public spotlight. Private individuals must prove only two points concerning fault:

- A medium acted negligently in failing to find that a statement was false.
- The statement defamed the private individual.

This public-private label is significant because public figures in libel suits must prove actual malice, a much more difficult argument than simple negligence. The courts have established the following three criteria in actual-malice decisions:

- Was publication of a story urgent (e.g., breaking news), or was there time for the reporter to check the facts?
- Was the source of a story reliable or suspect?
- Was the story probable on its face or improbable enough to warrant further investigation?

## ONLINE INSIGHTS > **COPYRIGHT**

Observers note that the Web is a vast copying machine. Once anything is published anyplace, it is effectively published everyplace.

For consumers, that's wonderful. It makes the Web a treasure trove of riches, mostly free for the taking. However, for artists and producers — particularly those who produce creative works such as music, films and novels — the Web is a curse that has cost them millions in lost revenue.

It is critical for you as an editor to understand basic copyright laws to avoid violations. First, you and your reporters cannot use the works of others willy-nilly — any more than others may use your material without limitations. Second, copyright involves all media and all platforms. Third, simply crediting the source of the copyrighted material is no protection against claims of violation.

Of course, the best way to protect yourself and your media outlet is to get permission from the copyright holder. This may involve your paying some kind of compensation. However, most often media outlets rely on the "fair use"

provisions of the copyright law, which center on the following four items:

1. The purpose and character of the use. The prevailing notion is that media borrowings of copyrighted material are "in the public interest." To qualify for this provision, the medium must add text, audio, graphics or video that comment or expand on the original.
2. The nature of the copyrighted work. This deals with whether or not a work is factual or fictional, published or unpublished.
3. The amount and substantiality of the portion used. Neither the number of words nor the length of borrowing is specified by the law. The key here is to limit the use to no more than is required to make the point.
4. The effect of the use on the value of the work. The courts here weigh how much the borrowing may reduce the market value of the protected material.

For information about piracy of content from your media outlet, see the "SOPA, PIPA and Dealing With Piracy" breakout.

A final couple of provisions concerning libel are worth mentioning. First, you cannot libel a group of individuals large enough that individual identities are not obvious; that number usually is 25.

Second, you cannot libel a dead person.

As noted previously, truth is absolute defense to libel. However — and this is a critical point — you must *prove* in court the facts in question.

# Legal Concerns — Privacy

Technology has made it easier today for more people to know more about you than ever before. As a result, the demand for personal privacy — the right to be left alone — has never been greater.

The distinction between public and private figures also plays a role in the right to privacy. The First Amendment Handbook says that public figures "are said to have voluntarily exposed themselves to scrutiny and to have waived their right of privacy, at least in matters that might have an impact on their ability to perform their public duties."[4] On the other hand, to limit intrusions into their lives, private individuals have more frequently hauled media into court, and courts generally have supported their claims.

Understand that private individuals can forfeit much of their right to privacy when they thrust themselves into the media spotlight. Then, they are considered public figures — at least insofar as the public issue is involved.

You can violate privacy in most states in four ways:

- Intrusion.
- Disclosure of private facts.
- False light.
- Misappropriation.

Three common types of intrusion are trespass, secret surveillance and misrepresentation. You can't go onto private property without the owner's consent, and you can't harass a person. Although you're restricted from using either bugging equipment or hidden cameras, anything you see or hear while positioned in a public place is legal as long as you don't use technology to increase your perception. Finally, misrepresentation means you can't lie or misrepresent yourself. However, this doesn't prohibit undercover reporting if a disguise isn't used for trespass or other illegal activities.

Whereas libel often involves details that are false, disclosure of private facts deals with those that are true. Private facts suits may follow disclosure of facts about a person's private life that may be highly offensive and embarrassing to a reasonable person. Moreover, their publication is not of legitimate public concern.

One defense to private facts suits is privilege, which protects fair and accurate reporting of public records, including police reports, judicial proceedings and birth certificates. Another defense is newsworthiness, which applies to public figures for almost everything and to everyone if the report concerns recent criminal behavior.

False light, according to the First Amendment Handbook, happens when all the following circumstances are true:

- Information published about a person is false or places the person in a false light.
- Information is considered highly offensive to a reasonable person.
- Information is published "with knowledge or in reckless disregard of whether the information was false or would place the person in a false light."[5]

Although false-light invasion of privacy is similar to defamation, the key distinction is that the plaintiff doesn't need to prove injury or damage to reputation.

The last privacy violation is misappropriation. Here, a person's name or likeness is used without permission for commercial purposes. This is not usually a concern for editors since they tend not to deal with the commercial content of their media.

Bob Steele of the Poynter Institute for Media Studies prepared the following privacy checklist, "Respecting Privacy Guidelines":

- What is my journalistic purpose in seeking this information? In reporting it?
- Does the public have a justifiable need to know? Or is this matter just one in which some want to know?
- How much protection does this person deserve? Is this person a public official, public figure or celebrity? Is this person involved in the news event by choice or by chance?
- What is the nature of the harm I might cause by intruding on someone's privacy?
- Can I cause considerable harm to someone just by asking questions, observing activity or obtaining information even if I never report the story?

## ONLINE INSIGHTS > **SOPA, PIPA AND DEALING WITH PIRACY**

The longtime defense for artists and others is copyright, which protects intellectual property and creative performance from being used without permission — and without reasonable compensation. (See the "Copyright" breakout.) The blanket term for such online illegal activity is piracy.

To protect copyrighted material online, Congress attempted during 2011–12 to pass the Stop Online Piracy Act and the Protect Intellectual Property Act. Both targeted foreign websites that infringed on copyright, especially those that hosted illegal copies of films and other media. However, opponents worried that neither of the bills protect enough against false accusations. Some observers warned that provisions of the legislation could shut down an entire website because it had a link to a suspect site.

More than 10,000 websites protested against the bills on Jan. 18, 2012, with many shutting down services for the day. Wikipedia and Reddit shut down, whereas Craigslist, Google and others protested by blacking out parts of their sites, asking visitors to sign online petitions and encouraging them to contact members of Congress. As a result of the blackout and unprecedented public response, lawmakers shelved the bills, at least for the time being.

As an online editor, you must be concerned with piracy of both the work you produce and the work you use. In other words, if other media outlets are stealing your stories and using them verbatim, that's an infringement of copyright. Or, as noted in the "Copyright" breakout, if you or one of your reporters posts copyrighted works of others, that's an infringement of copyright, too.

If you discover content from your media site is being unfairly used — without either permission or compensation — you can follow these four steps, all of which are supported by the 1998 Digital Millennium Copyright Act:

1. Contact the website owner and serve notice of the infringement.
2. Send a "take-down notice" to the online service provider.
3. Send a "take-down notice" to the company that registered the site's domain.
4. Send a "take-down notice" to search engines.

Should these steps fail, your next step is to get your attorney involved and potentially file a lawsuit.

- How can I better understand this person's vulnerability and desire for privacy? Can I make a better decision by talking with this person?
- What alternative approaches can I take in my reporting and my storytelling to minimize the harm of privacy invasion while still fulfilling my journalistic duty to inform the public? For instance, can I leave out some "private" matters while still accurately and fairly reporting the story? Or can I focus more on a system failure issue rather than reporting intensely on one individual?[6]

# Ethical Concerns — Codes of Conduct

Many journalistic organizations give their members voice in shaping the professional conduct they expect of themselves, organized into what organizations call their code of ethics. Violations of ethical codes will not draw either imprisonment or fines; however, these codes define how professional journalists should act in the performance of their duties.

The most popular code of ethics belongs to the Society of Professional Journalists. Their code is available online at http://spj.org/ethicscode.asp. The four major admonitions in the code are the following:

**FIGURE 4-2** The Society of Professional Journalists.

- Seek truth and report it.
- Minimize harm.
- Act independently.
- Be accountable.[7]

Other journalistic codes of ethics also are available online:

- American Society of Newspaper Editors Statement of Principles. http://asne.org/content.asp?pl=24&sl=171&contentid=171.
- Associated Press Managing Editors Statement of Ethical Principles. http://www.apme.com/ethics/.
- Code of Ethics and Professional Conduct of the Radio-Television News Directors Association. http://www.rtdna.org/pages/media_items/code-of-ethics-and-professional-conduct48.php.
- Online News Association Values Statement and Code of Ethics. http://journalists.org/wp-content/uploads/2011/09/ona_code_of_ethics_2010_03.pdf
- Society of American Business Editors and Writers Code of Ethics. http://sabew.org/about/codes-of-ethics/sabews-code-of-ethics/

As an editor, you should understand these codes and practice them in your professional lives. At the same time, many of the concerns about ethics and professional behavior would be minimized if editors worried less about whether they *can* do something and more about whether they *should* do something.

# Ethical Concerns — Diversity

As a copy editor, you must be aware of the ethical demands for diversity in stories you handle. Diversity respects the need for multiple perspectives and voices that cut across gender, race, ethnicity, age, religion, culture, sexual orientation and physical, mental and emotional abilities.

Included in the guidelines under "Seek truth and report it" of the SPJ Code of Ethics are provisions that speak to the need for reporting that is diverse and inclusive:

- Tell the story of the diversity and magnitude of the human experience boldly, even when it is unpopular to do so.
- Examine their own cultural values and avoid imposing those values on others.
- Avoid stereotyping by race, gender, age, religion, ethnicity, geography, sexual orientation, disability, physical appearance or social status.
- Support the open exchange of views, even views they find repugnant.
- Give voice to the voiceless; official and unofficial sources of information can be equally valid.

Among online resources that can assist you and reporters in expanding diversity in coverage is the SPJ "Rainbow Diversity Sourcebook" at www.spj.org/divsourcebook.asp.

Using this, you enter search terms or click boxes for the area of expertise you are seeking. Submit the request and the site's database returns appropriate sources.

In addition to sources that represent various perspectives, you need to be vigilant that stories use inclusive language. Language both reflects and determines how we think about people. Inclusive language affirms the value of the many conditions, circumstances or traits that comprise human diversity.

Cut references to a person's sex, race, ethnicity or other personal traits or characteristics — such as gender, sexual orientation, age or a disability — when they are irrelevant to the story. Check for consistency in descriptions of members of a group. Edit story details that single out women to describe their physical beauty or clothing, that note a disabled person's use of some aid or that refer to the race of the only minority member of a group unless it is at his or her request.

A variety of specialized style guides help to address issues of inclusive language. Among those available online are the following:

- Newswatch Diversity style guide: www.ciij.org/publications_media/20111205–95034.pdf

- Gay, lesbian, transsexual and transgender style guide: http://www.nlgja.org/resources/stylebook_english.html

- Disability style guide: http://www.ciij.org/publications_media/20050328–151849.pdf

- Asian-American style guide: http://www.aaja.org/aajahandbook/

- Guidelines for countering racial, ethnic and religious profiling: http://www.spj.org/divguidelines.asp

We will discuss inclusive language further in Chapter 11, "AP Potpourri."

For additional information, consult online editing resources in the Appendix.

# PART 2

# AP Style

## CHAPTER 5

# Abbreviations and Acronyms

*"Editing is both an art and a craft, calling for much patience, an infinite capacity for detail, and even some inspiration. And because editors serve several masters — the publisher, the writer, and the document itself — the task demands a nice balance of self-confidence and humility."*

~Anonymous

Abbreviations are shortened forms of words. Acronyms are specialized abbreviations comprised of words formed from the initial parts of names, often the initial letters. See the difference in the following:

- *Mo.* is the abbreviation for Missouri. The abbreviation usually is pronounced as the full word.

- *UNICEF* is the acronym for United Nations International Children's Emergency Fund, and you pronounce it using all the letters. By the way, while it still carries the same acronym, it is now the United Nations Children's Fund.

- *FBI* is the acronym for the Federal Bureau of Investigation. You pronounce it by sounding out each of the letters.

Both types are handy and sometimes necessary short forms for terms that journalists use. Keep in mind: Seldom are you *required* to use abbreviations or acronyms. Avoid their overuse, especially where the results would be "alphabet soup."

Although this chapter covers the most common categories, check the stylebook for other abbreviations or acronyms.

Remember, too, that these rules apply to both print and online media.

## Academic Degrees — Do not abbreviate

You will frequently be dealing with this style rule if you edit college media or stories about education. Instead of abbreviating, write bachelor's degree, master's degree, doctorate and so on and include the discipline of the degree, if appropriate, as in the following:

- *John earned a master's in psychology while Maria had a doctorate in English.*
- *A bachelor's degree usually is not enough to allow someone to teach college courses.*

## Addresses — Abbreviate Ave., Blvd. and St. only with numbered addresses; spell out all other similar words

The simplest way to apply this rule is to memorize the three that you should abbreviate with numbered addresses — Ave., Blvd. and St. Always write out the rest. In addition, abbreviate compass points only with numbered addresses.

Because addresses are a common method by which journalists help to identify people and to locate places in their stories, you can count on plenty of practice. See how these examples follow the rule:

**FIGURE 5-1**

- *4 Winchester Court*
- *2618 N. Main St.* but *North Main Street*

# Months — Abbreviate months with six or more letters when they are used with a specific date

AP calls for these forms, the same you learned in elementary school:
- *Jan.*
- *Feb.*
- *Aug.*
- *Sept.*
- *Oct.*
- *Nov.*
- *Dec.*

Never abbreviate a month without a date, and abbreviate only the longer months with a date, as in the following:
- *Aug. 10 and Aug. 10, 1962*
- *June 30 and June 30, 2008*

Note that commas always go before and after the year when it is presented with the day, as in the following:
- *Maria Sanchez came to the United States on May 13, 2002, with her parents and two brothers.*

# Organizations — Abbreviate only *after* the story has used the full organization name

Because you can't know that your readers are familiar with all abbreviations and acronyms, this rule ensures that they'll understand and still gives you the freedom to shorten on second reference. Consider this example: *The Country Music Association vision statement says it is "dedicated to bringing the poetry and emotion of Country Music to the world."*[1] *As part of that role, CMA hosts an awards show each June in Nashville, Tenn.*

However, AP style notes exceptions to this rule when organizations are better known by their abbreviations and acronyms. Then, the abbreviation or acronym is acceptable on all references, as in the following examples:
- *CIA*
- *FBI*
- *YMCA*

If you're unsure if an organization is better known by its abbreviation or acronym, look it up in the stylebook.

**FIGURE 5-2** All states except the eight shaded in this map are abbreviated when run with a city.

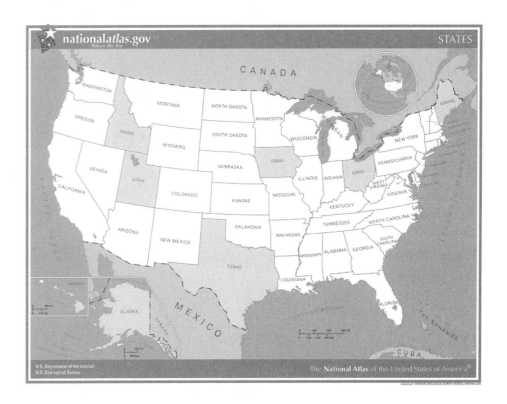

Finally, never put an abbreviation or acronym in parentheses following its full name. If you fear readers will not understand the abbreviation or acronym on second reference, don't use it.

# State Names — Abbreviate all but eight state names, using upper and lower case and set off with commas when used with a city, town or village

This rule expects one of two things: You will either memorize the eight states you shouldn't abbreviate, or you will check the stylebook every time you present a state with a city, town or village.

Here are the eight that you never abbreviate:

- *Alaska*
- *Hawaii*
- *Idaho*
- *Iowa*

- *Maine*
- *Ohio*
- *Texas*
- *Utah*

Don't assume you know the abbreviations of the remaining states. U.S. Postal Service abbreviations are two-letter forms that are all caps without periods. AP abbreviations are upper and lower case and followed by periods. Here are the ones that differ from the postal forms:

- *Ala.*
- *Ariz.*
- *Ark.*
- *Calif.*
- *Colo.*
- *Conn.*
- *Del.*
- *Fla.*
- *Ill.*
- *Ind.*
- *Kan.*
- *Mass.*
- *Mich.*
- *Minn.*
- *Miss.*
- *Mont.*
- *Neb.*
- *Nev.*
- *Okla.*
- *Ore.*
- *Tenn.*
- *Wash.*
- *W.Va.*
- *Wis.*
- *Wyo.*

Finally, whereas first references to cities usually require their state names, the following are examples of city names that can stand alone on first reference within stories:

- *Atlanta*
- *Boston*
- *Chicago*
- *Dallas*
- *Detroit*
- *Houston*
- *Las Vegas*
- *Los Angeles*
- *Miami*
- *Minneapolis*
- *New York*
- *Philadelphia*
- *Pittsburgh*
- *St. Louis*
- *San Francisco*
- *Washington*

The full list of cities that run without their state is in the *datelines* entry in the AP Stylebook.

# Text Messaging

Abbreviated forms from both text messaging and instant messaging are likely to find their way into copy, as in the following:

- *2* — Shortened form of *to* or *too,* as in the following: *I want that song 2.*
- *4* — Shortened form of *for.*
- *BFF* — *Best friend forever.* May be used sarcastically.
- *BRB* — *Be right back.*
- *C* — Shortened form of *see,* as in the following: *C U tonight.* Also may be lowercase.
- *G2G* — *Got to go.*
- *IDK* — *I don't know.*
- *IMO/IMHO* — *In my opinion, in my humble opinion.*

- *LOL — Laugh out loud or laughing out loud.* This suggests a sender considers something funny.
- *NSFW — Not safe for work.* This typically refers to material that is inappropriate for office/workplace reading or viewing, often referring to pornographic material.
- *POS — Parent over shoulder.* Used during an instant message exchange between teenagers and children, this warns that a parent is approaching the sender's computer.
- *R —* Shortened form of *are,* as in, R U ready? Also may be lowercase.
- *ROFL — Rolling on the floor laughing.* A stronger form of LOL.
- *thx, tnx —* Shortened form of *thanks.*
- *U —* Shortened form of *you.*
- *Y —* Shortened form of *why.*

# Titles — Abbreviate and capitalize certain titles when used *before* full names, whether inside or outside direct quotations

You should use such abbreviations only on first reference and drop them thereafter. Six titles follow this rule:

- *Dr.* for *doctor.*
- *Gov.* for *governor.*

- *Lt. Gov.* for *lieutenant governor.*
- *Rep.* for *representative.*
- *the Rev.* for *reverend.* (Note that the article *the* precedes this abbreviation for *reverend.* Also, this is the only abbreviation used for religious titles.)
- *Sen.* for *senator.*

This rule also applies to some military designations — and, consequently, to both police and fire department ranks — as in the following examples:

- *Gen.* for *general.*
- *Sgt. Maj.* for *sergeant major.*
- *Pfc.* for *private first class.*
- *Rear Adm.* for *rear admiral.*
- *Staff Sgt.* for *staff sergeant.*
- *Cpl.* for *corporal.*

Refer to the stylebook entry *military titles* for a full list of military ranks and their abbreviations, if any.

The stylebook is steadfast in its effort to discourage use of courtesy titles — *Mr., Miss, Mrs., Ms.* The rare exceptions are for direct quotation or when a woman requests it. See the *courtesy titles* entry in the stylebook for further guidance.

As you deal with questions involving capitalization of titles in stories, refer also to Chapter 6, "Capitalization."

# Political Parties

When giving political party affiliation of members of Congress and state legislatures, AP allows use of a short form. That begins with the party abbreviation as a single capitalized letter, with no period, using the following: *D* for Democrat, *R* for Republication and *I* for Independent.

For members of Congress, the party abbreviation is followed by a hyphen and home state — abbreviated following the preceding guidelines — and enclosed in commas, as in the following: *Sen. Christopher "Kit" Bond, R-Mo., was first elected to the Senate in 1986.*

For state legislators, the party abbreviation is followed by home city, as in the following: *Rep. Timothy Jones, R-Eureka, was the speaker of the Missouri House of Representatives in 2012.*

*GOP* is an acceptable form for the *Republican Party*, but only on second reference.

# Others

The following cover some common abbreviations and acronyms that fall outside of the previous categories:

- Never abbreviate *attorney general.*
- Abbreviate and capitalize *Jr.* or *Sr.* following an individual's full name on first reference, and don't use commas to separate either term from the name, as in *Martin Luther King Jr.*

**FIGURE 5-4** Republican Party logo.

**FIGURE 5-5** Democratic Party logo.

- Abbreviate the terms *Co.*, *Corp.*, *Inc.* and *Ltd.* following the corporate entity's name, and don't use commas to separate the terms from the names, as in *the Coca-Cola Co.*, *Microsoft Corp*, *Apple Inc.* and *Schlumberger Ltd.* A recent AP change: *Wal-Mart Stores Inc.* is the official name of the company, but *Walmart* is the style to use for its retail stores. When *corporation* is in a name any place besides the end, don't abbreviate, as in *the Corporation for Public Broadcasting*. See the stylebook entry *company names* for a listing of 125 major U.S. companies.
- Never abbreviate *department*.
- Never abbreviate *fort* in names of cities and military installations, as in *Fort Smith, Ark.,* or *Fort Leonard Wood, Mo.*
- *GPA* in all caps is an acceptable form for *grade point average*, but only on second reference.
- Use *mpg*, as in *miles per gallon*; *mph*, as in *miles per hour*; and *kph*, as in *kilometers per hour*. The abbreviations, lowercased without periods, are acceptable in all references.

- Abbreviate *saint* in names of saints, cities and other places, as in *St. Francis of Assisi*, *St. Louis* and *Mount St. Mary's College*. Two exceptions are *Saint John* and *Sault Ste. Marie*.
- *TV*, as in *television*, is all caps without periods and is acceptable in all references, whether it is a noun or adjective.
- *United States* — The abbreviation *U.S.* is acceptable as either a noun or adjective in all references. Use periods when abbreviating in text but no periods in headlines.

For abbreviations not here or in the AP Stylebook, use the first abbreviation in Webster's New World College Dictionary.

For additional information, consult online editing resources in the Appendix.

# ABBREVIATIONS AND ACRONYMS *exercise 1*

**DIRECTIONS:** Correct *abbreviations and acronyms* errors in the following exercises. Some may be correct. Check the spelling of all names in the Heartland Directory.

1. Heartland, Missouri, is proud of its heritage as a political and cultural center in the state and its reputation as one of the 100 best small towns in the U.S.

2. The city is near the geographic center of the state, which is about one mi. west of High Point, an unincorporated community 50 miles south of Heartland in southern Moniteau Cty.

3. Doctor Andrea Olson, Heartland Chamber of Commerce president, frequently boasts about the area's largest employer, Heartland Widgets Incorporated, which has its corporate headquarters and main manufacturing facility in the city.

4. The company has distribution centers in Garden City, Ks.; Franklin, Kent.; Mena, Ark.; and Hamburg, Ia.

5. In addition, Dr. Olsen cites other national corporations that have regional offices in the community, including Coca-Cola Co., ConAgra Foods Incorporated, Dell Inc., MetLife Incorporated and Whirlpool Corporation.

6. Because Heartland is only 30 miles from the state capital in Jefferson City, regular visiting VIPs are Governor Jay Nixon and Lieutenant Gov. Peter Kinder.

7. Well-known residents of the city are Reverend Amanda Quitman, a popular national radio evangelist; retired U.S. Sen. Alvin Rand, D.-Missouri; best-selling romance novelist Elizabeth Karr; and national skateboarding champion William E. "Willie" Evinger Jr.

8. Heartland also has more museums per capita than any other city outside of New York City, N.Y., and Boston, MA.

9. Not surprisingly, December is the busiest month for the community, mostly because of its annual Xmas parade, which officials claim is the biggest in the Midwest.

10. The city can also claim to be the smallest in the country with a network T.V. station, KHTD-TV, an ABC affiliate.

**Additional exercises are available online at** www.oup.com/us/rosenauer.

## CHAPTER 6

# Capitalization

*"English grammar is 'common-law,' not constitutional —
it's a veritable hackle-schmackle of dribs and drabs."*

~James Harbeck

Capitalization covers a good deal of territory. For the most part, AP advises against capitalizing any more than you must. Instead, follow the basic principle of capitalizing proper names and proper nouns. These are nouns that name a particular person, place or thing and include the common nouns that are an integral part of the name, as in the following:

- *Bill, Marian, Patrick, Sarah*

- *General Motors, Verizon, Marlboro, First Street Graphics*

- *Ethiopia, United States, Missouri, Heartland*

- *Missouri River, Bannister Mall, South Carolina, Faraon Street*

Although you're likely to learn how to capitalize terms you use frequently, your best bet is regularly to check the stylebook.

Few of you have problems capitalizing words that are proper nouns. However, the following cover AP entries for some of the terms that may *not* follow the basic principle mentioned previously.

**FIGURE 6-1**

# Addresses

Capitalize *Avenue, Alley, Boulevard, Circle, Drive, Road, Street, Terrace* and the like when used as part of a formal street name. Lowercase when used alone or with two or more streets, as in the following: *Sixth Street* but *Sixth and Seventh streets* or *Frederick Boulevard* but *Frederick and Noyes boulevards.*

# Agencies

The general principle that AP applies to agencies, especially state and local agencies, is that you always capitalize them if they are the formal name of the agency, whether or not the reference includes their location, as in the following:

- *Heartland Police Department* and *Police Department* (referring to the Heartland department), but lowercase *police* or *department*
- *Missouri State Highway Patrol*, *State Highway Patrol*, and *Highway Patrol* (referring to the Missouri agency), but lowercase *patrol* or *a highway patrol*
- *Heartland City Council* and *City Council* (referring to the Heartland council), but lowercase *the council, council members, city councils*
- *Heartland School District* and *School District* (referring to the Heartland district)

Note that you should capitalize the terms *city* and *state* only when part of proper names. Used alone or as simple modifiers that indicate the level of jurisdiction, the two always are lowercase, as in the following: *state auditor's office, state of Missouri, city funds, city government, city of Heartland.*

Beyond these, check specific entries in the stylebook to confirm usage.

# Buildings

Capitalize the proper name of a building, including the terms *building*, *tower*, *center* or other common nouns when they are part of the formal name, as in the following:

- *Flatiron Building*
- *Coit Tower*
- *Taj Mahal*
- *Chrysler Building*
- *Space Needle*
- *John Hancock Center*

Never abbreviate *building* or the other such terms.

# Compositions — Names of Books, Movies, Television Programs and Other Works

AP calls these *compositions*. Capitalize (and enclose in quotation marks) the main words in names of books, movies, plays, songs, poems, works of art, radio and TV programs and similar things.

Follow several basic guidelines for capitalization of composition titles:

- Capitalize the main words, including prepositions and conjunctions with four letters or more.
- Capitalize articles *the, a* and *an* as well as words shorter than four letters when they are the first or last words in titles.

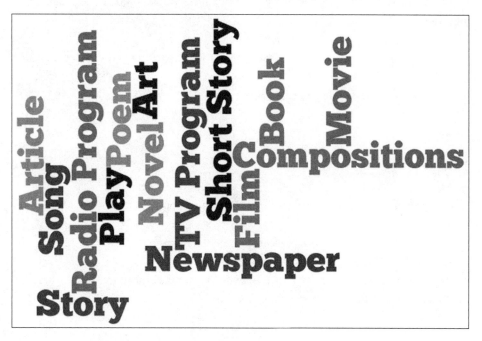

**FIGURE 6-2** A variety of publications comprise what AP considers compositions.

- Enclose all titles in quotation marks *except* the following: almanacs, the Bible, dictionaries, directories, encyclopedias, gazetteers, handbooks, magazines, newspapers, software and the like.

See how the guidelines apply to the following examples:

- "The Grapes of Wrath," "Rabbit Run," "South of Broad"
- "Gone With the Wind," "The Longest Day," "Harry Potter and the Half-Blood Prince"
- "My Fair Lady," "The Glass Menagerie," "Mama Mia"
- "Sentimental Journey," "I Want To Hold Your Hand," "Keeps Gettin' Better"
- "The Mona Lisa," "American Gothic," "Nighthawks"
- "Captain Midnight," "Hopalong Cassidy," "Prairie Home Companion"
- "The Andy Griffith Show," "Lost," "Law & Order: Special Victims Unit"

For further guidance, particularly in the use of quotation marks for composition titles, see Chapter 16, "Quotation Marks, Question Marks and Exclamation Points," or the AP entry for *composition titles.*

# Congress

Capitalize *U.S. Congress* and *Congress* (standing alone) when referring to that body. However, *congressional* is lowercase unless part of a formal title, as in *"Congressional Record."*

# Constitution

Capitalize *Constitution* with or without the *U.S.* in all references to the *U.S. Constitution.* Capitalize the term only with the name of a state or nation in all other uses, such as the following:

- *Missouri Constitution, French Constitution*
- *Surprisingly, a constitution quite similar to the U.S. Constitution is that of the Russian Federation, written in 1993.*

Lowercase *constitutional* in all uses.

# Department

Lowercase names of academic departments, except for proper nouns and adjectives, as in the following:

- *history department* and *department of history*
- *English department* and *department of English*

Capitalize the formal names of government departments, including those where the title is flopped and the *of* is dropped, as in the following:

- *Department of Agriculture, Agriculture Department*
- *Missouri Department of Revenue, Missouri Revenue Department*

Lowercase department when it is a modifier for academic titles, as in the following:

- *department Chairman Jahi Mangua*

# Directions and Regions

Lowercase compass directions: *north, south, east, west, southern Missouri, eastern Idaho, western United States.*

Capitalize specific geographic regions, as in the following:

- *The North defeated the South in the Civil War.*
- *Flannery O'Connor is a Southern writer.*
- *He spent time in the Midwest before traveling south.*
- *Courageous pioneers settled the Old West.*
- *The wind was blowing west across South St. Paul.*

# Fields of Study

Although schools at every level may capitalize the different fields of study or subjects in their curriculum, these always should be lowercase unless they are proper nouns, as in the following: *algebra homework, chemistry book, English studies, French class, history major, law courses, math tutor, psychology enrollments, Russian literature* and the like.

# Foods

Most foods are lowercase, except when a proper noun is part of its name, as in *Italian dressing, Waldorf salad* and the like. However, some entries like *french fries* and *manhattan cocktail* are lowercase because, as the stylebook says, they don't depend on a proper noun or adjective for their meaning.

Note that a handy feature of the online AP Stylebook is the *Food Style* category accessed by clicking *View Style Categories* on the home page. A pull-down menu gives quick access to more than 275 food entries, ranging from *a la carte* to *zip-close bag*. Each entry covers capitalization and punctuation.

# Heavenly Bodies

Capitalize the names of planets, stars, constellations and so on, as in *Jupiter, Betelgeuse, Canis Major,* and the *Big Dipper.* However, lowercase the name of our star, the *sun.* With comets capitalize only the proper noun element, as in *comet Hale-Boppe* or *Halley's comet.*

# Historical Periods and Events

Capitalize names of accepted epochs in archaeology, geology and history, as in the following:

- *the Bronze Age*
- *the Dark Ages*
- *the Middle Ages*

Also capitalize popular periods and events, as in the following:

- *the Exodus* (referring to the Jewish departure from Egypt)
- *the Renaissance*
- *the Boston Tea Party*
- *Prohibition*
- *the Great Depression*

Lowercase century, as in *the 21st century.*

Lowercase *ice age* and similar items because they do not refer to a single period.

# Indians

Preferred terms for those in the United States are *American Indian* or *Native American,* but it's better to specify the name of the tribe, as in the following:

- *Her father is a Cherokee chief.*
- *Jarod's great-great-grandfather was a Chippewa.*

# Legislature

Capitalize when a state name precedes it. Retain capitalization when the reference is to a particular state legislature, as in the following:

- *The Missouri Legislature overrode the governor's veto. In response, the governor lashed out against the Legislature.*

Lowercase generic and plural uses of legislature, as in *midwestern legislatures.*

# Online References

The much greater use of email and the World Wide Web means that journalists will more frequently find references to them in copy they write and edit. This is especially true if you are editing online media, of course.

Some of the more common AP entries you should check are as follows:

- *email*
- *domain names*
- *home page* [Two words, lowercase.]
- *Internet*
- *text, texting, texted*
- *text messaging* (See Chapter 5, "Abbreviations and Acronyms," or the stylebook entry *text messaging/instant messaging*.)
- *URL* (Acronym for *Uniform Resource Location* or *Internet address*.)
- *Web*
- *website* (One word, lowercase.)
- *Web page*
- *webcast* (One word, lowercase.)
- *webmaster* (One word, lowercase.)

# Plurals

In all plural uses, lowercase common noun elements, as in the following:

- *Democratic and Republican parties*
- *Massachusetts and Pennsylvania avenues*
- *departments of Labor and Justice*
- *Central and Northeast high schools*

See Chapter 8, "Plurals," for additional guidance.

# Political Parties

Capitalize both the name and the word *party* when part of the organization's name: *Democratic Party, Republican Party* and the like. Capitalize the following, and similar usages, when they refer to a specific party or its members:

- *America First Party*
- *Communist*
- *Conservative*
- *Democrat*
- *Liberal*
- *Peace and Freedom Party*
- *Republican*
- *Socialist*

Lowercase political philosophies, such as the following:

- *communism*
- *communist*
- *conservative*
- *fascism*
- *fascist*
- *liberal*

# Religious References

Capitalize proper names of monotheistic, pagan and mythological deities, as in the following:

- *God*
- *Allah*
- *Vishnu*
- *Jesus Christ*
- *the Father*
- *the Son*
- *the Holy Spirit*
- *the Chosen One*
- *Apollo*
- *Pallas Athena*

Lowercase *god* or *goddess* when referring to polytheistic deities. Also, lowercase all pronouns that refer to deities.

# Room

Capitalize *room* when the reference includes its number, as in *Room 222 of Taylor Hall.*

# Seasons

Lowercase *fall*, *winter*, *spring* and *summer* unless part of a formal name, as in *Winter Olympics* or *Spring Fling.*

# Time

Capitalize *Central Daylight Time* and similar; however, lowercase *standard time* when it is alone. Lowercase and use periods with no space for *a.m.* and *p.m.* Check the stylebook entry *time zones* for additional guidance.

Avoid the redundancy of *1 p.m. in the afternoon* and similar phrases; use one or the other following context, but prefer *a.m.* and *p.m.* because each is shorter.

# Titles

Capitalize formal titles before a name, but lowercase all titles in other uses, including when commas set off the name, as in the following:

- *Cooper County Prosecuting Attorney Aaron R. Smith*, but lowercase *Aaron R. Smith, Cooper County prosecuting attorney*
- *Pope Benedict XVI*, but lowercase *the pope* or *the pontiff* (which is always lowercase because it's not a formal title)
- *defense attorney Paul Peters*
- *professor Wilhelmina Nivens* (AP says to lowercase all uses of *professor* except *Professor Emeritus* when used before a name.)
- *The Heartland police chief, Chris Anderson, said that. . . .*

For additional guidance, see Chapter 10, "Titles," or the *composition titles* entry in the stylebook.

# Other Entries of Interest

Consult the following specific entries in the stylebook for additional guidance:

| | |
|---|---|
| *animals* | *legislature* |
| *brand names* | *months* |
| *building* | *monuments* |
| *committee* | *nationalities and races* |
| *Congress* | *nicknames* |
| *datelines* | *non-U.S. governmental bodies* |
| *days of the week* | *non-U.S. legislative bodies* |
| *directions and regions* | *organizations and institutions* |
| *family names* | *planets* |
| *food* | *plants* |
| *geographic names* | *police department* |
| *governmental bodies* | *religious references* |
| *heavenly bodies* | *seasons* |
| *historical periods and events* | *trademarks* |
| *holidays and holy days* | *unions* |

# CAPITALIZATION *exercise 1*

**DIRECTIONS**: Correct *capitalization* errors in the following exercises. Some may be correct. Check the spelling of all names in the Heartland Directory.

**1.** The first Winter snowstorm swept into the midwest Friday, and Heartland caught the brunt of it.

**2.** Snow began falling early Friday and had left 12 inches before ending in most areas around 3 P.M.

**3.** The national weather service issued a winter weather advisory by 10 a.m. Friday, calling for strong winds and bitter cold through Saturday.

**4.** The Heartland Public Works Department has been working nonstop since 4 a.m. Friday on emergency snow routes throughout the City.

**5.** "We probably won't begin clearing residential streets until Saturday morning," assistant Public Works director Tommy Lance said, "Because of the strong winds drifting snow back over the emergency routes."

**6.** The Heartland police department said that most drivers were doing a good job handling the wintry weather, though several minor accidents were reported.

**7.** "A real problem area was the intersection at ninth and Douglas Streets because of the steepness of the grade," said Capt. Earl Bryant, department shift commander.

**8.** Anna Graves, Heartland Memorial Hospital Public Relations Director, said that the Emergency Room stayed busy with various weather-related injuries, the most serious of which was a heart attack suffered by a 77-year-old Heartland man.

**9.** Friday classes had been canceled late Thursday for the Heartland school district, as well as for outlying schools, in anticipation of the heavy snow.

**10.** Hy-Vee Stock Clerk Stanley Kramer said that customers had cleared most staples from the shelves by early afternoon Friday, and snow shovels and ice melt were hard to find anywhere in town.

**Additional exercises are available online at** www.oup.com/us/rosenauer.

## CHAPTER 7

# Numerals

*"I fear three newspapers more than a hundred thousand bayonets."*

~Napoleon

In your everyday writing, your use of numerals likely is something you think little about. Standard American grammar isn't much concerned with whether you write "$2.00," "$2," "two dollars" or even "2 dollars."

However, as with most aspects of AP style, how you present numerals as a journalist is much more regulated, with the standard style goal that all journalists do it the same way. Fortunately, a handful of guidelines can cover most numerals.

The granddaddy of all numerals guidelines is quite simple: Write out numbers less than 10 but use figures for 10 and above. The only trick here is that this old timer has exceptions, most of which are covered in the next section.

## Exceptions to Less-Than-10 Rule

Write out numbers less than 10, but use figures for the following exceptions.

- Addresses — Always use figures for address numbers, as in the following:
  - ▶ *4 Winchester Court*

- Ages of people, places and things
  - ▸ *His son will be 6 in August.*
  - ▸ *Fire destroyed the 4-year-old building.*
  - ▸ *My shoes were only 2 years old.*
- Cents — Always use figures with cents; write out and lowercase cents rather than use the ¢ symbol, as in the following:
  - ▸ *A pack of chewing gum once cost 5 cents.*
  - ▸ *Here's my 2 cents worth of advice.*
- Dates — Always use figures without *nd, rd, st* or *th*, as in the following:
  - ▸ *President Roosevelt told the nation that Dec. 7, 1941, is a day that will live in infamy.*
  - ▸ *His birthday is April 13.*
- Dimensions — Always use figures; write out and lowercase the dimension reference (inches, feet, yards, kilometers and so on), as in the following:
  - ▸ *The woman was 7 feet 1 inch tall.*
  - ▸ *She was a 7-foot 1-inch woman.*
  - ▸ *A standard print size for photographs was 5 by 7 inches.*
  - ▸ *Make sure you buy a 5-by-7 frame for that photo.*
  - ▸ *The storm dumped 8 inches of rain on the metro.*

Note: AP style cautions that the use of the apostrophe to indicate feet and quote marks to indicate inches, as in 6'2", is acceptable only in technical contexts.

- Dollars — Always use figures and the $ symbol, except for casual references, as in the following:
  - ▸ *The price of a ticket for the early bird movie is $7.50.*

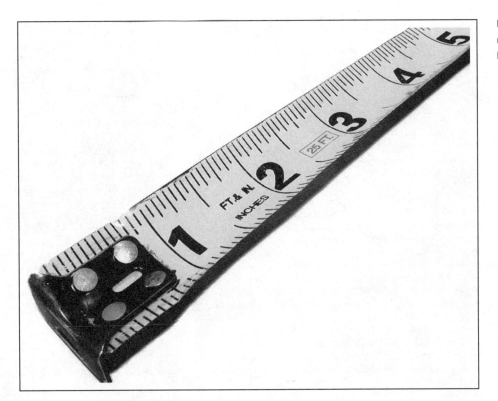

**FIGURE 7-2** If one can physically measure something, the stylebook has guidelines for how to write it.

► *Give me a buck and the sandwich is yours.*

► *The dollar is no longer the strongest currency in the world.*

Note: For whole dollars do not use double zeroes, as in the following:

► *The total bill for dinner came to $22.*

• Highways — Always use figures and capitalize the highway designation, as in the following:

► *U.S. Highway 36 runs across northern Missouri.*

► *The improvements to U.S. 36 during the past 10 years have been significant.*

► *Interstate 70 runs a slight diagonal route across Missouri, from Kansas City on the west to St. Louis on the east.*

► *Many baseball fans recall the I-70 World Series in 1985 when the Royals beat the Cardinals four games to three.* (Note that abbreviating interstate, as in I-70, is acceptable only on second reference.)

Note: When a letter is part of a highway designation, capitalize the letter and do not use a hyphen, as in the following:

► *We traveled the entire length of a scenic coastal highway, State Route A1A, from Key West to Callahan, Fla.*

• Percentages — Always use figures and, as needed, use decimals rather than fractions; write out and lowercase *percent* (which is one word), as in the following:

► *Employees at Twain State University received a 3 percent salary increase.*

► *The unemployment rate for the state rose in July to 9.3 percent.*

Note: For percentages under 1, precede the decimal with a zero, as in the following:

► *The July jobless figure represented a 0.6 percent jump over the previous month.*

**FIGURE 7-3** The stylebook offers clear guidance for using numerals that deal with temperature.

- Proportions — Always use figures without punctuation, as in the following:
  - ▶ *Thomas Alva Edison was the one who said that genius is 1 part inspiration to 99 parts perspiration.*
- Scores — Always use figures, with a hyphen between winning and losing scores, as in the following:
  - ▶ *The Kansas City Royals shut out the St. Louis Cardinals 11–0 in the last game of the 1985 World Series.*
  - ▶ *Tiger Woods struggled to win the match with a 1-under-par score.*
- Speeds — Always use figures, as in the following:
  - ▶ *Her car crept along at 3 mph; even the wind was faster at 6 mph.*

Note: Avoid long, hyphenated speed constructions, as in the following:

  - ▶ *Avoid — The 137-mile-per-hour speed of the winner at the 2010 Daytona 500 was in a Chevrolet driven by Jamie McMurray.*
  - ▶ *Prefer — The winner at the 2010 Daytona 500 was Jamie McMurray, who drove an average speed of 137 mph.*

- Temperatures — Always use figures, but write out *zero*; use the word *degrees* rather than the symbol ° and the word *minus* rather than the minus sign for temperatures below zero, as in the following:
  - ▶ *The high for today will be 9 degrees following an overnight low of minus 7.*
  - ▶ *A 4-degree increase in the average worldwide temperature could melt Greenland's glaciers.*
  - ▶ *Wind chill can become dangerous when temperatures drop below zero.*

Note: Do not use apostrophes with temperatures, as in the following:

  - ▶ *The average temperature in Heartland, Mo., during July 2012 was 72 degrees, well below the usual averages in the upper 80s.*

- Times — Always use figures except for *noon* and *midnight*, which are preferred references; use colons to separate hours from minutes, but avoid the double-zero at the top of the hour; and a.m. or p.m. require periods, as in the following:
  - ▶ *He had been ready for his 11 a.m. appointment since 9:15 a.m.*
  - ▶ *Betty preferred eating lunch at noon and certainly no later than 12:30 p.m.*

Note: Although the usage *9 o'clock* may be acceptable, AP style prefers a.m. or p.m.

Also, avoid the redundancy of *3:30 p.m. in the afternoon*. Although *3:30 in the afternoon* may be acceptable, AP style prefers the shorter form.

# Numbers Beginning Sentences

Write out all numbers that begin sentences *except* for years. This guideline is fairly simple and straightforward, as in the following:

- *Twenty-five dollars was the average price for those shoes.*
- *1968 was the year Robert Kennedy was assassinated.*

At times you may wish to change the sentence to avoid some long number constructions, as in the following:

- Avoid — *Three hundred and thirty-five thousand dollars was the cost for the house overlooking Table Rock Lake.*
- Prefer — *The cost for the house overlooking Table Rock Lake was $335,000.*

# Fractions

Spell out amounts less than one and use hyphens between the words, as in the following:

- *one-half*
- *seven-eighths*

Use figures for numbers larger than one and put a space between the whole number and the fraction, as in the following:

- *2 1/2 cups*
- *5 7/8 inches*

# Millions, Billions

Use figures and the terms *million* or *billion* and decimals to no more than two places rather than writing out all figures in large numbers, as in the following:

- *1 million votes* versus *1,000,000 votes.*
- *$3.75 billion* versus *$3,750,000,000.*

Note that a hyphen is not used to join the number and *million* or *billion*, as in the following:

- *The Missouri Legislature settled on a $23 billion budget for 2010.*

# Ordinal and Cardinal Numbers

Ordinal numbers indicate the order in a ranked sequence or series and follow the mega-rule given at the beginning of this chapter, as in the following:

- *fifth*
- *22nd*
- *333rd*

Cardinal numbers, such as *5, 22 or 333*, are used in counting to indicate quantity or in identification but do not indicate order. For guidelines involving cardinal numbers not covered here, consult specific entries in the "AP Stylebook," including those listed following:

- *act numbers*
- *aircraft names*
- *amendments to the Constitution*
- *betting odds*
- *century*
- *channel*
- *chapters*
- *congressional districts*
- *course numbers*
- *court decisions*
- *court names*
- *decades*
- *decimal units*
- *district*
- *earthquakes*
- *election returns*
- *fleet*
- *formula*
- *handicaps (sports)*
- *latitude and longitude*
- *mile*
- *No. (as in No. 1 or No. 2 and so on)*
- *page numbers*
- *parallels*
- *political divisions*
- *ratios*
- *recipes*
- *room numbers*
- *scene numbers*
- *serial numbers*
- *sizes*
- *spacecraft designations*
- *telephone numbers*
- *weights*
- *years*

## ONLINE INSIGHTS > "GOOGLE IT"

The term google has become ubiquitous, often interchanged with "searching the Web." No wonder, since it is the leading search engine and so much more. Consider the following additional Google services — all of which are free to use.

**Google AdSense** — Google's online advertising network that allows content publishers to embed a piece of code to display Google ads on their sites. The ads are selected based on the content of the page. Ad revenue is split between Google and the publisher in an undisclosed proportion, generally believed to be two-thirds to the publisher.

**Google AdWords** — Google's text-based flagship advertising product, which provides the lion's share of the company revenue. Ads are displayed on Google's own sites based on search terms that users type in, and advertisers pay only when the users click on them. The search terms, called keywords, are purchased by advertisers.

**Google Buzz** — Buzz is Google's attempt to counter Twitter and Facebook by leveraging the social graphs from users' email accounts. A more sophisticated version of Gmail "status updates," Buzz allows users to post updates about what they are doing, link to what they are reading and post their current locations. The service can integrate with other Google services, as well as feed into Twitter.

**Google Docs** — A free online service offered by Google, comprising word processing, spreadsheet, presentation and other software, all of which is "in the cloud." Users can work collaboratively on documents, editing them simultaneously.

**Google Earth** — This site allows you to travel through a virtual globe and see satellite imagery, maps, terrain, 3-D buildings and the like.

**Google Images** — This Google search service indexes more than 10 billion images from websites around the world.

**Google Maps** — This Web-based mapping service powers many map-based services, including Google's Maps website, Google Ride Finder, Google Transit and maps embedded on many third-party websites. In addition to providing street maps, Google Maps offers a route planner and urban business locator.

**Google News** — Google News is a computer-generated news aggregation site that locates news stories from media around the world and groups similar stories according to readers' personalized interests.

**Google Translate** — This free translation service provides instant translations between 58 languages, including words, sentences and Web pages.

**Google URL Shortener** — Comparable in most ways to the longstanding service at bitly.com. Both are free, both shorten long URLs for microblogging and both offer data about who has clicked the shorter URL, including their countries, their browsers, their operating systems and where they were referred from (such as twitter.com).

**Google Videos** — Similar to Google Images, users can search for and watch millions of videos with this service, including TV shows, movie clips, music videos, documentaries and personal videos.

**Google Wave** — An online collaborative space introduced by Google in which people can communicate and work together in real time; it resembles a "souped up Instant Messenger." Participants can add rich text, images, attachments, videos and maps to create a multimedia collaboration. A playback option allows new users to get up to speed on projects and creates an environment that is both real-time and asynchronous.

*— Some of the preceding content from "A Roadmap for Journalism x Technology," Version 1.0, released June 22, 2010, under a Creative Commons Attribution Share-Alike 3.0 License.*

# Math and Conversions for Editors

Just because a reporter plugs numbers into a story doesn't mean you accept them on faith. Check the math.

One of the most common errors in stories is that numbers don't add up. Checking those can be as simple as counting the names of victims in a story that says six people died in an auto accident. A little more demanding — though still easy to check — is a budget story that says the City Council awarded $135,000 in block grants to six local agencies. First, count the number of agencies in the story to confirm that six are listed. Second, add the awards made to each to be sure the total matches what the reporter wrote.

## Percentages and Decimals

If you get a bit queasy when the subject of percentages comes up, you're not alone. Nevertheless, percentages are vital in many stories, especially because percentages often are clearer in the minds of readers than the real numbers of things.

To convert percentages to decimals, remember that 100 percent is 1.00. Thus, any percentage smaller than 100 percent will be less than that number. Take the percentage and move the decimal two places to the left. So, 59 percent becomes .59, and 212 percent becomes 2.12.

When you're working with decimals, you typically should round up or down to only two places because most figures in journalism don't need more critical focus. So, .7544 will be .75, and 2.4876519 will be 2.49.

Caution: A 200 percent increase is not double the amount; it's triple. Remember that a 100 percent increase adds to an item to itself. So, if the number of hoodies sold at the campus bookstore increased 200 percent this semester over last, and last semester it sold 367, then the total this semester is 1,101 (367 times three).

- *To figure the actual number for a percentage of something, change the percentage to a decimal and multiply times the item.*

    For example, if teens bought 58 percent of the 132,000 songs sold on iTunes last month, that number would be 76,560 (132,000 times .58).

- *To figure one thing as a percentage of another, divide the first by the second and multiply by 100.*

    For example, let's say you want the percentage of freshmen among students at Heartland Christian School. Freshmen number 200, and the total number of students is 650. So the answer is 30.77 percent (200 divided by 650 = .30769 times 100). Thus, a story might read, "About 30 percent of the students at the high school are freshmen."

- *To figure the percentage change from one item to another, calculate the difference and divide it by the first item.*

    For example, say the total number of children in Heartland Christian School was 550 last year, whereas the total this year is 650. So the change was 18.18 percent (650 minus 550 = 100 divided by 550 = .1818 × 100). In this case, a story might read, "Enrollment at Heartland Christian increased just over 18 percent this year."

- *If you know that one number increased by a certain percentage and you want to know the increased number, multiply the number by [the percentage plus 100 percent, converted to decimals].*

    For example, if the total number of children at Heartland Christian School is 650 this year, and the principal believes the enrollment will increase 12 percent next year, next year's enrollment should be 728 (650 times [12% + 100% or 1.12] = 728).

- *To figure the new amount if you know that original amount decreased by a certain percentage, multiply the original by <100 percent minus the percentage>.*

    For example, if the total number of children at Heartland Christian School is 650 this year, but school officials are preparing for a 9 percent drop in enrollment, next year there should be 591 students (650 times [100% – 9% or .91] = 591.5). By the way, it's typical in such stories to use just the whole number and drop the decimal. We all know there's no such thing as half a student.

## Averages

Two kinds of averages are commonly found in stories, the mean and the median:

- *Mean is the arithmetic average — the one with which most of you are familiar — and is figured by adding up all the numbers and dividing by the number of numbers. For* example, the number of runs scored by the baseball team in its first five games is 6, 2, 0, 9 and 5. These total 22. Divide by 5 (the number of numbers) and the average number of runs scored is 4.4.

- *Median, on the other hand, is the middle value in a series of numbers* and is quite useful when a series has some considerably higher and/or lower numbers. *To figure the median, write all the numbers in order from low to high, add 1 to the total number of numbers and divide by 2. This will be the median number.* Thus, the median score for the ball team just mentioned is 5 (5 + 1, then divided by 2 = third number in the low-to-high series of 0, 2, 5, 6, 9).

## Distance, Time and Rate

Distance, time and rate are common in stories. First, make sure your numbers are consistent; that is, you're comparing apples to apples, so to speak. For example, if your rate is in miles per hour, then your distance needs to be miles and the time needs to be hours.

Consider the following common conversion formulas:

- If time is minutes, you must convert it to hours first with this formula:
  *Hours = minutes divided by 60.*
     So, 45 minutes divided by 60 equals .75 hour, and one hour 20 minutes, or 80 minutes divided by 60 equals 1.33 hours.
- To convert kilometers to miles, use this formula:
  *Miles = kilometers multiplied by .62.*
     Thus, 40 kilometers multiplied by .62 equals 24.8 miles.
- To convert miles to kilometers, use this formula:
  *Kilometers = miles multiplied by 1.61.*
     Therefore, 50 miles multiplied by 1.61 equals 80.5 kilometers.
- Use the following formulas to compute distance, time and rate.
  *Distance = rate multiplied by time.*
     If a vehicle is traveling 50 mph for 35 minutes, then *first* convert the minutes to hours (35 divided by 60 equals .58). Then, multiply 50 times .58 to get 29 miles, the distance the vehicle would travel in 35 minutes.
  *Time = distance divided by rate.*
     To find how long it will take for a vehicle traveling 30 mph to go five miles, divide five by 30 to get .17 (that's .1666666666 rounded up). To change that portion of an hour to minutes, multiply .17 by 60 to get 10.2 minutes. In most stories, it would be appropriate to write "just over 10 minutes."
  *Rate = distance divided by time.*
     To find the rate — or speed — a vehicle is traveling, divide the distance by the time, as in 110 miles divided by two hours 15 minutes (2.25) equals 48.89 mph. Such an exact rate would be unnecessary for most stories, so writing "nearly 50 mph" likely would be acceptable.

## Area Measurements

Area measurements — including perimeter, area and circumference — are another common element in a variety of stories.

Perimeter is the distance around a figure:

- *Perimeter = the total of a figure's sides.*

  So, a rectangle that is 45 feet by 20 feet would have a perimeter of 130 feet (45 + 45 + 20 + 20). The perimeter of a triangle that is 7 feet by 9 feet by 12 feet is 28 feet (7 + 9 + 12). The perimeter of a regular polygon (a figure with three or more straight and equal-length sides connected end to end) that is 5 feet on each of its five sides is 25 feet (5 + 5 + 5 + 5 + 5).

  Area is the amount of surface a two-dimensional figure covers and is given in square units, such as square feet or square miles.

- *Area of rectangles and squares = length times width.*

  Thus, the area of a rectangle that is 4 yards long and 7 yards wide is 28 square yards (4 times 7 = 28). Similarly, the area of a square that measures 12 feet on each side is 144 square feet (12 times 12 = 144).

- *Area of triangles = one-half the product of the base times height.*

  Therefore, the area of a triangle with a base of 6 and a height of 9 would be 27 (6 times 9 = 54 divided by 2).

  Circumference is the perimeter of a circle. Diameter is the length of a straight line that extends from the edges of a circle through its center. Radius is half the diameter. Part of the formula here involves pi (pronounced "pie"), which is a fixed number, 3.14.

- *Circumference = radius squared times pi (3.14).*

  So, the perimeter of a circle with a diameter of 8 feet would be 50.24 square feet (8 divided by 2 = 4, 4 × 4 = 16, 16 × 3.14 = 50.24).

  For additional information, consult online editing resources in the Appendix.

# NUMERALS *exercise 1*

**DIRECTIONS:** Correct *numeral* errors in the following exercises. Some may be correct. Check the spelling of all names in the Heartland Directory.

1. A six-year-old boy was reported missing from his home around 3:00 p.m. Friday, according to Heartland Police.

2. Sean Addington had been playing with 2 neighborhood children outside his home at 308 Floyd Ave. when his mother, Jean, noticed he was missing.

3. After checking with neighborhood children, who said that they had not seen Sean since 2:30 p.m. that afternoon, Jean Addington searched the area.

4. Unable to locate him, she phoned police, who dispatched three squad cars from the Second and Third precincts.

5. Officers searched a twelve-block area around the home but failed to locate the boy.

6. At that point police set up a command post at the intersection of 3rd and Floyd streets.

7. A dozen additional officers from the Heartland Police Department, Cooper County Sheriff's Office and Troop F of the Missouri Highway Patrol joined the search.

8. 15 members of the Lambda Chi Alpha fraternity at Twain State University heard of the search and volunteered to assist officers.

9. For 3–1/2 hours law enforcement officers and volunteers canvassed every house within 1 mile when the boy finally was located at the home of his uncle, Billy Addington, 3122 Dover St., police said.

10. A Heartland police spokesman said that this is typical of missing-children reports, where 95% are located with friends or relatives.

# NUMERALS *exercise 2*

**DIRECTIONS:** After consulting this workbook or other resources, answer the following exercises involving *use of math.*

1. You're checking the numbers for a crowd estimate in a story on a political rally. Assume that it was a loose crowd in which each person takes up about 10 square feet, and they were in a courtyard that measures 200 feet by 300 feet. What is the crowd estimate the reporter should have used?

2. Using the Forbes Magazine list of the top-earning musicians for 2009 (see following), check the number in a story in which the reporter gives the average (mean) earnings of the group:

   a. Madonna, $110 million

   b. Celine Dion, $100 million

   c. Beyonce Knowles, $87 million

   d. Bruce Springsteen, $70 million

   e. Kenny Chesney, $65 million

   f. (tie) Coldplay, $60 million

   g. (tie) Rascal Flatts, $60 million

   h. (tie) AC DC, $60 million

   i. The Eagles, $55 million

   j. Toby Keith, $52 million

3. Using the same information, check the reporter's figures for the median earnings.

4. While editing a story on movie attendance, you note the reporter writes that movie theater ticket sales for 2008 were $1.45 billion and increased 17.5 percent the following year. What should the story say 2009 sales are?

5. A story says Spanish-speaking residents in Heartland number 1 in 15. If Heartland's population is 48,400, how many speak Spanish?

6. A reporter writes that a water tower on the south side of Heartland holds 750,000 gallons. If it is half empty, how long will it take a 500-gallon-per-minute pump to fill the tower?

7. In a story on Heartland public transportation, the reporter writes that a bus averages 22 mph running 12 miles through the city's northeast sector. What should the reporter say is the average number of minutes to complete that route?

**8.**    A crime story says that a shooting victim was born April 2, 1949. How old is that victim now?

**9.**    A story on summer jobs in the Heartland area covers how much teens at the municipal golf course make. The typical student earns $7.25 an hour for 30 hours a week. The golf course manager says that 21.5 percent is withheld for taxes. How much should the story say the teen takes home each week?

**10.**    Using the information from #9, what is the total the student will take home during the 12-week job?

**Additional exercises are available online at** www.oup.com/us/rosenauer.

## CHAPTER 8

# Plurals

*"I am almost sure by witness of my ear, but cannot be positive, for I know grammar by ear only, not by note, not by the rules. A generation ago I knew the rules — knew them by heart, word for word, though not their meanings — and I still know one of them: the one which says — but never mind, it will come back to me presently."*

~Mark Twain, "The Autobiography of Mark Twain" (1924)

Most of the time forming plurals is relatively easy. Because it's familiar to you, you don't encounter problems. However, forming the plural of some words doesn't always follow standard expectations and procedures. Those can trip you up.

We will start with the easy and work our way to the more challenging.

## For Most Words

This familiar pattern works for most words: Just add *-s*.

**FIGURE 8-1** This shot shows the Washington Times newsroom, the second oldest paper in the U.S. capital. Its circulation is nearly 94,000 versus more than 500,000 for the Washington Post.

# For Words Ending in *-ch, -s, -sh, -ss, -x* and *-z*

Still pretty easy and familiar, you form these plurals by adding *-es*, as in the following:

- *arches, batches*
- *aliases, lenses*
- *ashes, wishes*
- *harnesses, kisses*
- *annexes, foxes*
- *blintzes, klutzes*

Note that *monarchs* is an exception to the rule.

# For Words Ending in *-is*

This is getting a little less common and a little more tricky. Here, change the *-is* to *-es*, as in the following:

- *crisis/crises*
- *nemesis/nemeses*
- *parenthesis/parentheses*
- *synopsis/synopses*
- *thesis/theses*

# For Words Ending in *-y*

You form plurals for words ending in *-y* in one of two ways:

1. If the *-y* is preceded by a consonant or *-qu*, change the *-y* to *-i* and add *-es*, as in the following:
   - *amenity/amenities*
   - *brewery/breweries*
   - *casualty/casualties*
   - *embassy/embassies*
   - *history/histories*
   - *malady/maladies*
   - *soliloquy/soliloquies*

   The stylebook lists occasional exceptions to this rule, such as *bialy/bialys*.
2. For all others just add *-s*, as in the following:
   - *abbey/abbeys*
   - *galley/galleys*
   - *kidney/kidneys*

# For Words Ending in *-o*

If the *-o* is preceded by a consonant, form the plural by adding *-es*, as in the following:
- *banjo/banjoes*
- *cargo/cargoes*
- *mango/mangoes*

Simple enough, but the following are exceptions to this rule:
- *albino/albinos*
- *duo/duos*
- *logo/logos*
- *piano/pianos*
- *ratio/ratios*
- *salvo/salvos*
- *solo/solos*
- *trio/trios*
- *zero/zeros*

# For Words Ending in *-f*

For most words ending in *-f*, change the f to v and add *-es*, as in the following:
- *calf/calves*
- *elf/elves*
- *hoof/hooves*
- *leaf/leaves*
- *loaf/loaves*
- *scarf/scarves*
- *wolf/wolves*

A few exceptions to this rule are *belief/beliefs, brief/briefs, dwarf/dwarfs, reef/reefs* and *roof/roofs*. Check the dictionary for others.

# For Words With Latin Endings

English uses quite a few Latin words, many of which end in *-a, -um* or *–us*. Form their plurals in one of several ways.
- Change the *-us* to *-i*, as in the following:
  ▶ *alumnus/alumni*
  ▶ *bacillus/bacilli*
  ▶ *fungus/fungi*
  ▶ *locus/loci*
  ▶ *nucleus/nuclei*
  ▶ *stimulus/stimuli*
- Among exceptions to this rule are *cactus/cactuses, genus/genera, hippopotamus/ hippopotamuses, incubus/incubuses, prospectus/prospectuses* and *syllabus/ syllabuses.*
- Change the *-a* to *-ae*, as in the following:
  ▶ *alumna/alumnae* (These are the female forms for *alumnus*.)
  ▶ *larva/larvae*
  ▶ *nebula/nebulae*
- An exception to this rule is *formula/formulas*.
- Form the plural of most words ending in *-um* by adding *-s*, as in the following:
  ▶ *atrium/atriums*
  ▶ *condominium/condominiums*
  ▶ *geranium/geraniums*
  ▶ *podium/podiums*
  ▶ *stadium/stadiums*
- Exceptions to this rule are *addendum/addenda, curriculum/curricula* and *medium/ media.*

# For Compound Words

Form the plural of compound words by adding *-s*. The trick is to decide just where to add the *-s*.

For compound words that are single words without hyphens, just add *-s* at the end. A few may be troublesome, as in the following:
- *cupful/cupfuls*
- *handful/handfuls*
- *tablespoonful/tablespoonfuls*

For words that are separated or hyphenated to form the compound, add *-s* to the most significant word in the group, as in the following:

- *also-rans*
- *attorneys general*
- *bills of fare*
- *chiefs of staff*
- *courts-martial*
- *go-betweens*
- *higher-ups*

- *lieutenant colonels*
- *mothers-in-law*
- *notaries public*
- *presidents-elect*
- *runners-up*
- *secretaries of state*

# For Proper Names

To form the plural of proper names, you usually will just add -*s*. However, you handle two forms differently.

To form the plural of proper names ending in -*es*, -*s* or -*z*, add -*es*, as in the following:

- *Joneses*
- *Ramirezes*
- *Williamses*

To form the plural of proper names ending in -*y*, add -*s*, as in the following:

- *Kennedys*
- *Willoughbys*
- *On the map they found two Kansas Citys, one in Missouri and the other across the river in Kansas.*

# Others

To form the plural of figures, add -*s*, as in the following:

- *The 1990s saw the beginning of the dot-com marketplace.*
- *The temperatures will be in the 90s on Saturday.*
- *His shoes were size 15s.*

To form the plural of single letters, add '*s*, as in the following:

- *Sheila earned two A's and three B's in the fall semester.*
- *Minding your p's and q's means minding your manners.*
- *The Oakland A's were the Kansas City Athletics from 1955 to 1967.*
- *How many s's are in Mississippi?*

On the other hand, to form the plural of multiple letters, add -*s*, as in the following:

- *Learning the ABCs is an important lesson for kindergarteners.*
- *Benjamin left a trail of IOUs in residence halls across campus.*
- *The president had a reception for campus VIPs.*

# PLURALS *exercise 1*

**DIRECTIONS**: In the blank after each word in the following, write the *plural* form *preferred* by AP style or, as appropriate, by Webster's New World College Dictionary.

1. vertebra _____

2. cupful _____

3. bill of fare _____

4. crisis _____

5. church _____

6. Jones _____

7. wolf _____

8. piano _____

9. son-in-law _____

10. larva _____

11. history _____

12. fungus _____

13. IOU _____

14. loaf _____

15. roof _____

16. hobo _____

17. bus _____

18. kiss _____

19. hoof _____

20. hoax _____

**Additional exercises are available online at** www.oup.com/us/rosenauer.

## CHAPTER 9

# Commonly Misspelled and Misused Words

*"It is a damn poor mind indeed which can't think of at least two ways to spell any word."*

~Andrew Jackson

Some people are naturals when it comes to being able to spell correctly, it seems, while others must work at it. Whether you are in the former or latter camp, spelling is an essential expectation of all good reporters and editors, as is using the correct word. In this chapter we'll cover a long list of commonly misspelled and misused words. It's not likely you'll memorize them all; however, you should acquire their spellings as you go along, rather like picking up shells on the seashore and tucking them into your pocket.

Of course, nearly all of us are quite familiar with the spell check features of popular computer word-processing software, such as Microsoft Word. The squiggly red line that appears under some words you type says that they are not in Word's dictionary. That can be helpful. However, the squiggly line won't show up for words correctly spelled but misused in the context. For those you have to check and learn as you go.

The following list, although not exhaustive, covers many of the more common misspelled and misused words, as well as brief definitions and examples where appropriate. Most of these preferences come from the stylebook. The rest, marked with asterisks, follow the preferred spelling in Webster's New World College Dictionary. All of the meanings reflect Webster's definitions to help you pick which word fits.

**a lot, allot\*** — *A lot* is an idiom meaning many or a large number and is always two words, as in the following: *The mayor had a lot on his mind. Allot* is a verb meaning to give or assign shares or to apportion, as in the following: *Meg had to allot a certain amount of money to paying her bills each month.*

**aboveboard**

**accept, except** — *Accept* is a verb meaning taking something offered or receiving willingly, as in the following: *He accepted the Emmy on behalf of the cast. Except* is often used as a preposition meaning leaving out or omitting, as in the following: *Everyone except Pete was present.*

**accommodate**

**acknowledgment**

**admissible**

**adverse, averse** — *Adverse* is an adjective meaning unfavorable or working in an opposite direction, as in the following: *The candidate weathered adverse public opinion. Averse* is an adjective meaning opposed or not willing, as in the following: *While vegetables are good for you, many of us are averse to eating Brussels sprouts.*

**adviser (not advisor)**

**aesthetic**

**affect, effect** — *Affect* is having an effect on or influencing and is more commonly used as a verb, as in the following: *His presence did little to affect the outcome. Effect* is a result and is more commonly used as a noun, as in the following: *The effect of his presence was negligible.* However, used as an occasional verb, *effect* means to bring about, as in the following: *John effected the changes immediately.*

**afterward (not afterwards)**

**aid, aide** — *Aid* is a verb meaning giving help or assisting, as in the following: *He aided the injured player.* As a noun *aid* is the help given, as in the following: *The player appreciated the aid. Aide* is a noun meaning an assistant, as in *the general's aide.*

**air bag**

**air base**

**airfare**

**airmail**

**airstrike**

**airtight**

**airways**

**allege**

**all right** — Though *alright* has gained popular acceptance, it is not grammatical and never allowed by AP style.

**allusion, illusion** — *Allusion* is a noun meaning indirect or casual reference, as in the following: *Her allusion to his past went unnoticed by all except Paul. Illusion* is a noun meaning a false or deceptive appearance, as in the following: *That he was wealthy was a grand illusion.*

**amid (not admidst)**

**anxious, eager*** — *Anxious* is an adjective meaning to be nervous or fearful, as in the following: *Eddie was anxious about his dental appointment. Eager* is an adjective meaning to be excited, as in the following: *Julie is eager to go to the game arcade Saturday.*

**archaeology**

**averse, adverse** — See *adverse, averse.*

**backward (not backwards)**

**bale, bail*** — *Bale* is a noun or verb meaning a large bundle of something like cotton, hay and the like or the act of making such a bundle, as in the following: *The huge hay bales rolled off the trailer and onto the highway. Bail* is a noun or verb meaning money or a bond guaranteeing that a released defendant will appear for trial or the act of securing the release, as in the following: *The man charged with embezzlement posted bail immediately after the hearing.*

**barroom**

**bazaar, bizarre** — *Bazaar* is a noun meaning a shop or marketplace for selling various goods, as in the following: *Ellen loved to visit the bazaars in Middle Eastern countries. Bizarre* is an adjective meaning odd in manner or appearance, even grotesque, as in the following: *The bright lighting threw bizarre shadows on the walls.*

**bellwether**

**besiege**

**bigwig**

**bizarre, bazaar** — See *bazaar, bizarre.*

**bobblehead**

**bourbon**

**broccoli**

**cannon, canon*** — *Cannon* is a noun meaning a piece of artillery, as in the following: *The regiment fired cannons to honor their fallen comrades. Canon* is a noun meaning rules, laws or principles, especially of a church, as in the following: *The man was excommunicated following Roman Catholic canon law. Canon* also is the complete works of an author.

**canvas, canvass\*** — *Canvas* is a noun meaning a tightly woven, coarse cloth used for tents and sails, as in the following: *Brent touched the tent's canvas side, whereupon the rain began seeping in. Canvass* is a verb or noun meaning to examine, discuss or look over carefully, as well as moving through an area seeking votes or opinions or the act of doing so, as in the following: *My volunteers began canvassing our neighborhood to encourage everyone to vote for our council candidate.*

**capital, capitol\*** — *Capital* is a noun meaning the city that is the official seat of government or cash and property in a business context, as in the following: *The capital of Missouri is Jefferson City. Capitol* is a noun meaning the building where Congress or a legislature meets, as in the following: *A must-see for any visit to Washington, D.C., is the Capitol.*

**catalog**

**censer, censor, censure** — *Censer* is a noun meaning ornamental container in which incense is burned, as in the following: *The priest swung the smoky censer around the casket. Censor* is most often used as a verb meaning to examine documents and remove objectionable material, as in the following: *The Army censored letters sent home from the secret base.* When used occasionally as a noun, *censor* is the person who does the review and removal. *Censure* is a noun or verb meaning strong disapproval or condemnation, as in the following: *The Senate censured the senator from Idaho for his unethical activities.*

**changeable**

**changeover**

**chauffeur**

**chickenpox**

**child care**

**churchgoer**

**claptrap**

**cloture, closure** — *Cloture* is a noun meaning a parliamentary procedure that ends debate and calls for an immediate vote, as in the following: *Williams voted cloture on the issue of the censure. Closure* is a noun meaning an end or a conclusion, as in the following: *Not finding and burying her body left the family without closure.*

**coattails**

**collide** — Two or more objects must be moving to *collide*, as in the following: *John's car collided with the freight train.*

**compatible**

**complacent, complaisant** — *Complacent* is an adjective meaning self-satisfied or smug, as in the following: *William was complacent about his wife's needs. Complaisant* is an adjective meaning willing to please or obliging, as in the following: *Sheila's main problem was that she was too complaisant about sharing what would make her happy.*

**complement, compliment** — *Complement* is a noun or verb meaning adding something or something added to make a whole, as in the following: *Jamie's quick wit was an* *interesting complement to Isabel's droll sense of humor. Compliment* is a noun or verb meaning something said or saying something in praise or admiration, as in the following: *He had problems knowing how to accept a compliment.*

**compose, comprise, constitute** — *Compose* is a verb meaning to put together or combine, as in the following: *Elliott composed a letter to his parents. Comprise* is a verb meaning to include or to consist of, as in the following: *Jeans and T-shirts comprised his wardrobe. Constitute* is a verb meaning to set up or to establish, as in the following: *His actions constituted a breach of his contract.*

**consensus**

**contagious**

**contemptible**

**council, counsel** — *Council* is a noun meaning a group chosen or called together for discussion or consultation — particularly a local elected body with legislative powers, as in the following: *He sought to be elected to the Heartland City Council. Counsel* is a noun or verb meaning a mutual exchange of ideas or advice as well as giving such ideas or advice, as in the following: *The judge advised the man to seek counsel before saying anything more.*

**criterion, criteria** — The singular and plural, respectively, of the nouns meaning standards or measurement, as in the following: *The professor listed five criteria for students to follow.*

**czar (not tsar)**

**day care**

**daylong**

**daytime**

**diarrhea**

**dilemma**

**disc, disk** — *Disc* is a noun referring to phonograph records or laser-based devices, as in the following: *My favorite disc jockey was Wolfman Jack. Disk* is a noun referring to computer and medical contexts, as in the following: *The computer chewed up Cynthia's disk.*

**discreet, discrete** — *Discreet* is an adjective meaning wise or prudent, as in the following: *Margot was discreet about her affairs. Discrete* is an adjective meaning separated into distinctive parts, as in the following: *The lines on the pavement encouraged discrete lineups. Indiscreet* and *indiscrete* suggest lacking in each of these.

**disburse, disperse\*** — *Disburse* is a verb meaning to pay out or spend, as in the following: *The paymaster disbursed the monthly paychecks to the platoon. Disperse* is a verb meaning to scatter in all directions or to distribute widely, as in the following: *The unruly crowd dispersed as soon as police fired canisters of tear gas.*

**drunkenness**

**dual, duel** — *Dual* is an adjective meaning having or composed of two parts, as in the following: *Glenda retained dual citizenship in both Switzerland and the United States.*

*Duel* is a noun or verb meaning a formal fight between two people, originally armed with deadly weapons or the act of doing so, as in the following: *Aaron Burr killed Alexander Hamilton in a duel in 1804.*

**eager, anxious*** — See *anxious, eager.*

**easygoing**

**effect, affect** — See *affect, effect.*

**emigrate, immigrate** — *Emigrate* is a verb meaning leaving one country and taking up residence in another, as in the following: *Millions of poor Irish peasants emigrated from Ireland following the potato famine in 1845. Immigrate* is a verb meaning to come into a new country, usually with the goal of settling there, as in the following: *The decision by these Irish to immigrate to the United States didn't solve all of their problems.*

**en route**

**ensure, insure** — *Ensure* is a verb meaning to make sure, to guarantee or to protect, as in the following: *Savings connected to the stock market did not ensure the retirees that they would have sufficient funds. Insure* is a verb meaning taking out a contract to be paid money following the loss of life, property or other, as in the following: *Missouri law requires drivers to insure their vehicles.*

**entitled, titled** — *Entitled* is a participle meaning given an honor or right, as in the following: *The coupon entitled her to get a free hamburger. Titled* is a participle meaning giving a title to something, as in the following: *The movie was titled "Run Silent, Run Deep."*

**exaggerate**

**except, accept** — See *accept, except.*

**farther, further** — *Farther* is an adjective or adverb meaning more distant or more remote, as in the following: *His frog hopped farther than the other 10 in the contest. Further* is an adjective or adverb meaning more deeply or to a greater degree, as in the following: *Minnie was further along in her studies than her sister Winnie.*

**faze, phase** — *Faze* is a verb meaning to disturb, typically used in the negative, as in the following: *Her anger didn't faze the police officer a bit. Phase* is a noun or verb meaning stages or forms in a cycle or series or to carry out such, as in the following: *The company had to phase in the salary increases.*

**fewer, less** — *Fewer* is used for individual items. So if the copy refers to people or things in the plural, use *fewer* as in the following: *Fewer people today agree that honesty is the best policy. Less* is used for bulk or quantity, particularly those things than can't or don't have a plural, as in the following: *Less money is being invested in savings today than ever.* Also, *less* is used with numbers when they are on their own and with expressions of measurement, time, money or distance, as in the following: *The town square is less than two miles from the elementary school.*

**field house**

**firefighter**

**flack, flak** — *Flack* is a noun, considered slang, meaning someone who works as a press or publicity agent, as in the following: *The flack from the local casino paid regular visits to the newsroom. Flak* is a noun meaning the shots from anti-aircraft guns, though often it is used to suggest a flurry of criticism, as in the following: *It was the spokesman's job to take the flak from pushy reporters.*

**flail, flay** — *Flail* is a noun or verb meaning a tool to thresh grain or to swing arms widely (the action of one using the tool or appearing to do so), as in the following: *Harriett flailed her arms as she tried to stop traffic. Flay* is a verb meaning to strip skin using a whip or the figurative use in tongue-lashing a person, as in the following: *Elmer flayed the children for wrecking the car.*

**flair, flare** — *Flair* is a noun meaning a natural talent, aptitude or knack, as in the following: *Marie had a flair for picking the right outfits for those occasions. Flare* is a noun or verb meaning to blaze suddenly and brightly, the flash or light that causes it and a sudden outburst, as in the following: *Tempers flared between the mayor and a councilman at Monday's meeting.*

**flaunt, flout** — *Flaunt* is a verb meaning to make a gaudy, showy even outlandish display, as in the following: *Some people flaunt their wealth even when many people are starving. Flout* is a verb meaning to mock, reject or defy, as in the following: *The mayor was criticized for flouting the law.*

**flier, flyer** — *Flier* is a noun that AP prefers to be used for either aviators or handbills whereas *flyer* is the proper name of some trains or buses.

**flounder, founder** — *Flounder* is a noun meaning a fish, as in the following: *He'd never seen a fish quite as odd or ugly as a flounder. Founder* is a verb meaning to stumble, bog down or fill with water (with ships), as in the following: *Lacy foundered as she headed for the straightaway. Founder* also is a noun meaning one who founds or establishes.

**fluorescent**

**forego, forgo** — *Forego* is a verb meaning to go before or to precede, as in the following: *Willie needed to forego the rest of the kids heading to the restroom. Forgo* is a verb meaning to overlook, neglect or do without, as in the following: *Lacking any money, he had to forgo drinking beer with his buddies.*

**foul, fowl** — *Foul* is an adjective or adverb meaning loathsome or so offensive to cause disgust, as in the following: *A foul odor came from the cooler. Fowl* is a bird, often referring to a chicken or turkey, as in the following: *If Sally had the choice of fish or fowl, she always chose fish.*

**fuselage**

**fusillade**

**gage, gauge** — *Gage* is a noun or verb meaning a pledge or something deposited to ensure an action, such as a fight, or the act of doing so, as in the following: *His only gage was his grandmother's wedding ring. Gauge* is a noun or verb meaning a standard measurement, a device for measuring or the act of measuring, as in the following: *The doctor gauged the ability of the injured man to handle the pain.*

**gibe, jibe, jive** — *Gibe* is a noun or verb meaning to jeer or taunt or the act of doing so, as in the following: *Alan was angry when Betty gibed him about his hair.* *Jibe* is a noun or verb meaning to change the course of a ship or to be in agreement or harmony, as in the following: *Even though he tried repeatedly, he couldn't get the accounts to jibe.* *Jive* is a verb meaning to speak in an insincere or flippant way, as in the following: *Zane was always ready to jive her kids about their musical tastes.*

**gobbledygook**

**goodbye**

**gray (not grey)**

**grisly, grizzly** — *Grisly* is an adjective meaning terrifying or horrible, as in the following: *This was Jennifer's first time reporting a grisly murder.* *Grizzly* is an adjective meaning having hair graying or streaked with gray, often applied to a species of bear, as in the following: *The grizzly bear stood 7 feet tall, towering over the frightened hunter.*

**hangar, hanger** — *Hangar* is a noun meaning a building housing aircraft, as in the following: *Jason couldn't afford keeping his Cessna in the hangar.* *Hanger* is a noun meaning a person who hangs or a thing on which objects are hung, as in the following: *When he opened their closet, all he saw were empty hangers.*

**hardy, hearty*** — *Hardy* is an adjective meaning bold, daring or courageous, as in the following: *He dreamed of being a hardy sailor on Ahab's ship.* *Hearty* is an adjective meaning friendly, cordial or enthusiastic, as in the following: *Otto's handshake was as hearty as his laugh.*

**headlong**

**hemorrhage**

**hideaway**

**hoard, horde*** — *Hoard* is a noun or verb meaning a supply (of money or goods) stored and kept in reserve, sometimes hidden, as well as the act of doing so, as in the following: *The rumor about gas shortages encouraged some people to hoard extra fuel.* *Horde* is a noun meaning a wandering or nomadic tribe or group, as in the following: *The horde of barbarians attacked the small Roman outpost.*

**hot line**

**hourlong**

**illusion, allusion** — See *allusion, illusion*.

**immigrate, emigrate** — See *emigrate, immigrate*.

**imply, infer** — *Imply* is a verb meaning to contain, hint or suggest, as in the following: *Meryl implied that the accident was my fault.* *Infer* is a verb meaning to derive by reasoning or draw as a conclusion, as in the following: *Paul inferred from my actions that I was angry.* Essentially, only a sender can *imply* something in a message, and only a receiver can *infer* something.

**impostor**

**inasmuch as**

**incite, insight*** — *Incite* is a verb meaning to urge someone to action or to stir up, as in the following: *The angry words of the speaker incited the crowd to leap to their feet.* *Insight* is a noun meaning the ability to see the inner nature of something, as in the following: *His letters offered additional insight into his love for her.*

**inquire, inquiry (not enquire, enquiry)**

**insure, ensure** — See *ensure, insure.*

**It's, its** — *It's* is a contraction for it is, as in the following: *It's getting close to closing time. Its* is the possessive pronoun, as in the following: *The dog licked its paw.*

**jibe, jive, gibe** — See *gibe, jibe, jive.*

**judgment**

**knickknack**

**kowtow**

**less, fewer** — See *fewer, less.*

**likable**

**livable**

**magnate, magnet*** — *Magnate* is a noun meaning an important or influential person, as in the following: *John Rockefeller was an oil magnate who was among the wealthiest men in the world.* *Magnet* is a noun meaning any material with the power to attract like material, as in the following: *The spilled syrup was like a magnet, drawing hundreds of ants to the pantry.*

**malarkey**

**manageable**

**mantel, mantle** — *Mantel* is a noun meaning a shelf or slab, often surrounding a fireplace, as in the following: *Teddy accidentally knocked the glass bird off the mantel.* *Mantle* is a noun meaning a loose cloak that symbolizes authority, often used figuratively, or anything that cloaks or conceals, as in the following: *Dillon strutted around the classroom wielding his piece of chalk like a mantle.*

**marshal, martial** — *Marshal* is a noun or verb meaning a military officer or federal law enforcement agent or to arrange or manage people or things, as in the following: *Gordon marshaled his resources to prepare for the big day.* *Martial* is an adjective meaning related to war and fighting or showing a readiness to fight, as in the following: *The president declared martial law in the riot-torn area.*

**medium, media*** — *Medium*, as related to journalism, is a single news, information or entertainment outlet, as in the following: *The Heartland News-Observer is the only daily print medium in Cooper County.* *Media* is the plural form.

**minuscule (not miniscule)**

**naive**

**nationwide**

**negligee**

**newsstand**

**nighttime**

**nowadays**

**palate, palette, pallet** — *Palate* is a noun meaning the roof of the mouth, as in the following: *Rachel burned her palate on the hot pizza. Palette* is a noun meaning the board on which an artist arranges and mixes paints, as in the following: *The old landscape artist used a palette that was aged and worn. Pallet* is a noun meaning a low platform on which goods or materials are arranged for storage or transportation, as in the following: *Empty pallets were stacked in the warehouse from floor to ceiling.*

**passed, past\*** — *Passed* is the past participle of the verb pass meaning to go or move from one place to another, sometimes referring to dying, as in the following: *The two passed each other in the hall every morning. Past* is usually an adjective or noun meaning a period preceding now, gone by or ended as well as the time to which that refers, as in the following: *The past can live to haunt one who refuses to live in the present.*

**pedal, peddle** — *Pedal* is a noun or verb meaning a lever operated by one's foot or the act of using it, as in the following: *Keith loved to pedal his bike along the river. Peddle* is a verb meaning going from place to place selling products, as in the following: *The old man eked out a living peddling the trinkets he made.*

**permissible**

**phase, faze** — See *faze, phase.*

**pore, pour** — *Pore* is a verb meaning to gaze intently or study carefully, as in the following: *Terry pored over his study notes. Pour* is a verb meaning to cause to flow in a stream or to emit or discharge, as in the following: *Arnie poured out his sorrows over the loss of his cat.*

**premier, premiere** — *Premier* is an adjective or noun meaning chief or foremost, as in the following: *His smile was his premier attribute. Premiere* is a noun, adjective or verb meaning the debut of a performance, a leading lady in a performance or the act of presenting something for the first time, as in the following: *Don Lillie's play "Marlowe" premiered during spring 2009.*

**principal, principle** — *Principal* is an adjective or noun meaning first in rank or authority or someone or something in that position, as in the following: *The principal figure in the murder case was actually a little old lady. Principle* is a noun meaning the ultimate source or cause or fundamental truth, as in the following: *The first principle in medicine is to do no harm.*

**rack, wrack** — *Rack* is a noun meaning a frame for holding or displaying things. Similarly, *rack* is a verb meaning to arrange or torture on that frame, as in the following: *His body was racked by pain.* Informally, *to rack up* means to accumulate or score. *Wrack* is a noun meaning destruction or a wrecked ship, as in the following: *The shore was strewn with wrack from the storm.*

**ravage, ravish** — *Ravage* is a noun or verb meaning the act of destroying violently, as in the following: *His health was ravaged by age, alcohol and hard work.* *Ravish* is a verb meaning to seize or carry off forcibly, to rape or to enrapture, as in the following: *Cee Cee's beauty was ravishing.*

**regardless (not irregardless)**

**reign, rein** — *Reign* is a noun or verb meaning power or rule holding sway, especially by royalty, as in the following: *The reign of the House of Windsor began in 1917.* *Rein* is a noun or verb meaning the narrow strap of leather used to guide a horse or the act of using it, as in the following: *Grant reined his horse as it arrived at the stable.*

**resistible**

**restaurateur**

**screen saver**

**scurrilous**

**serviceable**

**steppingstone**

**storyline**

**storyteller**

**supersede**

**their, there, they're\*** — *Their* is a pronoun that is the possessive form of they, as in the following: *Their books were stolen from their unlocked car.* *There* is an adverb denoting place, as in the following: *Vera loved the Ozarks and went there whenever she had the chance.* *They're* is a contraction for they are, as in the following: *They're a gruesome twosome.*

**throwaway**

**timeout**

**titled, entitled** — See *entitled, titled.*

**toward (not towards)**

**trooper, trouper\*** — *Trooper* is a noun meaning a state police officer or cavalry soldier, as in the following: *The trooper walked up to Zoe's car after stopping her for speeding.* *Trouper* is a noun meaning a veteran actor, as in the following: *Wilhelm was a trouper who began working on a vaudeville stage.*

**trusty**

**upward (not upwards)**

**wartime**

**weather vane**

**weeklong**

**who's, whose** — *Who's* is a contraction for who is, as in the following: *Karen is a friend* *who's always ready to offer a soft shoulder to cry on.* Whose *is a possessive pronoun, as in the following:* That is a professor whose students tremble in fear.

**wintertime**

**workweek**

**worldwide**

**wrack, rack** — See *rack, wrack.*

**yesteryear**

**zigzag**


For additional information, consult online editing resources in the Appendix.

# MISSPELLED AND MISUSED WORDS *exercise 1*

**DIRECTIONS:** Circle the correct choice in the sentences following.

1. The state [trooper, trouper] drove [passed, past] the stalled car [enroute, en route] to a call about cattle on a highway.

2. Because it was [day time, daytime] and because he saw no [fewer, less] than a half a dozen such cars each shift, he had to [forego, forgo] stopping but made a mental note to check back on it.

3. After an [hour long, hourlong] stop assisting with the [loose, lose] cattle, he drove back to the [site, sight] of the stalled car.

4. He had learned [its, it's] important to approach such situations with careful [judgement, judgment].

5. What he found was quite [bazaar, bizarre], even considering [a lot, allot] that he has seen [now a days, nowadays].

6. At such moments what one sees and what one knows he should see don't always [gibe, jibe], and even he wasn't sure it wasn't an [allusion, illusion].

7. In the [back seat, backseat] he spotted a [sizable, sizeable] leopard, which appeared to be sleeping.

8. Very little [fazed, phased] the veteran officer, but this went much [farther, further] than anything he had previously encountered.

9. Grabbing his radio, he called the dispatcher, [composing, comprising] his words carefully, and said, "[Your, You're] probably not going to believe this, but I've got a stalled car out here on Route 5 with a leopard in the back."

10. While he was not [adverse, averse] to a little ribbing, the [hardy, hearty] laughter and responses he got convinced him he would not be [anxious, eager] to return to headquarters following his shift.

**Additional exercises are available online at** www.oup.com/us/rosenauer.

## CHAPTER 10

# Titles

*"Put it before them briefly so they will read it, clearly so they will appreciate it, picturesquely so they will remember it and, above all, accurately so they will be guided by its light."*

~Joseph Pulitzer

Titles are among the most common methods journalists use to identify people in their stories; titles also help readers connect people in stories to what's going on. Therefore, because you can expect to deal with them regularly, become familiar with their capitalization, punctuation and presentation.

## The Golden Rule of Title Capitalization

This rule will cover most of what you need to know about capitalizing titles: Capitalize formal titles presented directly in front of an individual's name, but lowercase titles following names. Lowercase occupational or descriptive titles whether they are in front of or following names. See how the following illustrate the golden rule:

- *<u>President</u> Barack Obama met with the Boy Scouts who were visiting the White House.*
- *Waiting to visit with <u>first-year intern</u> Juan Gomez was <u>Chief of Surgery</u> Alena Young.*
- *During a hearing yesterday, <u>Circuit Judge</u> Allen Udahl admonished <u>defense attorney</u> Robert Holliday after his outburst.*

FIGURE 10-1

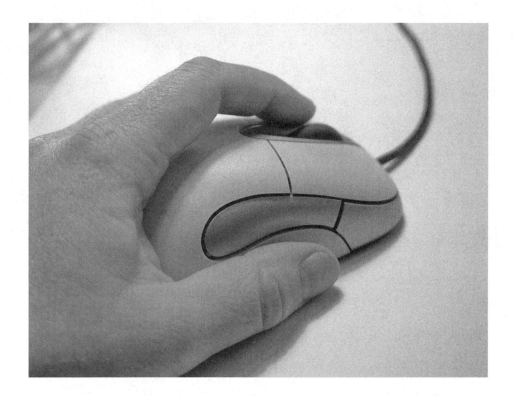

At times you may be unsure about whether a title is formal or occupational. According to the stylebook, a formal title "denotes a scope of authority, professional activity or academic activity."[1] The practice of the organization conferring the title determines whether it is formal or occupational. When in doubt, you can structure the sentence so that the title follows the name. Then, whether it is formal or occupational makes no difference. It's lowercase.

# Abbreviating Titles

Abbreviate and capitalize the following titles when they are used immediately before a name:

- *Dr.*, as in *doctor*.
- *Gov.*, as in *governor*.
- *Lt. Gov.*, as in *lieutenant governor*.
- *the Rev.*, as in *reverend*. (Note that the article *the* precedes this abbreviation for *reverend*. Also, this is the only abbreviation used for religious titles.)
- *Rep.*, as in *representative*.
- *Sen.*, as in *senator*.

In addition, abbreviate and capitalize many military titles used immediately before a name. Because they are numerous, check the *military titles* entry in the stylebook to see which you should abbreviate. Follow those guidelines for comparable titles used with police officers and firefighters. If needed for clarity, add *police* or *fire* in front of the rank, and always lowercase those terms. Consider these examples:

- <u>*Lt. Col.*</u> *Amanda Cox is commander of the military police unit.*

- *The highest enlisted rank in the Air Force is <u>chief master sergeant</u>.*
- *Among recent Congressional Medal of Honor recipients are <u>Pfc.</u> Ross A. McGinnis, <u>Lt.</u> Michael P. Murphy and <u>Sgt. 1st Class</u> Paul R. Smith.*
- *New to the department is <u>police Capt.</u> Gregory Uketui, who replaces <u>Cmdr.</u> Joan Connett as training officer.*

For other titles not listed here or in the *military titles* entry, do not abbreviate.

Finally, drop all titles in second and subsequent references.

# Government Officials

In stories with U.S. datelines, don't write *U.S.* in front of the titles of government officials. Add the *U.S.* for stories with international datelines or where you need it for clarity.

Two exceptions for adding *U.S.* to those stories with international datelines: Don't use it with the U.S. president and vice president.

# Past and Future Titles

Follow the golden rule previously, of course, for the main titles formerly held, about to be held or temporarily held. However, the terms that clarify those should be lowercase, as in *former*, *past*, *deposed*, *acting* and the like and the suffixes *-elect* and *-designate*.

Consider the following examples:

- *Alonzo was eager to meet <u>former President</u> Bill Clinton during a trip to New York City.*
- *At the same meeting was <u>President-elect</u> Barack Obama, who could not meet with Alonzo.*

# Long Titles

A premise of title placement is to put short titles in front of names and long titles following. Both of these options make reading easier and more natural.

For example, it's more comfortable to write *President George W. Bush* rather than *George W. Bush, president*. Likewise, it's a mouthful to write *Undersecretary of State for Political Affairs R. Nicholas Burns* rather than *R. Nicholas Burns, undersecretary of state for political affairs*. Both may be correctly capitalized according to the golden rule, but the latter flows better.

Keep in mind, too, that titles following names should be enclosed in commas.

Finally, inserting *a/an* or *the* in front of a title — whether it precedes or follows the full name — requires the trailing element, name or title, to be lowercased and enclosed in commas, as in the following:

- *<u>The undersecretary of state for political affairs,</u> R. Nicholas Burns, left for Thailand . . .*
  (Note the commas enclosing the trailing element, the name.)
- *R. Nicholas Burns, <u>the undersecretary of state for political affairs,</u> left for Thailand . . .*
  (Note the commas enclosing the trailing element, the title. Also, in this example and

**FIGURE 10-2** President Barack Obama addresses a joint session of Congress. Not surprisingly, the stylebook offers numerous entries covering government and politics.

the one preceding this, use of *the* indicates a unique title applying to only one person in an organization.)

- *An assistant professor of journalism at Twain State University,* Bill Bergland, will teach . . . (Note that the use of *a/an* suggests the person is not the only one holding such a title in an organization.)

# Doctor

Capitalize and abbreviate the title *doctor* on first reference in front of a full name when referring to someone with a medical degree or, as appropriate, an academic degree. Drop *Dr.* in subsequent references. When naming more than one *doctor*, the abbreviation *Drs.* is the form, as in *Drs. Charles H. Mayo and William J. Mayo.*

To avoid confusing readers, references to academic doctors should include their degrees and areas of study within a few sentences following.

# Legislative Titles

As you might expect, capitalize and abbreviate *Rep., Reps., Sen.* and *Sens.* when preceding full names on first reference. Lowercase and spell out in other references.

All other legislative titles should be capitalized in front of full names and spelled out in all references.

Drop legislative titles beyond first reference.

Capitalize specific organization titles presented before a full name on first reference, as in the following: *Speaker Newt Gingrich* and *Majority Whip James E. Clyburn.*

# Party Affiliation

Providing party affiliation of elected officials is appropriate in stories where the context supports it, but the stylebook says to avoid giving affiliation in all stories. Capitalize names of political parties, including the term *party* if it is typically used as part of the group's name.

The stylebook recommends four ways to indicate party affiliation:

- *Sen. Christopher "Kit" Bond, R-Mo., said . . .*
- *Democrat Sen. Claire McCaskill of Missouri met Thursday . . .*
- *Rep. Russ Carnahan was elected in 2005. The Missouri Democrat is . . .*
- *Rep. Kevin McCarthy of California, the Republican whip in charge of promoting the party agenda, . . .*

The first example just listed is what the stylebook calls the "short form." Several rules guide its use:

- Common party abbreviations are *D-* for Democrats, *R-* for Republicans and *I-* for independents. Present these without periods.
- Abbreviations of states in the short form should follow the standard style.
- Punctuation for the short form is the hyphen between the party and state; periods for state abbreviations, as needed; and commas before and after the entire form.
- In contexts where the home state of a federal senator or representative is clear, replace the state name in the short form with the hometown, as in *R-St. Louis.*
- For state legislators the short form should indicate party and hometown, as in *D-Heartland.*

**FIGURE 10-3** The AP Stylebook provides several entries to assist with editing stories that involve royalty, such as Queen Elizabeth II of England. Its entry on "nobility" is the most extensive.

# Religious Titles

The most common title for clergy on first reference in front of a full name is *the Rev.*, with lowercased *the* and capitalized *Rev.* Use the last name only on subsequent references.

The use of *the Rev. Dr.* is appropriate only when it is relevant for a person holding an earned doctorate. Also, use *the Most Rev.* and similar only if appropriate.

The first-reference title in front of full names of rabbis is *Rabbi*, with the title dropped subsequently. Similarly, *Sister* or *Mother* and *Brother*, as appropriate, are titles used on first reference with the full name and dropped thereafter.

For additional information about use of titles for clergy and other religious cases, check the *religious titles* entry in the stylebook.

# Royal Titles and Titles of Nobility

You're not likely to come across royalty and nobility in most of the stories you will edit. However, it's worth mentioning how to handle either when the situation arises.

First, the stylebook notes that most of its guidance concerning royalty and nobility follows the British tradition. You should begin there and modify for other countries.

Royalty, in this context, refers only to the royal family, whether living or deceased. Nobility involves the whole range of rank that is either inherited or conferred.

Beyond the standard practice of capitalizing *king*, *queen*, *duke* and the like when presented directly before names and lowercasing them when they follow, consult the stylebook entry *nobility* for guidance.

# Composition Titles — Names of Books, Movies and Other Works

Composition titles and TV program titles (in the next section) comprise a good chunk of the other types of titles you will find in stories. The stylebook entry *composition titles* covers the following works:
- *book titles*
- *computer game titles*
- *movie titles*
- *opera titles*
- *play titles*
- *poem titles*
- *album and song titles*

- *radio and television program titles*
- *lecture, speech and works of art titles*

Here are the standard AP guidelines for titles of these works:

- Capitalize all main words as well as prepositions and conjunctions of four or more letters.
- Capitalize articles — *a*, *an*, *the* — and words shorter than four letters when they are the first or last words of a title.
- Put quotation marks around such titles *except* for the following:

  - ▶ *the Bible*
  - ▶ *books that are primarily catalogs of reference material*
  - ▶ *almanacs*
  - ▶ *directories*
  - ▶ *dictionaries*
  - ▶ *encyclopedias*
  - ▶ *gazetteers*
  - ▶ *handbooks*
  - ▶ *software such as WordPerfect or Windows*

- Translate foreign titles into English except for most reviews of musical performances.
- Do not enclose in quotation marks the titles of magazines or newspapers. Examples of capitalization and punctuation of titles are the following:

  - ▶ *"The Grapes of Wrath"*
  - ▶ *"A Walk in the Woods"*
  - ▶ *"Halo"*
  - ▶ *"Super Mario Bros."*
  - ▶ *"Titanic"*
  - ▶ *"The Lion King"*
  - ▶ *"Carmen"*
  - ▶ *"Madame Butterfly"*
  - ▶ *"The Tempest"*
  - ▶ *"Guys and Dolls"*
  - ▶ *"The Raven"*
  - ▶ *"The Road not Taken"*
  - ▶ *"Hey Jude"*
  - ▶ *"Bridge Over Troubled Water"*
  - ▶ *"CSI"*
  - ▶ *"Two and a Half Men"*
  - ▶ *"The Gettysburg Address"*
  - ▶ *"Mona Lisa"*
  - ▶ *Kansas City Star*
  - ▶ *Webster's New World College Dictionary*

Note that AP style doesn't recommend use of italics for anything in news stories. This is mostly a throwback to a time when wire service and typesetting operations for newspapers couldn't handle italics. Therefore, while you italicize titles of larger or longer works, outside of journalism, AP uses quotation marks for most.

# Television Program Titles

Television program titles follow the basic guidelines listed previously as well as the following pointers:

- Put quotation marks around *show* and similar only if it is part of the program's formal title, as in *"The Man Show," "The Bob Newhart Show"* and *"The Jack Benny Program."*
- Use quotation marks for titles of episodes of TV programs, as in the following: *"And in the End,"* the final episode of *"ER"* and *"Requiem for a Lightweight,"* an episode of *"M\*A\*S\*H."*

# TITLES *exercise 1*

**DIRECTIONS:** Correct *titles* errors in the following exercises. Some may be correct. Check the spelling of all names in the Heartland Directory.

1.  Media Guru Marshall McLuhan coined the phrase "The medium is the message" in his 1964 book, Understanding media: The extensions of man.

2.  This idea that the medium that delivers a message influences how that message is perceived continues to be true today, according to Journalism Professor Vince Phillips.

3.  Phillips, who teaches multimedia courses at Kansas State University, spoke Monday to about 140 people in a talk titled The Evolution of Media from TV to the Web in Lee Hall at Twain State University.

4.  Early television, such as Hopalong Cassidy, which debuted in 1949 as the first network Western, challenged the stereotype that good guys always wear white hats but retained the notion that good guys always win.

5.  The 1950s series Superman suggested an upstanding, socially desirable, patriotic spin with its lead-in that said Superman "fights a never-ending battle for truth, justice and the American way."

6.  He explained that TV programs like M*A*S*H and Saturday Night Live often used humor to deliver commentary on important social issues.

7.  With the growth of the Web, television is being challenged as the leading medium by user-controlled social websites like "YouTube," "Facebook" and "MySpace."

8.  Phillips said the popularity of online news sites has hurt the newspaper industry to the extent that several major dailies have shut down, including the "Seattle Post-Intelligencer," "Tucson Citizen" and "Rocky Mountain News."

9.  Losses in numbers of viewers continue to plague even long-standing but still-powerful network news programs, with "NBC Nightly News" holding a slight lead over "ABC World News Tonight" and "CBS Evening News" trailing at third.

10. The online medium simply suits itself to many 21st-century readers, who get their daily news at The Drudge Report, AOL News, Yahoo News and Google News, Phillips said.

**Additional exercises are available online at** www.oup.com/us/rosenauer.

## CHAPTER 11

# AP Potpourri

*"I hate editors, for they make me abandon a lot of perfectly good English words."*

~Mark Twain

This chapter covers a variety of AP style references that don't fit neatly into the earlier chapters. Thus, it is a real potpourri, or mix, of material. Learning these may be more difficult, perhaps, because there's little here to hang your hat on, so to speak.

In addition, we will deal with issues involving inclusive language at the end of this chapter.

## Potpourri

Review the more than 70 entries that follow and get a sense of what each entails. Then, you can practice working with many of them in the exercises at the end of the chapter.

**academic degrees** — The stylebook tends to discourage references to a person's degree unless it's needed to establish one's credentials. Preference is to avoid abbreviations, using a form such as *Eileen Wilson, who has a master's in forensic science,* . . .

In addition, apostrophes are used in *bachelor's, bachelor's degree, master's* and *master's degree.* However, the preferred form for others is as follows: *associate degree* and *doctorate.* If the preferred form is inappropriate in the context, you may use *B.A., M.A. LL.D, Ph.D.* and the like. When referring to someone who holds a doctorate, you may use *Dr.* but only on first reference, and don't immediately follow the name with the abbreviation for the degree.

**accused** — Use *of*, and not *with*, this term, as in the following: *Daniels is accused of embezzling funds from the company account.* Avoid structures that suggest guilt before being tried, as in *the accused embezzler.*

**African-American** — This is acceptable for an American black person of African descent, as opposed to a black person from Haiti. Also acceptable is *black.*

**allege** — This term, and its forms *alleged* and *allegedly*, often are carelessly used by journalists. It is acceptable to use *alleged theft* or the like to suggest an act is unproved and not fact. Make clear somewhere in the story the source of a charge or allegation. Following an arrest but before charges, use the phrase *arrested on suspicion of* or similar.

Do not use *alleged* to describe an event known to have occurred, as in *the alleged assassination of John F. Kennedy,* especially if you mean the *alleged assassin of John F. Kennedy.* Note another example: *Jack Ruby allegedly shot Lee Harvey Oswald.* There's no allegedly about it; he did it live on national TV.

It is redundant and thus wrong, for example, to say any of the following:
- *The man was charged with allegedly murdering his wife.* Say instead, *The man was charged with murdering his wife.*
- *The prosecutor accused Johnson of allegedly accepting stolen property.* Say instead, *The prosecutor accused Johnson of accepting stolen property.*
- *Wilson was convicted of allegedly shooting her dog.* Say instead, *Wilson was convicted of shooting her dog.*

**almost never** — Don't use. Instead, say *seldom* or *hardly ever.*

**amendments to the Constitution** — These follow standard style for capitalization and use of numerals, as in *the First Amendment, the Fifth Amendment, the 12th Amendment, the 22nd Amendment* and so on. Don't use colloquial references to the Fifth Amendment, as in *He took the Fifth.*

**American Legion** — Capitalize this name as well as *the Legion* on second reference and *Legionnaires.* Likewise, members of the *Elks Club* are *Elks.*

**among, between** — Follow the standard guidelines that *between* involves two items and *among* involves more than two, as in the following:
- *The two bandits split the loot between themselves.*
- *The plan had been to divide the money among all five.*

**ampersand** — This mark (&) should not be used instead of *and* unless it is part of a company's formal name or a composition title.

**anchorman, anchorwoman** — Preferred form rather than *anchor* or *co-anchor.*

**angry** — Use *at* or *with*, as in the following:
- *Maryann was angry at the world.*
- *Charlie was angry with himself.*

**anniversary** — Avoid *first anniversary, one-year anniversary* or spans less than a year. Also, do not use *first annual.*

**anticipate, expect** — *Anticipate* involves expecting and preparing for something while *expect* does not involve any preparation, as in the following:

- *The Heartland Police Department expected 60,000 people for the Peach Blossom Parade.*
- *They anticipated it and brought in more officers.*

**army** — Capitalize when referring to U.S. forces. Lowercase for other nations' armies. The same is true for other military branches.

**arrest** — Be careful not to convict before trial with phrases such as *arrested for stealing funds*. As always, refer to the charge or the belief, as in *arrested on a charge of stealing funds* or *arrested on suspicion of stealing funds* (if charges have not been filed yet).

**association** — Never abbreviate but capitalize when part of a proper name, as in *National Rifle Association*.

**a while, awhile** — The first is a noun whereas the second is an adverb. Therefore, let the context be your guide, as in the following:
- *Zooey wants to wait for a while before leaving home.*
- *She will stay awhile if no one pesters her.*

**baby boomer** — Use lowercase without a hyphen.

**baby-sit, baby-sitting, baby-sat, baby sitter** — AP says to use the hyphen for the various verb forms but to drop it for the noun.

**because, since** — *Because* is used to suggest a specific cause-effect relationship, as in *He fell because of the broken stairs. Since*, however, points to a sequence of events, though not that one caused the next, as in *He watched the movie since he already was at the theater.*

**best-seller** — Always hyphenate.

**blond, blonde** — The first is used as the noun for males and as an adjective in all contexts. The second, *blonde*, is the noun for females.

**boats, ships** — A *boat* is a vessel of any size, though it usually suggests a smaller watercraft. A *ship* is a large, oceangoing vessel. A distinction often made is that a *boat* is a vessel small enough to be brought aboard a *ship*. Use the pronoun *it* when referring to either rather than the colloquial *she*.

**boy** — Appropriate until the 18th birthday; after that, use *man* or *young man*.

**boycott, embargo** — A *boycott* is an organized effort to avoid buying a product or service whereas *embargo* is a legal restriction concerning trade of a particular product.

**Boy Scouts** — This is the common reference to the *Boy Scouts of America*. Also, use *Cub Scouts*. Capitalize *Cubs* and *Scouts* when referring to boys who are members of these organizations.

**brand names** — Use actual brand names, which are capitalized, only when they are essential or add local color to a story. Otherwise, use generic terms, as in *cushioning material* versus *Bubble Wrap*, which is a registered trademark.

The reasoning behind this is a legal issue wherein owners of service marks or trademarks seek to protect their exclusive use. When brand names become the commonly used term, companies lose those exclusive rights, as with *linoleum, kerosene, trampoline, yo-yo* and others. Check the stylebook for particular terms to see if they are trademarked or generic.

**cabinet** — Capitalize the term when referring to a specific body of advisers of presidents, kings, governors and so on.

**can't hardly** — Avoid this because it suggests a double negative. Instead, use *can hardly*.

**catalog** — This is the spelling preferred by both the stylebook and the Webster's New World College Dictionary over the alternate, *catalogue*.

**chairman, chairwoman** — Capitalize this when it is a formal title in front of a person's full name. Do not use *chairperson, chair* or *co-chair* unless it is the organization's choice for formal title.

**character, reputation** — *Character* involves moral qualities whereas *reputation* involves how someone is regarded by others.

**children** — Use the following guidelines for stories involving children:
- Children under 16 can be called by their first names on second reference unless the story involves a serious matter, such as a murder case.
- For those aged 16 or 17, use your own judgment but prefer last names on second reference.
- Always use last names for those 18 and older.
- Avoid *kids* unless the less formal tone of a story invites it.

**city hall** — Capitalize this building when it is preceded by the name of a city or when the reference is clearly to a specific city's main municipal building. Lowercase in all plural and generic uses, as in the following:
- *The same architect designed Heartland and Columbia city halls.*
- *You can't fight city hall.*

**civil cases, criminal cases** — A *civil case* is one in which an individual, business or government agency files a lawsuit seeking damages from another individual, business or government agency for either breach of contract or wrongful act, injury or other damages not involving a contract. Thus, *civil lawsuit* is redundant.

A *criminal case* is brought by the state or federal government against an individual or entity charged with committing a crime.

**coed** — Although the preferred term is *female student, coed* may be acceptable as an adjective describing coeducational groups or institutions. No hyphen is used.

**collective nouns** — These are nouns that name groups, often composed of people, that take singular verbs and pronouns, as in the following: *audience, board, committee, company, council, family, herd, public, society, team* and the like.

However, team names and band names take plural verbs and pronouns.

The following illustrate the usage:
- *The committee meets on Fridays each week; it is composed of 12 people.*
- *The council is unwilling to bend on the issue of salary increases.*
- *The cattle herd that you bought is in the pen south of the building.*
- *The football team is ranked 14th in the nation.*
- *One hundred bushels per acre is a poor yield for that field. (A unit, singular.)*
- *One hundred bushels were lost when the wagon overturned. (Individual items, plural.)*

- *His data is incontrovertible.* (A unit, singular.)
- *His data were collected using online collection sites.* (Individual items, plural.)

**compared to, compared with** — *Compared to* is required when one intends to assert that two or more people or things are similar without requiring further elaboration, as in the following: *He compared his experiments with animal proteins to Louis Pasteur's experiments with milk.*

*Compared with* puts together two or more items to show similarities and/or differences, as in the following: *His take-home pay was $239, compared with $219 for his best friend.*

**continual, continuous** — Though similar, *continual* means steady repetition, over and over, as in the following: *Rachel's continual infidelity finally led to her husband's filing for divorce.*

*Continuous,* on the other hand, means uninterrupted or unbroken, as in the following: *A continuous line snaked out the door, down the block and around the corner.*

**contractions** — Although you should avoid excessive use of contractions, a review of many newspapers suggests that their use continues to become more popular.

**controversial issue/noncontroversial issue** — All issues, by definition, are controversial. Therefore, *controversial issue* is redundant, and *noncontroversial issue* is impossible.

**convince, persuade** — People may be *convinced that* or *convinced of* something; however, they must be *persuaded to do* something, as in the following: *Eduardo was convinced that Rachel cheated on him. She could not persuade him to believe otherwise.*

**damage, damages** — While *damage* is destruction of things, *damages* are awarded by courts to compensate someone for injury, loss and so on, as in the following: *Hurricane Katrina did an estimated $81 billion in damage across the Gulf Coast. Although some have tried, no homeowners have collected damages from the Army Corps of Engineers for its failed levies.*

**dangling modifiers** — When modifiers do not clearly and logically modify a word stated in a sentence, they are considered *dangling*, as in the following: *Walking across the park, the flowers were beautiful.* (Who was walking? Try this correction: *Walking across the park, I found the flowers were beautiful.*)

**demolish, destroy** — By definition each means to ruin completely. Therefore, something can't be *partly* or *totally demolished* or *destroyed.* The first, *partly*, is illogical, and the second, *totally*, is redundant.

**differ from, differ with** — *Differ from* means to be unlike whereas *differ with* means to disagree.

**disabled, handicapped, impaired** — As with many references, positive or negative, do not use these descriptions of a person unless they are pertinent to the story. In addition, when noting disabilities, avoid emotive verb forms, such as *afflicted with* or *suffers from.* Instead, say *has*, as in the following: *Michael J. Fox has Parkinson's disease.*

The preferred term for someone with a physical or mental disability is *disabled.* Do not use *handicap* to describe a disability. Do not use *mentally retarded.* For additional guidelines, see the stylebook entry.

**drunk, drunken** — *Drunk* is the term used after a form of the verb to be, as in the following: *Margot was drunk.* *Drunken* is the term used as an adjective in front of nouns, as in *drunken teen* or *drunken driving.* Follow the particular state usage concerning a violation for driving while drunk, often one of the following: *DUI, driving under the influence* or *DWI, driving while intoxicated.*

**each other, one another** — Simply, two people can look at *each other*, but more than two look at *one another.* If the number is unknown, either phrase is acceptable.

**elderly** — Use carefully and only when it is relevant. Acceptable in generic references, as in *legislation to assist the elderly.* Follow the same care using *senior citizen.*

**every one, everyone** — The first is correct when you refer to each individual item, whereas the second is a pronoun referring to all persons, as in the following:

- *Every one of my goldfish died.*
- *Everyone is sad about the loss of the goldfish.* (Note the singular verb.)

**felony, misdemeanor** — A *felony* is a serious crime whereas a *misdemeanor* is a minor crime. Although state definitions vary, at the federal level a *felony* is a crime that carries a penalty of more than a year in jail, and a *misdemeanor* carries a penalty of no more than one year. The term *felon* refers to anyone who has been convicted of a felony, regardless of whether the person has served any jail time. It is redundant to say *convicted felon.*

**female** — This is the preferred adjective rather than *woman*, as in *first female astronaut.*

**gentleman** — Not used and certainly not as a synonym for *man.*

**girl** — Appropriate until the 18th birthday; after that, use *woman* or *young woman.*

**Girl Scouts** — This is the common reference to *Girl Scouts of America* and also, *Brownies.* Capitalize *Brownies* and *Scouts* when referring to girls who are members of these organizations.

**hillbilly** — Avoid this term for an Appalachian or Ozark backwoods or mountain person because it usually is considered derogatory. Instead, use *mountaineer.*

**his, her** — Avoid use of the "generic *he*," that old, gender-biased assumption that a pronoun is male when the gender is unclear or indefinite. The best solution in most constructions is to make the noun antecedents and then their related pronouns plural, as in the following:

- Wrong: *A professor should know the names of his students.*
- Right: *Professors should know the names of their students.*

In addition, usually avoid general nouns that embed *man* in their construction, as in *fireman, mailman/postman, newsman* and the like. Instead, use *firefighter, postal carrier, reporter/journalist* and similar.

**Indians** — *American Indian* or *Native American* is preferred for those in the United States. Use the specific tribal name whenever possible. Also, avoid potentially offensive terms, such as *wampum, warpath, brave, squaw* and so on.

**lady** — Not used and certainly not as a synonym for *woman.*

**No.** — Use this capitalized abbreviation with a number, written as a figure, when referring to position or rank, as in *No. 2*.

**noon** — Stands by itself without *12* in front of it.

**OK** — Don't use *okay*. Other forms: OK'd, OK'ing and OKs.

**on** — Do not use in front of a date or day of the week except when the time reference is at the beginning of a sentence, as in the following:
- *The play "Marlowe" will open Thursday.*
- *John F. Kennedy was assassinated Nov. 22, 1963.*
- *On Sunday the congregation will gather at the park for joint services.*

**people, persons** — When referring to an individual, use *person*. *People* is the term for persons in plural contexts. *Persons* should be avoided unless part of a direct quotation or title.

**planning** — The term's definition already suggests future, so *future planning* is redundant.

**Realtor** — This term is trademarked and capitalized. Therefore, unless its use is relevant to the story, prefer *real estate agent*.

**redneck** — Avoid because it is considered derogatory as a reference to poor, white rural residents of the South.

**should, would** — *Should* suggests an obligation, whereas *would* suggests a customary action, as in the following:
- *You should eat at the new restaurant in the shopping center.*
- *We would eat at the Rib Crib everyday if we could.*

**slang** — Avoid slang terms unless in a direct quote or otherwise appropriate to the context of a story.

**sneaked** — Preferred for past tense of the verb *to sneak* rather than the colloquial form *snuck*.

**subjunctive mood** — The subjunctive is called for in situations that are contrary to fact or are expressions of doubts, wishes or regrets, often introduced by the conjunction *if*, as in the following:
- *If Norman were just two inches taller, he would be a great basketball player.*
- *She would have been killed if she were standing there.*
- *Alex wishes he were anywhere but in the physics class.*

**teen, teenager, teenage** — Avoid using *teen-aged*.

**theater** — This spelling is preferred over *theatre*, unless part of a proper name.

**today, tomorrow, tonight** — Prefer day of the week in stories, as in *7 p.m. Wednesday*. These are acceptable, though, in generic contexts, as in: *Teens today are much more technologically savvy.*

**trademark** — A *trademark* is a design, letter, symbol, word or similar used by a manufacturer as an exclusive reference to its products or services. Prefer the generic equivalent unless the trademarked term is relevant to the story. For more information on trademarks, including a media guide to their use, go online to the International Trademark Association at http://www.inta.org/TrademarkBasics/Pages/TMBasics.aspx.

**Uncle Tom** — Avoid its use because it is a potentially libelous term of contempt applied to a black person, suggesting the person is fawning or servile to whites to win favor.

**weather terms** — The following are the more common terms with definitions used by the National Weather Service. For additional guidance, consult the stylebook entry.

- *blizzard* — Considerable falling or blowing snow with wind speeds of 35 mph or more and near-zero visibility. Additionally, a *severe blizzard* is one with wind speeds 45 mph or more and a temperature of 10 degrees or lower.
- *cyclone* — The term may be used in the United States as a synonym for *tornado* and in the Indian Ocean for *hurricane*.
- *dust devil* — Also called a *whirlwind*, this is like a small, nondestructive *tornado*, with rapidly rotating wind that picks up dust or small debris.
- *gale* — Sustained winds ranging between 39 and 54 mph.
- *heavy snow* — Accumulation of 4 inches or more in 12 hours or 6 inches or more in 24 hours.
- *hurricane* or *typhoon* — A tropical *cyclone* with sustained surface winds of 74 mph or more. East of the international date line they are called *hurricanes*; west they are *typhoons*.
- *nor'easter* — Term referring to storms with winds blowing from the northeast that either exit or move north along the East Coast.
- *squall* — A brief, violent windstorm accompanied by rain or snow where the wind speed increases by at least 16 knots and rises to 25 knots or more, lasting at least one minute.
- *tidal wave* — Used incorrectly as a synonym for *tsunami*.
- *waterspout* — Tornado over water.

**Western** — Capitalize the film or book genre but lowercase the music style, often synonymous with *country*.

**whereabouts** — Always takes a singular verb.

**yesterday** — Use day of the week in stories, but acceptable in generic contexts.

**youth** — Appropriate reference to boys and girls aged 13 to 17. After that, use *man* or *woman*.

# Inclusive Language

As we saw in Chapter 4, "Legal, Ethical and Inclusive-Language Concerns for Copy Editors," journalists must glean from stories any *irrelevant* language involving race, gender, age, religion, ethnicity, geography, sexual orientation, disability, physical appearance or social status.

For example, consider the following lead from a robbery story: *A young black man is being sought for the robbery Tuesday of the Quick Shop on Main Street.* Here, the robber's

## ONLINE INSIGHTS > **ONLINE TERMS FOR EDITORS**

Your chances of working with online media are great and are likely to increase over time. Therefore, you should begin now acquiring an understanding of online terms that editors need to know.

The following is a partial list of the terms crowdsourced by the Hacks/Hackers, a grassroots group of hackers and journalists. *Crowdsourcing*, by the way, is a mass collaboration of individuals working together to solve a task. You can find the full "Hacks/Hackers Survival Glossary" online at http://hackshackers.com/resources/hackshackers-survival glossary/.

**app** — Short for application, a program that runs inside another service. Many mobile phones allow apps to be downloaded, leading to a burgeoning economy for modestly priced software. Can also refer to a program or tool that can be used within a website.

**blog** — One of the first widespread Web-native publishing formats, generally characterized by reverse chronological ordering, rapid response, linking and robust commenting. Although originally perceived to be light on reporting and heavy on commentary, a number of blogs are now thoroughly reported, and legacy media organizations have also launched various blogs. Originally short for "Web log," blog is now an accepted word in Scrabble.

**CMS (Content Management System)** — Software designed to organize large amounts of dynamic material for a website, usually consisting of at least templates and a database. It is generally synonymous with online publishing system. Free, open-source systems include Drupal, WordPress and Joomla.

**CSS (Cascading Style Sheets)** — Instructions used to describe the look and formatting for documents, usually HTML, so that the presentation is separate from the actual content of the document itself.

**embed** — A term meaning to place a specific piece of content from one Web page inside of another one. This is often done using an embed code (a few lines of HTML and/or JavaScript) that you can copy or paste. This is a common way for video content to be spread around the Internet and is increasingly being used for interactive components.

**Flash** — A proprietary platform owned by Adobe Systems that allows for drag-and-drop animations, program interactivity and dynamic displays for the Web. Apple has not allowed Adobe to create a Flash player for the iPhone operating system, which has created a feud between the two companies. HTML5 is emerging as an open alternative to Flash.

**HTML (Hypertext Markup Language)** — The dominant formatting language used on the World Wide Web to publish text, images and other elements. HTML can be considered code, but it is not a programming language; it's a markup language, which is a separate beast. The latest standard of HTML is HTML5, which adds powerful interactive functionality.

**HTML5** — The upcoming, powerful standard of HTML, which allows video to be embedded on a Web page. It is gaining in popularity compared to proprietary standards, like Adobe Flash, because it is an open standard and does not require third-party plug-ins. HTML5 will allow Web pages to work more like desktop applications.

**legacy media** — An umbrella term to describe the centralized media institutions that were dominant during the second half of the 20th century, including—but not limited to—television, radio, newspapers and magazines, all which generally had a unidirectional distribution model. Sometimes "legacy media" is used interchangeably with "MSM," for "Mainstream Media." Legacy media sits in contrast with social media, where the production and sharing is of equal weight to the consumption.

**mashup** — A combination of data from multiple sources, usually through the use of application program interfaces. An example of a mashup would be an app that shows the locations of all the movie theaters in a particular town on a Google map. It is mashing up one data source (the addresses of movie theaters) with another data source (the geographic location of those addresses on a map).

**mobile** — An umbrella term in technology that was long synonymous with cellular phones but has since grown to encompass tablet computing (the iPad) and even

## ONLINE INSIGHTS > **Continued**

netbooks. Sometimes the term is used interchangeably with "wireless." It generally refers to untethered computing devices that can access the Internet over radiofrequency waves, though sometimes also via Wi-Fi. Mobile technology usually demands a different set of standards — design and otherwise — than desktop computers and has opened up an entirely new area for geo-aware applications.

**platform** — In the technology world, platform refers to the hardware or software that other applications are built on. Computing platforms include Windows PC and Macintosh. Mobile platforms include Android, iPhone and Palm's Web operating system. More recently, in an extension of its commonly used definition, Facebook has created a "platform," allowing developers to build applications on top of it.

**RSS (Really Simple Syndication)** — A standard for websites to push their content to readers through Web formats to create regular updates through a "feed reader" or "RSS Reader." The symbol is generally a orange square with radiating white quarter circles.

**Scribd** — A document-sharing site that is often described as a "YouTube for documents" because it allows other sites to embed its content. It allows people to upload files and others to download in various formats. Recently, Scribd moved from Flash-based technology to HTML5 standards.

**SEO (Search Engine Optimization)** — A suite of techniques for improving how a website ranks on search engines such as Google. SEO is often divided into "white hat" techniques, which (to simplify) try to boost ranking by improving the quality of a website, and "black hat" techniques, which try to trick search engines into thinking a page is of higher quality than it actually is.

**SEM (Search Engine Marketing)** — A type of marketing that involves raising a company or product's visibility in search engines by paying to have it appear in search results for a given word.

**URL (Uniform Resource Locator)** — Often used interchangeably with the "address" of a Web page, such as http://hackshackers.com. While humans are familiar with URLs as a way to see Web pages, computer programs often use URLs to pass each other machine-readable content, such as RSS feeds or Twitter information.

**Web 2.0** — Referring to the generation of Internet technologies that allow for interactivity and collaboration on websites. In contrast to Web 1.0 (roughly the first decade of the World Wide Web) where static content was downloaded into the browser and read, Web 2.0 uses the Internet as the platform.

**widget** — This refers to a portable application that can be embedded into a third-party site by cutting and pasting snippets of code. Common Web widgets include a Twitter box that can sit on a blog or a small Google Map that sits within an invitation. Desktop widgets, such as ones offered for the Macintosh Dashboard or by Yahoo!, can be placed on the desktop of a computer, such as for weather or stocks.

**wiki** — A website with pages that can be easily edited by visitors using their Web browser, but generally now gaining acceptance as a prefix to mean "collaborative." Ward Cunningham created the first wiki, naming it WikiWikiWeb after the Hawaiian word for "quick." A wiki enables the audience to contribute to a knowledge base on a topic or share information within an organization, like a newsroom. The best-known wiki in existence is Wikipedia, which burst onto the scene around the year 2000 as one of the first examples of mass collaborative information aggregation. Other sites that have been branded "wiki" include Wikinews, Wikitravel and WikiLeaks (which was originally but is no longer a wiki).

*—From "A Roadmap for Journalism × Technology," Version 1.0, released June 22, 2010, under a Creative Commons Attribution Share-Alike 3.0 License.*

race is appropriate, especially as the reporter likely would include in the story other physical details — his height, hairstyle, clothing — to help apprehend him.

After the suspect's arrest, a lead might read: *Elliott Green, a 24-year-old black man, was arrested Friday and charged with robbing the Quick Shop on Main Street on Tuesday.* The suspect's name and age are relevant; however, his race is not. Cut it.

Some terms are unnecessarily gender specific. Review the following examples, the recommended substitution for each and whether the AP stylebook covers it:

- *actress* — > actor, performer. (The stylebook says it's OK to use actress for female performers who prefer it.)
- *businessman* — > executive, business person, manager, entrepreneur.
- *congressman* — > member of Congress, representative, legislator, senator. (The stylebook recommends congressman or congresswoman, as appropriate.)
- *councilman, councilwoman* — > councilmember. (The stylebook advises using either councilman or councilwoman, as appropriate.)
- *craftsman* — > craftsperson, artisan, crafter.
- *forefathers* — > ancestors, precursors, forebears.
- *foreman* — > supervisor. (The stylebook says to use foreman or forewoman, as appropriate.)
- *gentlemen's agreement* — > personal agreement, informal contract.
- *layman* — > layperson, lay, laity, lay person, lay member.
- *man-hours* — > work hours, staff hours, hours worked, total hours.
- *manhunt* — > a hunt for. . . .
- *mankind* — > humanity, human race, human beings, people, human family, humankind. (Although the stylebook says that mankind is OK if no other term is convenient, it recommends humanity, person or individual.)
- *man-made* — > artificial, handmade, of human origin, synthetic, manufactured, crafted, machine made.
- *manpower* — > work force, human resources, labor force, personnel, workers.
- *middleman* — > go-between, liaison, agent. (The stylebook says that middleman is acceptable.)
- *salesman* — > sales person, sales representative, salesclerk, seller, agent.
- *spokesman* — > representative. (The stylebook advises using spokesman or spokeswoman, as appropriate. If the gender is unknown, then representative is acceptable.)
- *workman* — > worker, laborer, employee.

Clearly, these examples illustrate that the stylebook doesn't address many common noninclusive terms. Religion, education and special-interest groups seem more active in promoting inclusive language. Nevertheless, even though the stylebook may allow you to use some noninclusive terms, you still have an ethical responsibility to cut them from stories when you can.

# AP POTPOURRI *exercise 1*

**DIRECTIONS:** Correct *AP style* errors in the following exercises. Some may be correct. Check the spelling of all names in the Heartland Directory.

1.  The blond coed, who is working on her bachelor of arts degree in English at Twain State University, has a problem making it to all of her classes because she has two kids.

2.  Drunk driving is a controversial issue today, especially among teen-aged drivers in Missouri.

3.  The boy often sneaked into the Heartland Theatre when it was showing R-rated films.

4.  The local TV anchorman was arrested for disorderly conduct while he was covering the peace rally in front of Heartland city hall.

5.  The Heartland City Council is meeting Monday to consider an ordinance authorizing the razing of Main Street Hardware, which was partially destroyed by fire in August.

6.  The Jones twins, compared to other close siblings, rarely quibbled among themselves.

7.  The attorney for the two scouts who were accused with setting fire to the Boy Scout cabins expected a quick trial.

8.  Baby-boomers now largely comprise the Legionnaires at American Legion Post 287.

9.  Prosecuting Attorney Aaron Smith on Friday charged Anson Williams, 22, with allegedly raping a 16-year-old woman.

10. If Mayor Karl Shearin were given good reasons, he might support future plans for the Cooper County Industrial Park.

**Additional exercises are available online at** www.oup.com/us/rosenauer.

# Style Mastery

The exercises in this chapter will test your mastery of AP style covered in chapters 5–11. Refer to those, as needed, to check the discussions, guidelines and rules.

# STYLE MASTERY *exercise 1*

**DIRECTIONS**: Correct errors involving *all aspects of AP style, including word choice and spelling,* in the following exercises. Some may be correct. No need to worry about punctuation, but check the spelling of all names in the Heartland Directory.

1. It's Fall, one of the prettiest times of the year for the Heartland Arboretum, located on the Twain State University Campus.

2. Maintenance staff will plant nine new species in the arboretum this month, thanks to a $2,700 donation from Mrs. John Spencer, outgoing president of the Twain State alumni association.

3. Spencer selected the trees from a list of desired species maintained by forester Horace Martine.

4. They include a Fraser Fir, Balsam Fir, Trident Maple, Sweet Birch, Monarch Birch, Chinese Pine, Quaking Aspen, Serbian Spruce and English Walnut.

5. Most of the stock is three years old, with heights ranging from four feet to seven feet tall.

6. Martin said he is anxious to begin planting soon since the new trees will be a stunning compliment to current varieties.

7. "We've had cites selected for each of these trees for the past two years," he said, adding that all trees on the desired list are planted following the master plan.

8. 105 tree species make up the arboretum, and Martin considers the specific needs of each as well as esthetic and practical criteria when planting them.

9. The arboretum is divided into 3 carefully maintained locations: Huck Finn Glen, Mark Twain Trail and Tom Sawyer Meadow.

10. Tom Sawyer Meadow, the largest area, is located in the northwest corner of campus on eleven acres of rolling hills while Huck Finn Glen is in the center of campus, and Mark Twain Trail is Southwest of Altman Stadium.

# STYLE MASTERY *exercise 2*

**DIRECTIONS**: Correct errors involving *all aspects of AP style, including word choice and spelling,* in the following exercises. Some may be correct. No need to worry about punctuation, but check the spelling of all names in the Heartland Directory.

1. Cotton candy, 4 H exhibits, tractor pulls, sideshows, the Ferris wheel and Country music are all regular features of county fairs.

2. So, when the week-long Cooper County Fair opens July 11th in Heartland, visitors can expect to see all those and more.

3. Hilda Jo Boudoin, president of the Cooper County Fair Board of Directors, says this year's line up is the best yet.

4. "Two thousand and ten was a great fair," she explained, "but this year's is premiere in every way imaginable."

5. A featured attraction for 2012 is the Sons of the Pioneers, in town for a one-night, special engagement from their Branson, MO., theatre.

6. Admission to the fairgrounds is free, but admission to Big Grandstand entertainment is $8 for adults and $3 for children under seven.

7. Carnival rides, operated by Lewellen Amusements Inc. of Andover, KS., include a Ferris wheel, Tilt-A-Whirl, Gravitron, Spider and more.

8. For unlimited rides, visitors can purchase either single-night arm bands at $12 for adults and $8 for children or run-of-fair arm bands at $50 for adults and $30 for children.

9. A half dozen food booths — with favorites such as hamburgers, hot dogs, gyros, cotton candy, caramel apples, chicken on a stick and ice cream — should offer plenty of choices to suit every palette.

10. Hours for the fair are 10 A.M. to 11 P.M. Monday thru Sunday.

# STYLE MASTERY *exercise 3*

**DIRECTIONS**: Correct errors involving *all aspects of AP style, including word choice and spelling,* in the following exercises. Some may be correct. No need to worry about punctuation, but check the spelling of all names in the Heartland Directory.

1. A 19-year-old Heartland boy died, and a New Franklin couple were injured Friday night at 9 p.m. in a two-car accident north of the city.

2. Edgar S. Black Jr., of 2618 Faraon Street, was killed, and David and Cyndi Smith received minor injuries.

3. Firemen from the Cooper County Rural Fire Department in New Franklin used the Jaws of Life to extricate Black from his vehicle.

4. An ambulance transported him to Heartland Memorial Hospital where Cooper County coroner Dianne Weams pronounced him dead.

5. David Smith, 48 complained of neck injuries, and Mrs. Smith, 44, reported some bruises on her head and arms.

6. The accident happened on Missouri highway 87 about three miles northwest of the city.

7. Black's car collided with Smith's car, which had stopped to turn east on County Rd. 342.

8. Corporal Seth Vaughn, of the Missouri Highway Patrol, said that none of those involved in the accident were wearing seat belts.

9. Cooper County Deputy Sheriff William Birdsong said, "Since this is the 3rd accident at this junction during the past two years, we're going to ask Highway Engineers to consider installing warning lights."

10. Black, the son of Mr. and Mrs. Edgar S. Black Sr., was a sophomore majoring in biology at Twain State University.

# STYLE MASTERY *exercise 4*

**DIRECTIONS**: Correct errors involving *all aspects of AP style, including word choice and spelling,* in the following exercises. Some may be correct. No need to worry about punctuation, but check the spelling of all names in the Heartland Directory.

1.  The Twain State University River Raiders win over the Northwest Mo. State University Bearcats Saturday set a new school record.

2.  The Raiders are 9 and 0 on the season following their 24-to-21 win, beating their previous best season of 8–1, set in 1997.

3.  The two teams had come into the contest nationally ranked, with the Raiders at No. 12 and the Bearcats at number five.

4.  The American Football Coaches' Association (AFCA) should release new figures for the Top 25 Division II Poll tomorrow.

5.  Twain Head Coach Jerry Jarvis believes their performance against Northwest should push them up in the standings, perhaps by as many as six spots — another record for the school.

6.  While both coach and team basked in the warmth of their win Sunday, it was business as usual on Monday as Twain State prepared for Saturday's game against another Mid-America Athletics Association team, Missouri Southern State University.

7.  Raider quarterback Alan Newhart said both offenses started slow Saturday, but each found its groove mid-way through the 2nd quarter.

8.  "When we face Southern," Newhart said, "we'll have to crank it up and come out scoring in the 1st quarter."

9.  Though the Lions are unranked, Jarvis said it would be critical to hold them to less yards than they've wracked up in their last three games.

10. Amidst all the hoopla surrounding that dual, the game likely will settle any questions concerning the Raiders' playoff potential.

**Additional exercises are available online at** www.oup.com/us/rosenauer.

# PART 3

# Punctuation and Usage

## CHAPTER 13

# Commas

*"The preferred tool for placement of commas is a pair of tweezers, not a salt shaker."*

~Audrey Dorsch

Comma usage is troublesome for many journalists. Some spend time fretting over whether a comma is needed here or there. Others insert commas willy-nilly. Still others seem to ignore them. The following cover the most common comma rules that you likely will need. Read them. Understand them. Practice them. Then, you will use commas correctly, at least most of the time.

For additional explanations and examples beyond these following, refer to the punctuation usage section of the stylebook — which is quite clear in its guidance — search online or check a Standard English handbook.

## Compound Sentences: Use a comma before a coordinating conjunction that joins two or more independent clauses (complete sentences)

Coordinating conjunctions include the following: *and, or, nor, but, for, yet, so*. Some contexts call for *either-or* and *neither-nor* pairings. All of these have subtle but specific meanings that help show the relationship of one clause to another.

Remember that an independent clause is one that can stand alone and includes at least a subject and verb and often a direct object, as in the following:

- *Marilyn lost her father to cancer last year, <u>and</u> she lost her only brother in a car accident this year.*
- *In that time either she has taken solace in the belief that they are in heaven, <u>or</u> she has grieved at their no longer being here with her.*
- *It is not easy to overcome depression, <u>nor</u> will life seem brighter soon.*
- *Marilyn often felt like it was the end of her world, <u>but</u> life goes on following personal tragedy.*
- *She deals with the losses each day, <u>for</u> she is a sensitive person.*
- *Marilyn thinks often about both of them, <u>yet</u> the pain has eased over time.*
- *Her family has helped her through this difficult time, <u>so</u> Marilyn is optimistic about her future.*

Note that the trend today, which AP style encourages, is to drop the comma between two *short* independent clauses, as in the following:

- *My ride is here <u>and</u> I must go.*
- *You won't like this <u>but</u> that's too bad.*
- *Henry is angry <u>yet</u> he remains calm.*

Some sentences with a single subject use coordinating conjunctions to connect compound predicates, that is, the verb and direct object package following a subject. These *do not take* commas before the conjunctions. Consider the following examples:

- *Claire sought to make things right <u>but</u> was ill-equipped to do so alone.*
- *Some movies like "It's a Wonderful Life" are classics <u>and</u> continue to delight audiences.*
- *Heavy snow blanketed the state <u>and</u> shut down travel in most areas.*

A word of caution: The seven coordinating conjunctions are the only words you can use to join two independent clauses with only a comma. Consider the following: *Marilyn is trying to build a closer relationship with her mother, however, that will take time.* This is a common error in which the writer seeks to join the two independent clauses with a comma and the conjunctive adverb *however*.

Two fixes are available. Either replace the comma before *however* with a semicolon or replace the *however* and comma following with the coordinating conjunction *but*.

# Elements in a Series: Use a comma to separate three or more elements in a series, except for the last element

Among the most common and easiest of these comma rules is the listing of related elements following one another, where the last is joined by conjunctions "and" or "or." Use commas following each element except the final one joined by the conjunction, as in the following:

- *His favorite pastimes are reading, fishing and photographing nature.*
- *John, Manuel, Pete and Stevie have been friends since second grade.*
- *His Swiss army knife can cut, clip, screw, drill and pick.*

Note that this is journalistic style; standard American grammar does *not* have writers drop the comma before the conjunction in elements in a series.

# Other Series: Use a comma to separate a series of adjectives modifying a single noun or a sequence of date or place elements

The stylebook calls such a series of adjectives *equal adjectives*. A good tip in applying this usage is that you should use commas if you can logically insert *and* between these equal adjectives. The following illustrate this rule:

- *He'd like to think that he is an intelligent, hardworking man.*
- *Sylvia is seeking a fulfilling, high-paying job following graduation in May.*

However, as the stylebook notes, do not use the comma if the last adjective before the noun "outranks" those preceding it, as in *expensive sports car*, where *sports car* is a noun phrase comparable to a single noun.

Another word of caution: Make sure the modifiers are adjectives. The rule does not apply to adverb-adjective series, as in the following:

- *Some friends have joked that he may be a very hardworking man but not a very intelligent one.* (Whereas *hardworking* and *intelligent* are adjectives, *very* is an adverb that modifies these adjectives. By the way, usually avoid use of *very*; it isn't as strong an adverb as some journalists would like to think.)
- *Regardless, he has been a gainfully employed professor since 1976.* (Like most words ending in *-ly*, *gainfully* is an adverb.)

In a sequence of date elements with month, date and year, precede and follow the year with commas. Similarly, precede and follow the state with commas in a sequence of place elements that includes the city and state. Consider the following:

- *Her vacation began on Friday, July 10, 2012, after she got off work.* (Sequence of date elements.)
- *He was born in Heartland, Mo., at Heartland Memorial Hospital.* (Sequence of place elements.)

# Introductory Elements: Use a comma to set off introductory elements (clauses, phrases and words), especially those containing a verb or verb form

Sometimes a sentence begins with dependent clause, phrase or word that delays the actual subject of the sentence. In such cases insert a comma between the introductory material and the main clause. However, you usually do not need a comma when the dependent clause follows the main clause. See how this rule works in the following:

- *If you are a good writer, you probably enjoy telling stories.* (Introductory dependent clause.)
- *Whenever you have a good story to tell, writing probably comes easily.* (Introductory dependent clause.)
- *However, when you don't have much to say, writing can be grueling.* (Introductory transition and introductory dependent clause.)
- *Often wasting a lot of time staring at a blank sheet of paper or computer screen, such writers may learn to dislike writing.* (Introductory participial phrase.)
- *To change this attitude, a weak writer must find something worth saying.* (Introductory infinitive phrase.)
- *Sadly, some of the worst writers don't even know their writing is weak.* (Introductory adverb.)

When the introductory element contains no verb or verb form and is short, use your own judgment about whether to follow it with a comma. Consider the following:

- *In her garage Margot set up a full-fledged auto repair shop.*
- *For fun Hank played pranks on his little sister.*

# Interrupting Elements: Use commas to set off an interrupting element from the rest of the sentence, especially nonessential clauses, phrases and words, as well as other interrupters

Nonessential elements are those that add noncritical information, although likely informative. Some of these are appositives, nouns or phrases that rename or further describe a noun, noun phrase or pronoun and follow the material they modify. Pronouns *which*, *who* or *whom* often introduce nonessential clauses. The pronoun *that* introduces essential clauses, which do *not* take commas. See how the examples here follow these guidelines:

- *His oldest brother, Steve, worked many years as a trucker.* (*Oldest* clearly defines one brother, so his name is nonessential.)
- *Carolyn, who is a social worker, is the oldest in her family.* (That Carolyn is a social worker isn't essential to understanding that she is the oldest.)
- *The state's annual budget, which passed 127–34 in the Missouri House of Representatives, calls for a $261 million cut in spending.* (Regardless of the actual vote, the cut remains the same; therefore, the vote is nonessential, and commas set it off.)
- *Ken Jones, of Heartland, is the leading candidate in the upcoming mayoral race.* (AP style says that whether the *of* is used or not, hometowns immediately following names are nonessential appositives and take commas.)

- *Jones, 60, is the former CEO of Heartland Widgets and has not previously held public office.* (Ages that immediately follow a noun or pronoun also are nonessential appositives, requiring commas.)
- *His brother Ron was the youngest in his family.* (The name here is essential to know which brother is the youngest; therefore, do not use a comma.)
- *Students flocked to see the 2009 film "Avatar."* (The name of the film is essential to know which 2009 film.)

Commas set off interrupters such as "yes" and "no." Also, a direct address needs commas, as in the following:

- *Yes, his sister Karen is his twin.* ("Yes" set off by comma. Note no commas around *Karen* because the name here is essential.)
- *No, dear readers, they are not identical twins.* (It uses both *no* and a direct address.)

# Attribution: Use commas to set off all attribution for direct quotations and attributions that do not *introduce* indirect quotations

Attribution identifies the source of content, including speaker or source and a related verb. Use commas to set off attribution of all direct quotations and attribution that follows indirect quotations. Do *not* use a comma to set off attribution that precedes indirect quotations. Consider the following:

- *Ann said, "I am ready to leave for class."* (Attribution introducing a direct quotation.)
- *"I'll grab some fast-food breakfast," she added, "or end up starving before lunch."* (Attribution within a direct quotation.)
- *"By the way, I'll be late for dinner," she said while walking out the door.* (Attribution following a direct quote.)
- *Regular meals are important, Ann believes, to maintain good health.* (Attribution within an indirect quotation.)
- *However, sometimes it is difficult to eat well while attending college, she explained to her parents.* (Attribution following an indirect quotation.)
- *She tells her friends that they should be careful in their own diets.* (Attribution introducing an indirect quotation *without* a comma.)

Note that commas (and periods) *always* go inside closing quotation marks.

# Large Numbers: Use commas with most numbers above 999

This is a standard practice for all large numbers. AP style lists several exceptions, though, including addresses, telephone numbers, room numbers, serial numbers and years. See this usage in the following:

- *Henry earned $4,500 at his job last summer.* (Number above 999.)
- *The population of Heartland, Mo., is 48,400.* (Number above 999.)
- *Her address is 12492 Winchester Court.* (Number above 999, but an address is an exception to the rule, so no comma.)

# Beyond the Rules

The preceding rules will cover most situations; however, when a rule doesn't clearly cover a situation, three more guidelines may help:

1. Never use a single comma between a subject and its verb.

    This is the easiest way to get out of some comma pickles where you're unsure of the specific rule. Either *no commas* or *two commas* always follow a subject.

2. When in doubt, leave it out.

    Commas can be tricky to use correctly. Some people learn — incorrectly — to put a comma wherever a reader pauses; actually, the reverse is true. If you cannot find a rule that tells you to use a comma, you are wise to leave it out.

3. Use a comma to prevent misreading.

Let your ear be your guide in applying this guideline, as in the following:

- "Let's eat, Grandma." *or* "Let's eat Grandma."
- Whatever will be, will be.

# COMMA *exercise 1 — compound sentences and elements in a series*

**DIRECTIONS**: Correct *comma* errors involving *compound sentences* and *elements in a series* in the following exercises. Some may be correct. Check the spelling of all names in the Heartland Directory.

1. Enrolling in college can be challenging frustrating and time-consuming.

2. Ask students and most will have something to say about their first experiences in registering.

3. Some will say that the task wasn't that bad so they can't understand the problems others faced.

4. The majority, though, will grimace at the memory and recount their registration battle stories.

5. Probably topping the list of complaints are the long lines lousy choices for class times closed classes and unappealing class choices.

6. Many schools work to improve enrollment experiences, especially for first-time students but the challenges can be difficult to overcome.

7. Three things that have made the task more efficient include computer processing of schedules online registration for current students and splitting new students into smaller, more manageable groups.

8. Nevertheless, even extensive planning and well-designed procedures can fail, and leave new students dissatisfied.

9. Many colleges are concerned about keeping new students happy so they often will use a combination of student staff professional staff and faculty members to provide lots of TLC.

10. In the end the personal touch likely is the best practice for new students need to know that somebody cares.

# COMMA *exercise 2 — other series*

**DIRECTIONS**: Correct *comma* errors involving *other series* in the following exercises. Some may be correct. Check the spelling of all names in the Heartland Directory.

**1.** Some students find history to be a dull boring subject.

**2.** Others, however, are fascinated by the time-consuming tedious chore of remembering facts involving dates, places and events.

**3.** Yet, all Americans should know that Dec. 7 1941 is an important date in our history.

**4.** Because many historians, including Peter N. Stearns, argue that "the past causes the present and so the future,"[1] students should understand what happened at Valley Forge Pa. and Oak Ridge Tenn.

**5.** Part of the problem even for bright dedicated students is often the way history is taught.

**6.** Some teachers stress only the potentially boring approach that has students memorize places and dates.

**7.** Nevertheless, the best history teachers can bring alive the May 10 1869 event at Promontory Summit Utah when the tracks of the Central Pacific and Union Pacific railroads finally met.

**8.** They often rely less on what can be lifeless meaningless textbooks and more on powerfully stimulating film, music and other resources.

**9.** With increasingly convenient, ready access to the Internet, for example, students can find an abundance of websites about railroad songs.

**10.** These can provide unique valuable insight into the lives and experiences of the thousands of men who helped to bring our nation together with the first transcontinental railroad.

# COMMA *exercise 3 — Introductory Elements*

**DIRECTIONS**: Correct *comma* errors involving *introductory elements* in the following exercises. Some may be correct. Check the spelling of all names in the Heartland Directory.

1. After running a red light at the intersection of 5th and Main Thursday afternoon a car driven by William Anderson struck a 6-year-old boy on a bicycle, according to Heartland Police reports.

2. Although he was not seriously injured the boy was taken by ambulance to Heartland Memorial Hospital.

3. When Heartland police Sgt. Mike Rose questioned Anderson he refused to discuss details of the accident.

4. Following a field sobriety test administered by Rose Anderson was arrested on suspicion of driving while intoxicated.

5. However he protested that he had not been drinking and struggled with Rose.

6. Subduing Anderson required the police officer to use his pepper spray, and he was able to handcuff the man.

7. Inside the squad car the suspect began kicking at a back window, forcing Rose to threaten use of the spray again.

8. Fortunately Anderson stopped kicking and remained calm as he was taken to Heartland Law Enforcement Center.

9. If convicted on the DWI charge Anderson could receive a $500 fine and spend up to six months in jail.

10. According to Cooper County Prosecutor Aaron Smith Anderson also may be charged with failure to stop at a stop sign and failure to yield right of way.

# COMMA *exercise 4 — interrupting elements*

**DIRECTIONS**: Correct *comma* errors involving *interrupting elements* in the following exercises. Some may be correct. Check the spelling of all names in the Heartland Directory.

1.  Construction begins Tuesday on a new Heartland School District middle school which was approved by voters in April.

2.  Cost for the 80,000 square foot building the first new school in the district since 1975 will be $21 million.

3.  Although the school will accommodate approximately 525 students when it opens in two years, its capacity is 650 enough to handle anticipated growth in the district for the next 10 years.

4.  The goal is to reduce overcrowding at Garfield and Roosevelt two of the district's middle schools.

5.  A state-of-the-art multimedia learning center considered by many voters as key to their support will be the best in this part of the state, officials have said.

6.  Another highlight of the new school is a basketball arena that will allow two games to be played simultaneously a benefit that none of the other middle schools can match.

7.  In addition, the energy-saving features of the new building will allow it to operate more cheaply than the current middle schools a cost reduction estimated to be at least 25 percent.

8.  The district also will see savings in removing seven temporary classroom units from the other middle schools which annually cost more than $10,000 each in lease payments.

9.  Staffing at the new school not yet officially named should total 40 certified teachers, two administrators and three clerical workers.

10. Although the majority of these teachers will be transferred from other schools, district officials have said they will need at least eight new positions each costing an average of $40,000.

**Additional exercises are available online at www.oup.com/us/rosenauer.**

## CHAPTER 14

# Semicolons and Colons

*"A semicolon is like a guy standing on a tightrope: he has to have things of equal weight on either side — that is, syntactically independent units. A colon, on the other hand, is like a pair of eyes looking expectantly: what's on one side depends on what's on the other side."*

~James Harbeck, Editors' Association of Canada member

Semicolons and colons often are misunderstood, misused and neglected. You might be able to live without them, but there's no reason you should. These two marks are handy and sometimes necessary for specific uses in journalism.

The general sense of semicolon usage is that it is a stronger separation than a comma but not as strong as a period. Material joined with semicolons tends to be closely related. Colons, on the other hand, serve primarily to introduce something. Of course, we will assume that the use of the colon to indicate clock time (as in 4:45 p.m.) can go without further explanation.

For additional explanations and examples beyond those following, refer to the punctuation usage section of the stylebook — which is quite clear in its guidance — search online or check out a Standard English handbook.

# Semicolons — Independent Clauses (Complete Sentences) Joined Without Coordinating Conjunctions

We know from Chapter 13 that you always can use a comma and coordinating conjunction to join two independent clauses (full sentences) and to show how they relate to one another. However, there are times when you may seek a tighter connection without the relationship signal offered by the conjunction, as in the following examples:

- *Andrea and Sam have known each other since 7th grade, and they have a special friendship.* (Two independent clauses joined by a comma and the coordinating conjunction *and*.)—> *Andrea and Sam have known each other since 7th grade; they have a special friendship.* (Two independent clauses joined by only the semicolon. See the difference?)

- *She wants a greater commitment from Sam, but he wants to play the field.* (Two independent clauses joined by a comma and the coordinating conjunction *but*.)—> *She wants a greater commitment from Sam; he wants to play the field.* (Two independent clauses joined by only the semicolon. Some writers might wish to signal the relationship between these two clauses by inserting the conjunctive adverb *however* followed by a comma, as in the following: *She wants a greater commitment from Sam; however, he wants to play the field.*)

# Semicolons — Elements in Series That Have Commas

This is an easy rule to follow. Although you normally use commas to separate elements in a series, use semicolons to separate each of the element groups when one or more of those groups already have commas. This makes clearer to readers the separation of the items. See how the following sentences illustrate this:

- *Robert was a young, successful engineer; had a lovely wife; and lived in a large, upscale home in the suburbs.*
- *However, to be totally happy, he wanted a cherry red, fully restored 1957 Thunderbird; a beachfront home at Oak Island, N.C.; and a mint condition, first edition of John Steinbeck's "The Grapes of Wrath."*

You also might use semicolons instead of commas to join long or otherwise complex elements in a series.

# Colons — Introduction of Lists

Using colons to introduce lists probably is the most common and familiar use for journalists. Essentially, what follows the colon expands on what precedes it.

A key requirement is that what precedes the colon is a complete sentence. If it isn't, drop the colon, as in this example: *Delilah went to the mall to get the following: a new sundress for vacation, the latest CD by Britney Spears, new batteries for her digital camera and some snacks for the long drive.* (Alternatively, you could write it this way: *Delilah went to the mall to get a new sundress for vacation, the latest CD by Britney Spears, new batteries for her digital camera and some snacks for the long drive.*)

# Colons — Separations for Explanations, Rules or Examples from Preceding Independent Clauses (Full Sentences)

This usage is similar to the preceding one; however, instead of introducing a list, the independent clause introduces an explanation, an amplification or an example. Capitalize the first word following the colon if it is a proper noun or begins an independent clause. See this rule applied in the following:

- *The message was clear: He needed to leave now.* (What precedes the colon is a full sentence that introduces what follows the colon, which is also a full sentence.)
- *He had only one option: drop the lawsuit.* (Here, the material preceding the colon is a full sentence that introduces what follows; however, because the material following is not a full sentence, do not capitalize *drop*.)

# Other Uses

Reporters sometimes use colons following a speech tag that introduces a direct quotation. However, AP has some clear distinctions for this usage. It says to use a comma following the tag if the quote is a single sentence within the same paragraph but to use a colon if the direct quote is long and within the same paragraph or if the direct quote that follows is a separate paragraph, as in the following examples:

- *Jones said, "We are not responsible for the screw-ups that led to the collapse of the building."* (Here, use just the comma following the speech tag that introduces a simple direct quote.)
- *Allison O'Brien said: "I am delighted to win this prestigious award. It represents for me the culmination of years of effort, and I am honored at being chosen by the panel of judges. It made all the long hours I put into my project well worth the sacrifice."* (The colon here follows the speech tag that introduces a long direct quote.)

Also use colons to present subtitles that follow titles, as in "Storycrafting: A Process Approach to Writing News."

# SEMICOLONS/COLONS *exercise 1*

**DIRECTIONS**: Correct *semicolon and colon* errors in the following exercises. Some may be correct. Check the spelling of all names in the Heartland Directory.

1. The Tucker family will serve as grand marshals for the 2013 Peach Blossom Parade, the parade rolls down Market Avenue May 4 at 10 a.m.

2. The parade theme this year is: "A Tribute to Heartland Families: The Heart of Our City."

3. "We thought the Tuckers would be perfect representatives, they are an original Heartland family," Peach Blossom Executive Director Mindy Wolfe said.

4. Martin Tucker is state representative for the 132nd District in the Missouri House and represents voters in the following counties, Cooper County, Moniteau County and parts of Morgan and Pettis counties.

5. Lavelle Tucker is a social worker for the Heartland School District; is the president of the Heartland Black Archives; and was Peach Blossom queen in 1988.

6. As Heartland's favorite parade, based on the People's Choice Awards; the Peach Blossom is an excellent opportunity for the community to give the Tuckers the recognition they deserve, said Ken Zaner, president of the Peach Blossom.

7. The couple has four sons: Mike, a defensive end for the Green Bay Packers, Martin "T," a top contender in the NFL draft this year, Bill, a sales representative for Heartland Widgets and Micah, a social science professor at Twain State University.

8. Zahner said: "This family embodies the spirit of this year's parade theme perfectly."

9. All parade entries are encouraged to reflect in their entries the theme for this year's Peach Blossom; "A Tribute to Heartland Families: The Heart of Our City."

10. For additional information and entry forms, contact Wolfe: by phone at 573–261–0422, by email at mwolfe@ peachblossom.com or online at www.peachblossom.com.

**Additional exercises are available online at** www.oup.com/us/rosenauer.

## CHAPTER 15

# Apostrophes

*"Inattention to the proper use of punctuation can inconspicuously help to undermine a civilization, because it weakens the mortar — language — that holds that civilization together."*

~Paul Wilson

Hold on to your hats because as simple as they may seem, apostrophes cover a lot of territory. As you review the uses for apostrophes, you should find many that you know. However, AP is specific about apostrophe use and may not follow some practices you have used previously. Many you can pick up quickly, especially after you've read the rules and examples and worked through the exercises following. For the rest check the stylebook whenever the need arises — always a good practice.

## Possessives

Using an apostrophe to indicate possession likely is its most frequent application. Before you think that you already know how to indicate possession, though, read on.

- Singular nouns not ending in *-s* — Add the *-'s*. The stylebook departs here from guidance in some handbooks, with AP saying that even if a word ends in a sound similar to *-s* (*-ce, -x, -z*), add the *-'s*, as in the following:
  - ▶ *customer's needs*

- ▶ *house's rafters*
- ▶ *ice's weight*
- ▶ *quiz's scores*
- Singular common nouns ending in *-s* — Like the previous rule, add the *-'s*, except when the word following begins with *-s*. Then, add the apostrophe, as in the following:
  - ▶ *fortress's occupants*
  - ▶ *fortress' stability*
  - ▶ *watercress's crunch*
  - ▶ *watercress' simple appearance*
- Singular proper names ending in *-s* — Add the apostrophe, as in the following:
  - ▶ *Sisyphus' boulder*
  - ▶ *William Carlos Williams' best poetry*
  - ▶ *Jesus' miracles*
  - ▶ *Arkansas' role*
- Plural nouns not ending in *-s* — Add the *-'s*, as in the following:
  - ▶ *men's club*
  - ▶ *people's right to know*
  - ▶ *deer's food preferences*
  - ▶ *geese's formation*
- Plural nouns ending in *-s* — Add the apostrophe, as in the following:
  - ▶ *dogs' dishes*
  - ▶ *cities' scourge*
  - ▶ *chairs' covers*
  - ▶ *flowers' scent*
- Nouns plural in form but singular in meaning — Add the apostrophe, as in the following:
  - ▶ *pants' length*
  - ▶ *eyeglasses' availability*
  - ▶ *gymnastics' most ardent supporter*
  - ▶ *scissors' cutting edge*

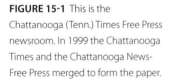

**FIGURE 15-1** This is the Chattanooga (Tenn.) Times Free Press newsroom. In 1999 the Chattanooga Times and the Chattanooga News-Free Press merged to form the paper.

# Contractions

Contractions are another familiar usage of the apostrophe; they are commonplace in informal speech and writing and more popular today than ever in publications and online. Just avoid excessive use.

For example, unless in a direct quotation, *ain't* is never acceptable.

Also, make sure that you avoid common contraction errors, such as using *it's* (contraction for *it is*) when the context calls for *it has*, as in the following:

- Incorrect: *It's been 10 years since the two saw each other.*
- Correct: *It has been 10 years since the two saw each other.*

# Single Letters

Forming the plural of single letters is straightforward: Add *-'s*, as in the following:

- *Sheila earned two A's and three B's in the fall semester.*
- *Minding your p's and q's means minding your manners.*
- *The Oakland A's were the Kansas City Athletics from 1955 to 1967.*

On the other hand, to form the plural of multiple letters, add *-s*, as in the following:

- *Learning the ABCs is still an important lesson for kindergarteners.*
- *Benjamin left a trail of IOUs in residence halls across campus.*
- *Campus VIPs typically are invited to the president's office.*

# Figures

To form the plural of figures, including references to decades, add *-s*, as in the following:

- *The 1990s were boom years for dot-com startup companies.*
- *Airbus A380s are the newest jumbo airliners on the market today.*
- *He stomped his size 12s onto the bug.*

Note: This is an exception to apostrophe guidelines in Webster's New World College Dictionary.

# Double Possessives

These are tricky beasts; fortunately, they're not too common. We know that possession is signified by either the *-'s* (or the apostrophe alone), as in *the country's treasury*, or with the preposition *of*, as in *the treasury of the country*. Double possessives involve phrases such as *a book of Brenda's*. Stylebook guidelines offer two conditions that must be met to use double possessive:

1. The word following *of* must refer to an animate (living) object.
2. The word preceding *of* must involve only part of the animate object's possessions.

Thus, consider the following:

- *A car of John's was in an accident near campus.* (The word following *of* is animate, and the word preceding *of* is only one of his possessions. Note the distinction between this and one of the following: *One of John's cars was in an accident* or *John's car was in an accident.*)

Bottom line, double possessives often sound odd to many of us. When they do, recast the sentence to eliminate them.

# Omitted Letters or Figures

Although the contractions just listed cover the most common occurrences of omitted letters, you may encounter several others, as in the following:

- *'Twas a night not fit for man nor beast.* (The apostrophe indicates a missing *i*, as in *it was.*)
- *Elvis was regarded as the king of rock 'n' roll.* (The apostrophes indicate missing letters, the *a* and *d*, as in *and.*)
- *Philip had worked hard to earn his reputation as a ne'er-do-well.* (The apostrophe indicates the missing *v*, as in *never.*)
- *Elmo ate a po'boy every day after class.* (Here, the apostrophe indicates the missing *or*, as in *poor.*)

Use the apostrophe to indicate omitted figures, as in the following:

- *Most members of the class of '12 were born in 1991.*
- *When we think of the Spirit of '76, we typically think of George Washington.*
- *The '60s were represented by free love, cheap pot and other gentle rebellions.* (Note the use not only of the apostrophe for the omitted *19* but also the lack of apostrophe for the plural form of year for the decade.)

Note: This is an exception to apostrophe guidelines in Webster's New World College Dictionary.

# Descriptive Phrases

When words are used more in a descriptive (or adjectival) sense rather than possessive, don't use either the *-'s* or apostrophe alone. This can be a little more troublesome when the words are plural. Consider the following:

- Prefer *the university extension office* rather than *the university's extension office.*
- Prefer *the teacher strike* or *the teachers strike* rather than *the teachers' strike.*
- *citizens band radio.* (This is a specific AP style entry.)

However, when a plural word in such contexts does not end in *s*, add the *-'s*, as in the following:

- *He joined a men's club.*
- *It is the people's right to defend their homes.*

# Plural Words

When you are referring to a word itself in the plural, use *-s* with no apostrophe, as in the following:

- *He was tired of dealing with dos and don'ts.*
- *Conflicts often erupt between the haves and the have-nots.*

Note: This is an exception to apostrophe guidelines in Webster's New World College Dictionary.

# Special Expressions

You will need to commit to memory a few phrases you may encounter, as in the following:

- *for appearance' sake*
- *for conscience' sake*
- *for goodness' sake*

# APOSTROPHES *exercise 1*

**DIRECTIONS**: Correct *apostrophe* errors in the following exercises. Some may be correct. Check the spelling of all names in the Heartland Directory.

1. Budget cuts topped the agenda at the Heartland School Board Tuesday night's meeting.

2. School officials and board members fine-tuned cuts and reductions due to last weeks levy and bond defeats, which left the district with a $380,000 deficit.

3. However, although the district scaled back to 37 its pre-election vow to cut 132 teachers, Director of Finance Melody Jones recommended elimination of 82 noncertified jobs.

4. Jones's goal was to stay as far away from the classroom as possible in working to balance the budget.

5. "There have been a lot of rumors circulating about teacher cuts, that we would make more than needed just for appearance's sake, and we wanted to end those once and for all," she said.

6. The budget cuts biggest impact will be on school maintenance.

7. District Superintendent Byron Munson said, "If Lindbergh School needs a new roof, we wont be able to do that. We just cant go there."

8. Students' needs will be what drives spending until additional revenue can be found.

9. Nevertheless, this years' budget will see an increase in the cost for school lunches, with many previously free lunches eliminated.

10. At it's meeting next month, the board will give final approval to the district budget.

**Additional exercises are available online at www.oup.com/us/rosenauer.**

## CHAPTER 16

# Quotation Marks, Question Marks and Exclamation Points

*"Great books are weighed and measured by their style and matter, and not the trimmings and shadings of their grammar."*

~Mark Twain, Speech at the Annual Reunion of the Army and Navy Club of Connecticut (April 1887)

Of the three punctuation marks we will cover in this chapter, the one you will deal with most frequently is the quotation mark. In addition, whereas question marks and exclamation points have narrow, specific uses — most of which you are quite familiar with — using quotation marks correctly involves a number of rules.

## Quotation Marks — With Other Punctuation

You will regularly be using quotation marks with other punctuation. Follow some simple, basic rules, and you should have few problems:

- Commas and periods always go inside closing quotation marks, as in the following:
  - ▶ *Near the end of his inaugural speech, President John F. Kennedy said, "Ask not what your country can do for you — ask what you can do for your country."*
  - ▶ *"Leadership doesn't stop at the hospital door," the badly wounded soldier said, "and I believe I can do a good job helping others deal with their injuries."*
- The other marks — semicolon, colon, dash and exclamation point — go inside the closing quote marks *if* they apply to the quoted material. Otherwise, they go outside, as in the following:
  - ▶ *His questions — "Who am I?" and "Where am I?" — revealed his lack of awareness of his surroundings.*
  - ▶ *"Have you read that J.D. Salinger book 'Catcher in the Rye'?" John asked.*
  - ▶ *Who wrote, "To thine own self be true"?*
  - ▶ *He loved da Vinci's "Mona Lisa"; however, he also loved pepperoni pizza with anchovies.*
- Quotations within quotations require that the interior quotation marks change from the standard double quotes (" ") to single quotes (' '), with all other preceding rules applying, as in the following:
  - ▶ *"I rather like the title 'The Happy Hooker' for my fishing essay," the freshman composition student said.*
  - ▶ *"His question 'Is there a God?' worried me," Andy's father said.*

# Quotation Marks — For Direct Quotations

Direct quotations — that is, the exact words of a person or publication — demand two things: attribution identifying the source and quotation marks surrounding the quoted material.

**FIGURE 16-1** This newsroom is where TV Z1 in the Czech Republic prepares and packages its news. Z1 was the first Czech private, 24-hour news channel.

Attribution most often is in the form a speech tag that includes the name or identification of the source (or an appropriate pronoun reference) and the verb. The preferred order of these elements in speech tags is *source + verb*. This is true whether the tag introduces, follows or is inserted in the middle of the quoted material. The only time you should change the source-verb order for a tag following a quote is when a source's name is followed by either a long title or other long descriptive phrase, as in the following:

- AVOID: *"Low enrollment in too many courses is killing the university budget," Dr. William Blakely, vice president for academic and student affairs, said.* (Although this follows preferred order, the long title separating the speaker and verb makes it hard to follow. How long is too long? Let your ear be the judge.)
- PREFER: *"Low enrollment in too many courses is killing the university budget," said Dr. William Blakely, vice president for academic and student affairs.* (Another benefit of this order is the use of one less comma in the structure.)
- AVOID: *"The plight of wild horses in many western states has been overlooked too long," Cecil Troutman, a leading expert who advises the U.S. Bureau of Land Management, said.* (As previously, the long description splitting the speaker and the verb makes it harder to understand.)
- PREFER: *"The plight of wild horses in many western states has been overlooked too long," said Cecil Troutman, a leading expert who advises the U.S. Bureau of Land Management.*

The preferred verb for speech tags is a form of the verb *to say*, as in *Elliott said.* Resist the urge to vary frequently the choice of speech-tag verb; *to say* is the most comfortable, neutral and least obtrusive, and using it exclusively throughout a story is fine. Another verb may be used when the context demands it, as when a question or a shout is quoted.

Even in feature stories, alternatives to the verb *to say* should be used with care. Too often they carry additional meaning that can be troublesome, as in *mumbled, complained* or *lied.* Such verbs may imply an opinion of the reporter, which may be appropriate only in commentary or analysis.

Avoid using *that* to introduce direct quotes, though you may do so with a partial quote, as in the following:

- *Grandma said that "I am just too old to worry about learning to use a computer."* (Here, strike *that* and add a comma following *said.*)
- *Grandma said that she had enough trouble dealing with other "new-fangled contraptions," like her TV remote control.* (This paraphrase includes some unique language from the speaker, which deserves to run in quotes.)

The exact words of a speaker always should go inside quotation marks. However, keep in mind that not *everything* a source says should be used exactly as spoken. You might as well just present readers with a transcript. Good reporting is more concerned with presenting what a speaker means than necessarily what a speaker says.

Few of us speak as clearly and as concisely as we might, especially in an interview. Sometimes, too, the exact comments are not appropriate to repeat. It is up to a good reporter and/or a good editor to decide what to quote exactly and what to paraphrase, keeping in mind that paraphrases, or indirect quotes, still are attributed to sources but are not enclosed in quotation marks, as in the following:

- *President Jimmy Carter said of Sen. Ted Kennedy at a 1979 White House dinner, "If Kennedy runs, I'll whip his ass."* (A memorable quote, which at the time raised quite a few eyebrows, even among the unshakeable White House press corps.)

- *President Jimmy Carter said at a 1979 White House dinner that if Sen. Ted Kennedy ran for the Democratic nomination, he would beat him soundly.* (This paraphrase loses all of the punch and power of the original remark. Many media in 1979 did not use the exact words given here. According to a Time magazine report at the time, Roger Mudd of CBS Evening News alluded to the president's remark without quoting it directly. On a screen behind him, though, was projected a copy of the New York Post's front-page headline carrying the quote. These days, the original is certainly the one to use.)

A few tips about paraphrasing are in order. First, good paraphrase doesn't come from changing just a word or two of the direct quote from the source. It involves writing a clearer, often shorter and more concise version of the original. Second, although not required, many paraphrases are presented with the speech tag first. In those instances, the tag is not followed by a comma but may be followed by *that*, as in the following:

- *Darby said he was eager to leave while there was still daylight.*
- *He explained that he wasn't afraid of the dark.*

Let your ear be your guide as to whether you use *that*.

When the speech tag follows a paraphrase, separate the statement from the tag with a comma as you do with direct quotes, as in the following:

- *He was eager to leave before nightfall, Darby said.*
- *He really wasn't afraid of the dark, he explained.*

Most of the time, avoid fragmentary quotes — that is, enclosing in quotation marks only a few words or a short phrase from a speaker — unless the material is unusual or used in an unfamiliar way.

Where to put the speech tag is another choice reporters and editors must make. Following the direct quote or paraphrase usually is best because that privileges what is said over who said it. However, placing the tag first may a better choice when 1) the speaker is a VIP or 2) when you are switching from one speaker to another.

Of course, you may put the tag in the middle of a quote or paraphrase for variety, but make sure you insert it at a natural break in the sentence or between sentences. If within a sentence, precede and follow the tag with commas. If between sentences, precede the tag with a comma and follow it with a period. See how the following illustrates these rules:

- *"We're willing to invest as much as we can," Williams said, "in order to protect the community from this outbreak of vandalism."*
- *"Our best resources, though, are residents," he said. "Your neighbors' eyes and ears are your No. 1 defense."*

While we are covering the use of quotation marks for direct quotes, it may be valuable to remind you of some other pointers in presenting direct quotes.

For example, the stylebook is quite clear in advising journalists never to change the wording in direct quotes even to correct minor errors in grammar, spelling or word usage. This is a strict approach, one that is always safer from both legal and ethical standpoints. Nevertheless, more than a few reporters and editors take careful liberties in making grammatical corrections to direct quotes.

A safe alternative, of course, is to paraphrase the direct quote to correct the error.

# Quotation Marks — With Composition Titles

AP style says to enclose in quotation marks those titles that would in non-journalistic writing be set in italics or enclosed in quotation marks. Titles for the following, which don't take quotation marks, are *exceptions* to that rule:

- *magazines*
- *newspapers*
- *the Bible*
- *books that are primarily catalogs of reference material*
- *almanacs*
- *directories*
- *dictionaries*
- *encyclopedias*
- *gazetteers*
- *handbooks*
- *software such as WordPerfect or Windows*

Note: Guidance in the online stylebook's Ask the Editor advises *not* to put quotation marks around formal titles of academic courses.

# Quotation Marks — With Nicknames, Irony and Unfamiliar Terms

Follow several guidelines for the use of nicknames:

- First, when a nickname replaces a given name because an individual prefers it, do *not* enclose it in quotation marks, as in *Jimmy Carter* or *Dizzy Dean*.
- Second, a nickname presented with an individual's full name should be enclosed in quotation marks, as in *William F. "Buffalo Bill" Cody, Louis "Satchmo" Armstrong, Frank "Old Blue Eyes" Sinatra*.
- Third, capitalize but do not enclose in quotation marks the nicknames of other things, such as states, cities, locations and the like, as in *The Show-Me State, Circle City, The Big Apple*.

Irony, which is saying one thing and meaning another, is another use for quotation marks. Quotation marks may make clearer that some terms are used ironically, as in the following:

- *He called her new hairstyle "special."*
- *People were unsure how to respond when the professor said the basket-weaving essay was "crafty."*

If words likely are unfamiliar to readers — for example, technical terms in a nontechnical publication — enclose them in quotation marks, but only on first reference, as in the following:

- *Sizes of digital files are measured in "bytes," a term coined in 1956 by Dr. Werner Buchholz.*
- *"Pixel" is the term used to measure the resolution of a digital photograph or other graphic image.*

# Question Marks

Journalists have no specialized way to use question marks; the guidelines are the same you'd find in a good writing handbook. However, to make sure we are all on the same page, follow this advice:

- Question marks should be placed at the end of a direct question, as in the following:
  - ▸ *What will the mayor do following his resignation?*
  - ▸ *The professor asked his students, "Are any of you afraid of the dark?"*
  - ▸ *"Can you believe it's the end of the semester already?" Angela asked her roommates.*
- Do not use question marks at the end of an indirect question, as in the following:
  - ▸ *The professor asked if any of his students were afraid of the dark.* (See how the preceding direct question is paraphrased, with both the quotation marks and question mark dropped here and in the next example.)
  - ▸ *Angela asked her roommates if they could believe it was already the end of the semester.*
- Question marks go inside closing quotes when the question applies only to the quoted material, as noted earlier.
- The question mark replaces the comma normally used between a direct quote and a speech tag that follows, as in the following:
  - ▸ *"Are you ready for some football?" singer Hank Williams Jr. asked before each "Monday Night Football" game.*
  - ▸ *"How many lives have been lost?" the governor wondered aloud as she surveyed the hurricane damage.*

# Exclamation Points

As with question marks, guidance is no different than that for use of exclamation points in nonjournalistic writing:

- Exclamation points follow material that expresses considerable surprise, shock, disbelief or other strong emotion, also termed interjections, as in the following sentences:
  - ▸ *"Damn!" the player uttered after dropping the ball.*
  - ▸ *Tiffany shouted, "Wally, don't you dare touch that pie!"*
- Don't overuse exclamation points. Therefore, mild interjections should be followed with just a comma or period, as appropriate, as in the following:

> ► *"Oh my." That was all the coach could say after the receiver dropped the winning touchdown pass.*
> ► *"Well, well, well," Wally said. "Look at this pie."*

- Exclamation points go inside closing quotes when the interjection applies only to the quoted material, as we noted previously.
- The exclamation point replaces the comma normally used between a direct quote and the speech tag that follows, as in the following:

  > ► *"Damn the torpedoes! Full speed ahead!" shouted Admiral David Farragut during the Civil War Battle of Mobile Bay.*

# QUOTATION MARK, QUESTION MARK AND EXCLAMATION POINT *exercise 1*

**DIRECTIONS**: Correct *quotation mark, question mark and exclamation point* errors in the following exercises. Some may be correct. Check the spelling of all names in the Heartland Directory.

1.  "This funding is a real financial shot in the arm in our battle against the H1N1 virus", Dr. David DuMont, Heartland director of public health, said.

2.  The "funding" DuMont was referring to is $78,000 in federal money that will be awarded to the city by the Missouri Department of Health and Senior Services to vaccinate residents against swine flu.

3.  A chunk of that money will go toward advertising, likely in the "Heartland News-Observer," alerting residents to the availability, times and locations of the vaccine.

4.  "We have to do all we can to publicize key information" said DuMont, "this is too serious to trust word of mouth."

5.  When the City Council votes at its first October meeting, we are confident in a quick, easy passage," the doctor said.

6.  Some residents, like Lillian Baker, who works the night shift at Heartland Widgets, were "worried about getting a shot."

7.  "What can I do, she asked, if I can't get out to the health office when they're giving the shots?"

8.  Her husband, Stanley, said, "Dagnabbit. I don't trust them. I don't get the regular flu shot either."

9.  Edward (Ned) Silcott, a bookkeeper at Brown Transfer Co., said, I'm frightened at all this talk of flu epidemic. I want my shot now if I can get it.

10. DuMont said that, "The first doses of the vaccine will be available in early October."

**Additional exercises are available online at** www.oup.com/us/rosenauer.

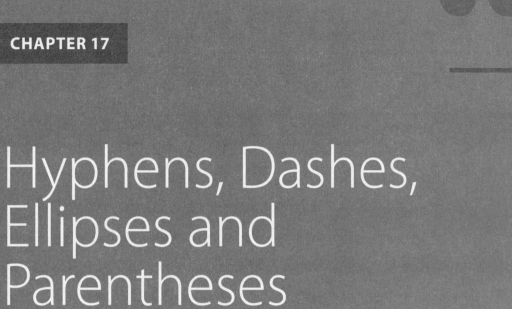

## CHAPTER 17

# Hyphens, Dashes, Ellipses and Parentheses

*"If you take hyphens seriously, you will surely go mad."*

~The Oxford University Press stylebook

We deal here with four punctuation marks that see varying frequency in journalistic writing. The first, hyphens, is the more commonly used, with dashes less frequent, ellipses occasional and parentheses rare.

Remember the basic role for the first two: Hyphens join and dashes separate. The job of the ellipsis, the singular form of the word, is to indicate omitted or missing material in a passage. Parentheses enclose text within other text with an opening parenthesis, the singular form of the word, and closing parenthesis.

Also, whereas you indicate the hyphen with the hyphen key and use it without spaces, typically you present the dash using two hyphens with a space before and after the pair. Some word-processing software automatically transforms the double hyphens into a dash, and you actually can type a dash using certain key combinations with many computers (on a Macintosh, for example, it's shift+option+hyphen).

An ellipsis, according to the stylebook, is three unspaced periods with a space before and after the trio. When the material preceding the ellipsis is a complete sentence, put a period after the last word, type a space and then type the ellipsis.

When another punctuation mark is needed — such as a comma, colon, question mark or the like — the order is the ending word, punctuation mark, space and then ellipsis, as in the following:

- *"Aren't you ashamed of yourself for what you did last night? . . . " she asked.* (The order here follows the recommended pattern, but note, too, that following the ellipsis are quotation marks that close the direct quote.)
- *"I regret my behavior at the meeting, . . . " Williams said.*

Finally, as most of you already know, parentheses are accessed using the *shift+9* key to open and *shift+0* key to close.

# Hyphens — Compound Modifiers

You may be surprised at how much is involved with hyphen usage. Nevertheless, if you check the stylebook for everything of which you're not absolutely, positively sure, you should do fine.

Joining compound modifiers is a common use of the hyphen. Keep in mind, though, that you need hyphens only when two or more adjectives that describe a single concept precede the noun they describe. The same combination following the noun usually does not use hyphens. An exception to this is when a form of the verb *to be* connects the subject to the modifiers.

Moreover, you never hyphenate adverb-adjective combinations. You can identify many adverbs from their *-ly* endings, such as *angrily*, the adverb form of the adjective *angry*. However, some adjectives carry the *-ly* suffix, such as *friendly*. If you're unsure about whether a word is an adjective or adverb, check the dictionary.

Consider these examples:

- *It was a hard-fought ballgame.* (The adjectives *hard* and *fought* work together for a single concept as opposed to a *hard ballgame* and a *fought ballgame*. Also, they precede the noun they modify.)
- *The ballgame was hard-fought.* (Same pairing and same single concept. The hyphen is retained because the adjective combination follows *was*, a form of the verb *to be*.)
- *The ballgame looked hard fought.* ([Same pairing and same single concept; however, because no form of the verb *to be* is used, no hyphens are used either.)
- *His ego was so large that he wore a 20-gallon hat.* (Again, the adjective combination is a single concept in front of the noun it modifies.)
- *His third-quarter touchdown was the last of the game.*
- *The last touchdown of the game came in the third quarter.*
- *He held a part-time job through the fall semester.*
- *He worked part time through the fall semester.*
- *Everyone heard his barely whispered curse.* (This is an adverb-adjective combination, so no hyphen is used.)
- *She had a very hot temper.* (Again, adverb-adjective combination.)

**FIGURE 17-1**

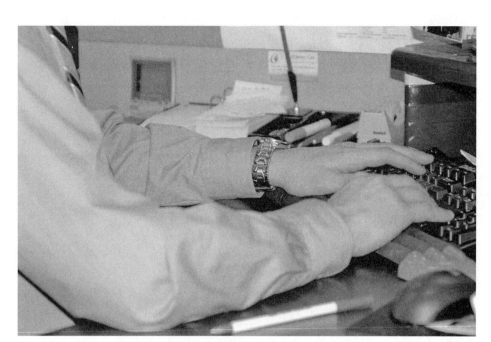

# Hyphens — Prefixes

The stylebook has 63 prefix entries, but the following are the more common:

- *anti-*
- *co-*
- *dis-*
- *ex-*
- *non-*

- *pre-*
- *pro-*
- *re-*
- *sub-*
- *un-*

The general practice is to avoid hyphenating prefixes. Yet, three instances call for use of a hyphen with prefixes:

- When a prefix ends in the same vowel that begins the word following except for *coordinate* and *cooperate*, as in *pre-election, pre-existing, semi-invalid, re-enact, re-entry.*
- When the word following the prefix is capitalized, as in *pro-Democrat supporters* or *anti-American protests.*
- With doubled prefixes, as in *sub-subparagraph.*

That said, there are exceptions. The stylebook has specific examples among its entries (see following), especially with common prefixes you will encounter; otherwise, consult Webster's New World College Dictionary. Your best bet, as always, is to check; don't guess. Look at the following exceptions:

- *pre-convention.* (This is an exception both to the preceding rules and to Webster's. See the *pre-* entry in the stylebook.)
- *extra-mild sauce.* (Guidance is in the *extra-* entry of the stylebook. This example illustrates one of the points there: Use a hyphen with *extra* when it is in a compound modifier that describes a condition beyond usual size, extent or degree.)

- *pro-war, pro-peace, pro-business, pro-labor* (Use the hyphen when forming words that show support for something.)

Sometimes prefixes with a hyphen help to avoid confusion, as in the following:

- *recover,* as in *get back,* versus *re-cover,* as in *cover again.*
- *reform,* as in *improve,* versus *re-form,* as in *form again.*
- *resign,* as in *quit,* versus *re-sign,* as in *sign again.*

# Hyphens — Suffixes

Suffixes tend to be somewhat less common than prefixes and, therefore, less troublesome. Verb forms of words with suffixes should be two words. The following suffixes are in the stylebook, unless otherwise indicated:

- *-added* (From Webster's, *value-added.*)
- *-designate* (As in *chairman-designate.*)
- *-down* (*breakdown, countdown, rundown, slowdown* but *sit-down.* When most of these are used as verbs, they are two words without the hyphen.)
- *-elect* (Always hyphenate such constructions, as in *president-elect, treasurer-elect.*)
- *-fold* (No hyphen, as in *twofold, fourfold, hundredfold.*)
- *-in* (Typically hyphenated, as in *drive-in, sit-in.*)
- *-less* (No hyphen, as in *gutless, heartless, waterless.*)
- *-like* (No hyphen unless the main element is a proper noun or the letter *l* would be tripled, as in *businesslike, carnivallike, God-like, shell-like.*)
- *-maker* (Examples from the stylebook include *automaker, carmaker, chip-maker, coffee maker, drugmaker, oddsmaker, pacemaker, policymaker, speechmaker.* If a word is not in the stylebook or Webster's, the stylebook entry *-maker* says to hyphenate noun and adjective forms, such as *music-maker, tire-maker, sausage-maker, ship-maker, space-maker* and *wire-maker.*)
- *-out* (*cop-out, fade-out, fallout, flameout, hide-out, pullout, walkout, washout.*)
- *-over* (*carry-over, holdover, takeover, stopover, walkover.*)
- *-persons* (The stylebook advises against using coined terms like *chairperson* or *spokesperson,* except in direct quotes.)
- *-up* (A sampling of the terms listed in the *-up* entry are *breakup, call-up, checkup, cover-up, follow-up, grown-up, holdup, mix-up, roundup, smashup, tie-up.*)
- *-wide* (No hyphen, as in *citywide, countrywide, nationwide, statewide, worldwide.*)
- *-wise* (No hyphen when the term means in the direction of or with regard to, as in *clockwise, lengthwise, otherwise.* When *-wise* means smart, use the hyphen, as in *penny-wise, street-wise.*)

# Hyphens — Ratios and Odds

Ratios are a concise way of showing the relationship between two quantities of something. Use figures with hyphens — not a colon as in nonjournalistic writing — when presenting them, as in the following:

- *The ratio of medically insured Americans to uninsured is about 6-to-1.* (Note that two hyphens are used in this context.)
- *Apples outnumbered oranges by a 2–1 ratio.* (When *ratio* or similar word follows the number, drop the *to.*)

To present betting odds, which are specialized ratios that try to predict the likelihood of something happening versus something not happening, always use figures with a hyphen, as in the following:

- *Odds were 3–1 that she'd say no to his proposal.*
- *On a 75–1 long shot, his $2 bet paid handsomely.*

# Hyphens — Fractions

You should spell out amounts less than one and use hyphens between the words, as in the following:

- *three-fourths*
- *seven-eighths*
- *one-sixth*

For amounts greater than one, use decimals where practical. Otherwise, when you present whole numbers with fractions, put a space between the two, as in the following:

- *2 1/8*
- *5 1/2*
- *1 3/4*

# Hyphens — Scores and Vote Tabulations

Use figures always, and put a hyphen between the winning and losing scores, as in the following:

- *The Kansas City Chiefs beat the St. Louis Rams 28–24.*
- *The Royals dropped another game, losing to the Yankees 9–7.*
- *The St. Louis Blues edged the Chicago Blackhawks 1–0.*

Always use figures for vote tabulations. When presenting results under 1,000 votes on each side, use the hyphen, as in the following:

- *The U.N. General Assembly voted 112–70 to fund the proposal.*
- *The Senate supported the nomination with a 61–39 vote.*

When the results are more than 1,000 votes on each side, replace the hyphen with *to.*

# Hyphens — Other

Some word pairings that stand as single concepts also take hyphens. The secret is to check the stylebook in such instances. However, the following cover most of those listed:

- *air-condition, air-conditioned* but *air conditioner, air conditioning*
- *baby-sit, baby-sitting, baby-sat* but *babysitter*

- *best-seller*
- *break-in* (The noun and adjective but not the verb, which is *break in*.)
- *breast-feed, breast-feeding, breast-fed*
- *carry-on*
- *carry-over*
- *chipmaker, chipmaking*
- *cloak-and-dagger*
- *cross-examine, cross-examination*
- *cross-section* (Only the verb form.)
- *cure-all*
- *die-hard*
- *double-click*
- *drive-in* (Only the noun form.)
- *first-grade* (Or *second-grade, 10th-grade* and so on. Also, *first-grader, second-grader* and so on.)
- *flare-up* (Only the noun form.)
- *flip-flop*
- *follow-up* (The noun and adjective, but not the verb, which is *follow up*.)
- *free-for-all*
- *freeze-dry, freeze-dried, freeze-drying*
- *get-together* (Only the noun form.)
- *globe-trotter, globe-trotting* (However, the basketball team is the *Harlem Globetrotters*.)
- *go-between*
- *grant-in-aid, grants-in-aid*
- *grown-up*
- *half-and-half*
- *hand-picked*
- *hang-up*
- *hard-boil, hard-boiled*
- *hard-liner*
- *hanky-panky*
- *helter-skelter*
- *hi-fi*
- *hip-hop*
- *hit-and-run* (The noun and adjective, but not the verb, which is *hit and run*.]
- *ho-hum*
- *home-school, home-schooled, home-schooler*, but *home schooling*
- *hurly-burly*
- *hush-hush*
- *know-how*
- *mix-up* (The noun and adjective, but not the verb, which is *mix up*.)
- *mock-up* (Only the noun form.)
- *mo-ped*
- *mop-up* (The noun and adjective, but not the verb, which is *mop up*.)

- *nitty-gritty*
- *pan-fry*
- *pell-mell*
- *point-blank*
- *pooh-pooh*
- *profit-sharing*
- *profit-taking*
- *push-button*
- *right-hander*
- *rip-off* (The noun and adjective, but not the verb, which is *rip off*.)
- *roly-poly*
- *runner-up, runners-up*
- *send-off* (Only the noun form.)
- *shake-up* (The noun and adjective, but not the verb, which is *shake up*.)
- *shut-in* (Only the noun form.)
- *shut-off* (Only the noun form.)
- *sit-in* (The noun and adjective, but not the verb, which is *sit in*.)
- *tie-in* (The noun and adjective, but not the verb, which is *tie in*.)
- *tie-up* (The noun and adjective, but not the verb, which is *tie up*.)
- *trade-in* (The noun and adjective, but not the verb, which is *trade in*.)
- *trade-off* (The noun and adjective, but not the verb, which is *trade off*.)
- *U-turn* (Note the capital *u*.)
- *vote-getter*
- *well-wishers*
- *wheeler-dealer*
- *whistle-blower*
- *write-in* (The noun and adjective, but not the verb, which is *write in*.)
- *year-end*

Some word pairings and groups *don't* take hyphens, as in *corn on the cob*.

Another pair of words commonly hyphenated outside of journalism that does not take hyphens following AP style is *vice president*.

And to keep you flipping eagerly through the pages, the stylebook has some word pairings that are single words, as in the following:

- *daylong*
- *headlong*
- *monthlong*
- *yearlong*
- *weeklong*

When you present compound proper nouns and adjectives, as with dual heritage, hyphenate the pairing, as in the following:

- *The Mexican-American Fiesta is held each August at St. Patrick's Catholic Church in Heartland.*
- *He was proud of his Anglo-Saxon heritage.*

However, the stylebook offers two exceptions to the hyphenation requirement for proper nouns and adjectives: *French Canadian* and *Latin American*.

Suspensive hyphenation involves contexts in which hyphenated words occur in sets of two or more, and the second part of the compound is used only once, as in the following:

- *Your assignment is to write a 300- to 500-word news story.* (As opposed to writing *a 300-word to 500-word news story.*)
- *Cut the wire into 2-, 6- and 10-inch lengths.* (As opposed to writing *2-inch lengths, 6-inch lengths and 10-inch lengths.*)

# Dashes — Abrupt Change

Dashes are used to separate. Keep in mind that the first word following a dash is lowercase, unless it's a proper noun or adjective. Probably the more frequent usage of dashes involves abrupt changes in thought or an emphatic pause in a sentence, as in the following:

- *The Heartland Chamber of Commerce held its regular weekly meeting — though it would be hard to call it regular — at the Chuck E. Cheese pizza parlor.* (Note the dashes preceding and following the interrupting thought. Also, a space precedes and follows each dash.)
- *The mayor will push for pay increases for Heartland workers — if the budget can be balanced.* (Because the interrupting thought is at the end of the sentence, only one dash is used.)
- *The girl — the one dressed in black and sitting in the corner of the classroom — had not attended class before.*

# Dashes — Series Within a Phrase

Use a dash in those contexts when a phrase that contains commas would normally be set off by commas, as in the following:

- *The Chamber of Commerce members — minus its president, vice president, secretary and treasurer — were confused at this turn of events.*
- *City employees — who include salaried, hourly and part-time workers — haven't had a pay increase in three years.*
- *The usual students dressed in black — Angela, Zach and Margot — did not know the new girl.*

# Dashes — Other

Occasionally, you can use a dash for attribution following a quote, as in the following:

- "You miss 100 percent of the shots you never take." — Wayne Gretzky.
- "To the man who only has a hammer, everything he encounters begins to look like a nail." — Abraham Maslow.

When you present a dateline, separate it from the text of the story with a dash, as in the following:

- *ST. LOUIS — The Heartland High School Marching Band won the prestigious Mid-America Music Award Saturday following three days of competition.*

# Ellipses

The only times you should encounter ellipses are when one or more words in a direct quote are deleted or when directly quoting a speaker who does not finish a thought. Used sparingly, careful cutting of a direct quote with ellipses marking where cuts occurred can improve what some speakers say.

However, remember that a well-written paraphrase is sometimes the better choice and does not call for ellipses. On rare occasions a partial quote may suit the clipped content better. At any rate try to avoid any possibilities that presenting less than the original quote would alter its meaning and/or context — an unforgiveable error for reporters and editors.

Use of ellipses may not be a frequent occurrence, perhaps, but you should know how to use them.

Let's see how you might apply these approaches to some excerpts from President Obama's address to a joint session of Congress on Sept. 9, 2009[1]:

- Passage 1: *"I want to thank the members of this body for your efforts and your support in these last several months and especially those who have taken the difficult votes that have put us on a path to recovery. I also want to thank the American people for their patience and resolve during this trying time for our nation."*

- Passage 2: *"One man from Illinois lost his coverage in the middle of chemotherapy because his insurer found that he hadn't reported gallstones that he didn't even know about. They delayed his treatment, and he died because of it. Another woman from Texas was about to get a double mastectomy when her insurance company canceled her policy because she forgot to declare a case of acne. By the time she had her insurance reinstated, her breast cancer more than doubled in size. That is heartbreaking, it is wrong and no one should be treated that way in the United States of America."*

- Passage 3: *"Now, add it all up, and the plan I'm proposing will cost around $900 billion over 10 years — less than we have spent on the Iraq and Afghanistan wars and less than the tax cuts for the wealthiest few Americans that Congress passed at the beginning of the previous administration. Most of these costs will be paid for with money already being spent — but spent badly — in the existing health care system. The plan will not add to our deficit. The middle-class will realize greater security, not higher taxes. And if we are able to slow the growth of health care costs by just one-tenth of 1 percent each year, it will actually reduce the deficit by $4 trillion over the long term."*

See how these passages are shortened using ellipses:

- *Obama said, "I want to thank the members of this body for your efforts and your support in these last several months. . . . I also want to thank the American people for their patience and resolve during this trying time for our nation."* (This is a clipped quote from Passage 2. Note that the retained portion of the original sentence is followed by a period, a space and then the ellipsis.)

- *The president on Wednesday said that cases where Americans lose their insurance coverage or have care delayed because of questionable insurance company tactics are "heartbreaking,"* adding that *"it is wrong and no one should be treated that way in the United States of America."* (This use of paraphrase and partial quotes from Passage 1 allows reporters to craft stories that don't just repeat the entire speech but enables them to focus in on particular points. The method avoids use of ellipses because it is clear in this context that the passages are partial quotes.)

- (This two-paragraph rendering of Passage 3 uses an ellipsis in the first paragraph and paraphrase with a partial quote in the second. Again, it's a matter of fashioning the speaker's comments into a news story that provides key points.):

> *"Add it all up, and the plan I'm proposing will cost around $900 billion over 10 years. . . . Most of these costs will be paid for with money already being spent — but spent badly — in the existing health care system," Obama said.*
>
> *He claims that his plan would not add to the deficit. Rather, he said, "if we are able to slow the growth of health care costs by just one-tenth of 1 percent each year, it will actually reduce the deficit by $4 trillion over the long term."*

# Parentheses

The stylebook advises sparing use of parentheses because they are jarring to readers. Better alternatives to parentheses often are paired commas or dashes around the parenthetical material or other structures that don't call for parentheses.

However, when a context offers no alternative, use parentheses.

Note: Whereas most nonjournalistic contexts call for parentheses around the area code of a phone number, as in *(573)619–8020*, AP style says to drop the parentheses and use a hyphen instead, as in *573–619-8020*.

# HYPHEN, DASH, ELLIPSIS AND PARENTHESIS *exercise 1*

**DIRECTIONS**: Correct errors involving *hyphens, dashes, ellipses and parentheses* in the following exercises. Some may be correct. Check the spelling of all names in the Heartland Directory.

1. "Even if you're on the right track, you'll get run over if you just sit there": Will Rogers, American humorist.

2. Such inspiration from Will Rogers might be just what the Heartland School Board needs if it hopes to avoid the possibility of a board teacher showdown.

3. With 3/4 of Heartland teachers voting last week to send an ultimatum to the board for increased salary and benefits in next year's contract, the teacher strike clock appears to be ticking.

4. One thing keeping some board members just sitting there on the issue of teacher compensation is the outspokenness of proteacher factions, including outside groups.

5. "I'll not be bullied by left wing groups that don't even have a dog of their own in this fight," board member Alton Everrett said.

6. He was referring to the continued presence of the National Education Association, which sought last fall to represent the 459 member teacher force at Heartland.

7. Currently, the Classroom Teachers Association is representing teachers by a 2 to one ratio, based on local voting in September.

8. Another obstacle to board action is the looming possibility of a 10- to 15-percent cutback in next year's state funding for schools.

9. Board President Roger Woolson encouraged the board to get past the obstacles and take a stand any stand that will get negotiations moving.

10. CTA spokeswoman Maria DiNozzo told the board that 10 and 15 member teacher groups, formed to solicit feedback from citizens, business owners and civic leaders, would provide reports at next month's board meeting.

**Additional exercises are available online at** www.oup.com/us/rosenauer.

## CHAPTER 18

# Irregular Verbs

*"First they came for the verbs, and I said nothing because verbing weirds language. Then they arrival for the nouns, and I speech nothing because I no verbs."*

~Peter Ellis

Verbs have three forms: present, past and participle. We use these to establish the tense or time of the action or state of being suggested by the verb. The form for regular verbs is to use the root in the infinitive for present and then to add *-ed* for the past and participle forms, as in the following:

- *Grover loves hot dogs.* (Present tense.)
- *He loved to eat them all the time.* (Past tense.)
- *In fact, he has loved them so much that he opened a hot dog shop.* (Present perfect tense using the participle *loved*.)
- *Grover had loved hot dogs even before so many great varieties were available.* (Past perfect tense using the participle *loved*.)
- *He likely will love them until he dies.* (Future tense using the root form *love*.)
- *When he dies, he will have loved hot dogs more than most people love them.* (Future perfect tense using the participle *loved*.)
- *The epitaph on his gravestone might read, "To eat a hot dog is to love a hot dog."* (Infinitive form.)

Understand that writers often use the participle of a verb to form the *perfect* tenses—past perfect, present perfect and future perfect—along with a helping or auxiliary verb, such as forms of the verb *to have*. That's the case in the preceding examples.

However, irregular verbs do not form the past and the participle by adding *-ed*. Instead, each verb uses distinct forms for the past and the participle (see list following).

Six popular irregular verbs are particularly troublesome: *to lay* or *to lie*, *to raise* or *to rise* and *to set* or *to sit*. The problems, as you can probably guess, involve the fact that each of these paired verbs is similar and often confused with its mate.

# To Lay or To Lie

Using *to lay* or *to lie* is less troublesome if you understand that the first is a transitive verb meaning to put or to place. It takes a direct object, as in the following:

- *She lay her books on the counter.*

    Its past tense is *laid*, as in the following:

- *She laid her books on the counter yesterday, too.*

    Its participle is *laid*, as in the following:

- *She always has laid her books there.*

    Its future is *lay*, as in the following:

- *She will lay her books on the counter unless company is coming.*

    *To lie* is intransitive; in other words, it cannot take an object. One of its meanings is to recline, as in the following:

- *Arnold lies on his daybed each day after lunch.*

    Its past tense is *lay*, as in the following:

- *He lay on the daybed for a week when he was sick last month.*

    Its participle is *lain*, as in the following:

- *Occasionally, he has lain in the daybed to read the newspaper.*

    Its future is *lie*, as in the following:

- *He will lie on the daybed unless his cat is already there.*

    Another meaning of the verb *to lie* is to tell an untruth, as in the following:

- *Some parents who are planning to divorce lie to their children.*

    Note that because this form is a regular verb, its past tense and participle is *lied*, as in the following:

- *Charlotte's parents lied to her about their financial problems.*
- *They likely have lied at other times to ease her worries.*

# To Raise or To Rise

*To raise* is to cause to rise, elevate or lift upward. As a transitive verb, it takes a direct object, as in the following:

- *A heavy rain often raises the level in the Heartland reservoir.*

  Because this is a regular verb, its past tense and participle is *raised*, as in the following:

- *Heavy downpour raised the level a full inch on Sunday.*
- *Days of heavy rains in 1993 had raised the reservoir to flood stage.*

  *To rise* is the irregular verb in this pair; it's intransitive, meaning it takes no object. It means steady, upward movement, as in the following:

- *Katy rises from bed promptly at 6 each morning.*

  Its past tense is *rose*, as in the following:

- *Even so, her mother rose before Katy.*

  Its participle is *risen*, as in the following

- *Both nearly always have risen before Katy's brother, Michael.*

# To Set or To Sit

*To set*, a transitive verb, means to put or to place something, as in the following:

- *He set his glass on the table.*

  Its past tense and participle are both *set*, as in the following:

- *Because he set his glass there, the moisture left a mark.*
- *Even though he had set glasses there before, they had never left marks.*

# Irregular Verb List

Webster's New World College Dictionary provides an extensive list of preferred irregular verb forms. You have three choices: learn the forms, check the irregular verb list in the Appendix or check Webster's.

**FIGURE 18-1** The newsroom at Georgetown University's The Hoya student newspaper, which has been the paper of record there since 1920.

Let's review some examples of several to make sure you have a handle on how to use the list:

- *To bite*
    - ▶ *Dogs really do bite the hand that feeds them.* (*Bite* is the present tense of the verb *to bite.*)
    - ▶ *Gail's dog bit her last week when she stuck her hand into his dog dish.* (Past tense is *bit.*)
    - ▶ *Never before had he bitten her.* (Participle is *bitten.*)
- *To find*
    - ▶ *As an editor I find errors and omissions in copy and correct them.* (*Find* is the present tense of the verb *to find.*)
    - ▶ *I found few errors in Anthony's story on the City Council meeting.* (Past tense is *found.*)
    - ▶ *Nevertheless, I have found some whopping errors in his other stories.* (Participle is *found.*)
- *To mistake*
    - ▶ *I sometimes mistake my brother's glasses for my own.* (*Mistake* is the present tense of the verb *to mistake.*)
    - ▶ *When I mistook them the other day, I ended up getting a headache before I realize my error.* (Past tense is *mistook.*)
    - ▶ *I have mistaken them so often that I should know better.* (Participle is *mistaken.*)
- *To show*
    - ▶ *Whenever he can, Jason shows his landscape photographs to his friends.* (*Shows* is the present tense of the verb *to show.*)
    - ▶ *Once he even showed them to his photography class at the university* (Past tense is *showed.*)
    - ▶ *He has shown them so much that he is earning quite a reputation as a local photographer.* (Participle is *shown.*)

For additional information, consult online editing resources in the Appendix.

# IRREGULAR VERB *exercise 1*

**DIRECTIONS**: Write in the blanks the correct forms of *irregular verbs* to complete the following exercises.

**Example**: He had [*to light*] _____LIT_____ the hurricane lamp after the radio station [*to broadcast*] _BROADCAST_ the storm warning.

**1.** Robin always [*to strive*, past tense] _____ to do her best, even if it [*to mean*, past tense] _____ spending extra time off the clock.

**2.** Jenny [*to lie*] _____ on the couch after she [*to overdo*] _____ raking the leaves in her yard.

**3.** He had not [*to ride*] _____ the snowmobile far before the wind had [*to blow*] _____ snow over the trail.

**4.** Telly had just [*to drive*] _____ up when the wind gust [*to fling*] _____ a large branch down on the garage.

**5.** Because Joan had [*to hide*] _____ Bob's letters, her father [*to forbid*] _____ her to see him anymore.

**6.** The evidence had [*to prove*] _____ that the girl [*to dive*] _____ into the shallow end of the pool after being warned by the lifeguard.

**7.** When Sergio had [*to drink*] _____ too much, he often [*to swim*] _____ in the pool at his condominium.

**8.** The little boy [*to cling*] _____ to his mother until he had [*to wring*] _____ every last tear from his eyes.

**9.** After the pipe [*to spring*] _____ a leak, the water level in the basement had [*to rise*] _____ slowly up the staircase to the door.

**10.** Having [*to forgive*] _____ her captors, Lisa [*to grow*] _____ silent.

**Additional exercises are available online at** www.oup.com/us/rosenauer.

## CHAPTER 19

# Problem Pronouns

*"If I had my choice I would kill every reporter in the world, but I am sure we would be getting reports from Hell before breakfast."*

~William Tecumseh Sherman

Pronouns. Ya gotta love 'em. They're great stand-ins for nouns in our writing, giving it more variety and less unnecessary repetition. Now, before your eyes glaze over and your mind begins wandering to something more appealing, we are not going to deal with all pronouns here. Likely you have a good handle on their use and can take care of most pronoun issues without any additional instruction.

However, some pronouns can be troublesome. Even if you don't typically have problems with pronouns, some of your reporters will, and it's up to you not only to fix the errors but also to help your reporters to stop repeating them. So, you will need to know enough to explain why.

In this chapter we will cover the following: *that* and *which*, *who/whom*, *whoever/ whomever*, *who's/whose* and *their/there/they're*. The stylebook may be of some help here, but its references to problem pronouns are limited.

Most of our focus involves words called relative pronouns, which begin subordinate clauses and connect them to nouns in sentences. The entire list includes the following: *that, who, whom, whoever, whomever, whose, which, whichever, where, when, whenever*

191

and *why*. However, we will deal only with those that tend to be more confusing and error prone.

## *That* and *Which*

Our first concern involving *that* and *which* is when to use each. You can go online and find many sites that discuss these two, but we can cover here what you need to know. Some grammarians and other usage experts willingly admit that many writers today don't see the need to distinguish between *that* or *which*. Yet, correctness in writing is always a worthwhile goal.

You will be in fine stead if you understand and apply the following rule: Use *that* to introduce essential, or restrictive, clauses and *which* for nonessential, or nonrestrictive, clauses. Although both clauses offer additional information, the material in an essential clause is important enough to the context that removing it threatens to change or confuse the meaning of the sentence.

Let's consider some examples:

- *The book that I was reading is on the coffee table.* (The clause introduced by *that* is essential to understand which book you are referring to.)
- *The book, which I was reading, is "In Odd We Trust" by Dean Koontz.* (Here *which* is required because the book is named in the main clause, and whether or not you were reading it doesn't change that.)
- *The Heartland High School football team that Jeff Johnson played on won only two games.* (You can't know which Heartland team won only two games without the information about Johnson; therefore, the clause is essential and must be introduced by *that*.)
- *The Heartland High School football team, which had a losing record last year, is now second in the state.* (Regardless of its record last year, removing that information from the sentence will not change its meaning.)

Another concern with *that* and *which* involves punctuation. The rule is simple: Don't use commas with essential clauses, correctly introduced by *that*, but always use commas for nonessential clauses, correctly introduced by *which*.

Finally, *that* and *which* deal with inanimate objects or animals not named. *Who* is used for people and animals with names.

## *Who/Whom* and *Whoever/Whomever*

The same rule listed previously for commas with nonessential elements applies here. Also, as noted earlier, *who* or *whom* introduce clauses dealing with people or named animals.

Beyond those rules, deciding whether a sentence requires *who* or *whom* (as well as *whoever* or *whomever*) can be a stumbling block for some journalists. The trick is to apply what we will call the "he-him rule": Replace the pronoun being considered, *who* or *whom*, with *he* or *him*. If *he* fits the context, use *who*, or *whoever*. If *him* works, use *whom* or *whomever*. Consider the following examples:

- *The captain of the team, who plays either tight end or safety, is Brad Weems.* (Replace *who* with *he*, as in *he plays*. It fits, so *who* is correct.)
- *The captain of the team, who we thought was a great tight end, is Brad Weems.* (Replace *who* with *he*, as in *we thought he was*. It fits, so *who* is correct. By the way, don't let such parenthetical elements as *we thought* throw you off.)
- *The captain of the team, whom fans called "Crazy Legs," is Brad Weems.* (Replace *whom* with *him*, as in *fans called him*. It fits, so *whom* is correct.)
- *Who is the best tight end on the Heartland High team?* (Questions can add a bit more confusion, so change the question to a statement first, and then apply the "he-him rule," as in *he is the best tight end*. It fits, so *who* is correct.)
- *Whom do the fans support as the best tight end on the Heartland High team?* (As in the preceding, change the question to a statement, as in *the fans support him*. It fits, so *whom* is correct.)

In the previous first three examples, the content of the sentence determines whether material is essential or nonessential, and commas are applied accordingly. Sometimes, though, it is the writer who makes that choice, as in the following, where using commas or not changes the intended meaning:

- *Football players who work out regularly tend to be healthier than other college students.*
- *Football players, who work out regularly, tend to be healthier than other college students.*

Both of these are correct. The only differences between each example are the commas. Yet, those differences have consequences in the meaning. In the first, without the commas, the reporter is using *who work out regularly* as an essential clause, suggesting that only those football players who work out regularly will be in better health than other college students. In the second example, with the commas, the reporter considers the clause nonessential; in other words, whether or not they work out, football players tend to be healthier.

# *Who's* and *Whose*

Misusing these two pronouns is a common error for some reporters; fortunately, it also has a simple fix.

*Who's* is a contraction for *who is*. Therefore, check whether it is used correctly by mentally replacing the *who's* with *who is* and see if it makes sense. If it does, you are good to go. If not, likely you need *whose*. By the way, avoid the careless use of *who's* as a contraction where the context calls for *who has* or *who was*. They're not the same.

*Whose*, on the other hand, is a possessive pronoun and when correctly used is always followed by a noun. Just to be sure, you can try replacing it mentally with *who is*. If that doesn't make sense, *whose* likely is OK.

Consider the following examples:

- *Jerry was wondering who's going to cover his shift on the soundboard.* (Replace *who's* here with *who is*. It fits. So, this is a correct use of the contraction.)

- *Shaun was not sure who's turn it was to fill in for Jerry.* (Replace *who's* here with *who is*. It doesn't work. So, try *whose*. Bingo!)
- *"Whose able to help out?" he asked.* (No noun follows *whose* here. Therefore, test *who is*. That works. The correct word is *who's*.)
- *No one remembered who's running the board when the schedule was made.* (Check this by trying *who is*. Maybe, but with the past tense verb *was* in the two parts of the sentence, the better answer is *who was*. Therefore, don't use the contraction.)
- *Linda, whose father also works the soundboard, finally volunteered to cover Jerry's shift.* (There's a noun, *father*, following *whose*. Also, *who is* doesn't fit here. Therefore, the use of *whose* here is correct.)

## *Their, There* and *They're*

*Their* is a possessive pronoun that indicates a particular noun belongs to *them*. You can check it for correctness by mentally replacing it with *our*, as in the following:

- *Their cat had a litter of kittens in our garage last spring.* (Replace *their* with *our*. No problem.)
- *The students were nervous about their midterm exam grades.* (Replace *their* with *our*. Again, no problem.)

*There* typically works in sentences as either an adverb or occasionally a noun, referring to a place or perhaps a more abstract location, as in the following:

- *When Kelsey started teasing Alan about the girl who dumped him, he warned her not to go there.* (Adverb.)
- *There are many people who don't eat enough vegetables.* (This is an adverb; however, limit use of *there* in this kind of context because it is wordy. A better version is *Many people don't eat enough vegetables.*)
- *Asked if she had ever been to Mexico, Sylvia said, "No, but I'd love to go there."* (Noun.)

*They're* is a contraction for *they are*. As with *who's* previously, you can mentally replace *they're* with *they are*. If it makes sense, that term is correct, as in the following:

- *The Smiths are so happy winning the lottery that they're building a swimming pool for their neighborhood.* (Replace *they're* with *they are*. It works. Use *they're*.)
- *"Well, they're certainly able to afford that," snuffed the local curmudgeon.* (Replace *they're* with *they are*. Yes, it makes sense. *They're* is the correct choice.)

# PROBLEM PRONOUN *exercise 1*

**DIRECTIONS:** Select the correct forms of *problem pronouns* in the following exercises.

**1.** [Their/There/They're] ready to head out to dinner as soon as they find out [who's/whose] driving.

**2.** For [who/whom] is this book being reserved?

**3.** [Whoever/Whomever] is first to finish will get the prize.

**4.** [Their/There/They're] looking for the student [who/whom] will throw out the first pitch for the baseball team's season opener.

**5.** Jason didn't know [who/whom] would go [their/there/they're] with him.

**6.** I don't know [who/whom] to trust because of [their, there, they're] shady pasts.

**7.** [Their/There/They're] are too many people [their/there/they're] because [their/there/they're] bus is running late this morning.

**8.** [Their/There/They're] last free book should go to [whoever/whomever] comes in the door next.

**9.** In [who/whom] should children trust if [their/there/they're] are no positive role models in [their/there/they're] lives?

**10.** Donnie wanted to beat up [whoever/whomever] turned him in for smoking in the restroom.

**Additional exercises are available online at** www.oup.com/us/rosenauer.

## CHAPTER 20

# Prepositions

*"The growing acceptance of the split infinitive, or of the preposition at the end of a sentence, proves that formal syntax can't hold the fort forever against a speaker's more comfortable way of getting the same thing said — and it shouldn't."*

~William Zinsser

Prepositions deal with connections involving location, time and actions or movement. Their role in English is essential, showing the relationships between and connecting ideas. The preposition usually introduces a prepositional phrase, beginning with the preposition and followed by its object — a noun or pronoun — along with related words.

## Unnecessary Prepositions

It is said that Winston Churchill, corrected for ending a sentence with a preposition, responded, "The rule which forbids ending a sentence with a preposition is the kind of nonsense up with which I will not put." This is perfect grammar. It is also perfect nonsense. We know we never would write that sentence, choosing instead the following: *This is the sort of nonsense I will not put up with.*

Purists cringe at such sentences that end with a preposition; however, most grammarians and educators prefer a less strict rule: Don't use *unnecessary* prepositions *anywhere* in a sentence. That's the approach we will take here.

**FIGURE 20-1** Winston Churchill.

Consider the following examples:

- *Her stand on military intervention in Iraq is something I can't agree with.* (Purists will ding this usage, but most reporters and editors are OK with it.)

- *Her stand on military intervention in Iraq is something with which I can't agree.* (This is the purist's solution, one that is grammatically better than the one preceding it. However, it tends to sound more formal and might be too formal for the context in which you are writing. Ah! See the prepositional usage in that sentence? The first temptation may be to write, " . . . might be too formal for the context you are writing," but it needs the preposition *in*, so perhaps " . . . might be too formal for the context you are writing in." Frankly, that isn't awful and certainly doesn't violate the rule to avoid ending a sentence with *unnecessary* prepositions. However, such decisions tend to be personal and contextual. As always, *listen* to the writing to see which choice sounds best.)

- *Where did Wilbur get that sandwich at?* (Incorrect usage. No need for the preposition *at*. Write it this way: *Where did Wilbur get that sandwich?*)

- *Take your feet off of my desk.* (Incorrect usage. Drop the preposition *of* and write, *Take your feet off my desk.*)

- *Where did Marian go to?* (Incorrect usage. You don't need the preposition *to*. Write instead, *Where did Marian go?*)

- *My mother always liked to cut my meat up into small pieces.* (Incorrect usage. The correct alternative, dropping the preposition *up*, is this: *My mother always liked to cut my meat into small pieces.*)

# Wordy Prepositions

Keeping your prepositions simple — and appropriate for context, of course — is the goal. Wordy prepositions are cumbersome and clutter rather than clarify writing. Reporters may use them because they *seem* to make what they're saying more important.

Look at this list of wordy, cumbersome prepositions that can and *should* be replaced by their simpler counterparts, which may not always be prepositions:

- Avoid *as a result of*                                    Use *because.*
- Avoid *at a later date*                                   Use *later.*
- Avoid *at that point* or *at that point in time*          Use *then, now.*
- Avoid *by means of*                                       Use *by.*
- Avoid *by virtue of*                                      Use *by, under.*
- Avoid *despite the fact that*                             Use *although, even though.*
- Avoid *during the course of*                              Use *during.*
- Avoid *for the amount of*                                 Use *for.*
- Avoid *for the purpose of*                                Use *for, under.*
- Avoid *in accordance with*                                Use *by, under.*
- Avoid *in an attempt to (deny)*                           Use just infinitive *to deny.*
- Avoid *in an efficient way* (and similar)                 Use just adverb *efficiently.*
- Avoid *in close proximity to*                             Use *near.*
- Avoid *in connection to*                                  Use *about.*
- Avoid *in excess of*                                      Use *more than.*
- Avoid *in favor of*                                       Use *for.*
- Avoid *in order to (win)*                                 Use just infinitive *to win.*
- Avoid *in relation to*                                    Use *about, concerning.*
- Avoid *in the event that*                                 Use *if.*
- Avoid *in the immediate vicinity of*                      Use *near.*
- Avoid *in view of the fact that*                          Use *since, because.*
- Avoid *inasmuch as*                                       Use *since, because.*
- Avoid *the manner in which*                               Use *how.*
- Avoid *until such time as*                                Use *until.*
- Avoid *with respect/reference/regard to*                  Use *about, concerning.*
- Avoid *with the exception of*                             Use *except.*

# Idiomatic Use of Prepositions

American English relies on particular prepositions being used with particular nouns and verbs. So, besides the sentence-ending preposition concern previously, you may find problems with a reporter's choice of preposition for a given context. This is more troublesome for non-native speakers, but prepositions trip up even some American-born and -raised writers from time to time. Bottom line, most of us rely on our ears to tell us if a preposition fits a context; in other words, use of prepositions is largely idiomatic, based more on usage than exact definition.

First, let's consider a handful of prepositions that tend to cause more than their share of trouble:

- *at* vs. *by* — When referring to time, use *at* for exact times something is done, and *by* for times no later than something will be done, as in the following:
  - ▶ *The group will gather for dinner at 7 p.m.*
  - ▶ *We will leave for the restaurant by 7 p.m.*

- *beside* vs. *besides* — *Beside* means "by the side of," whereas *besides* means "in addition to" or "as well," as in the following:
  - ▶ *Jeff stood beside the stream and took a picture.*
  - ▶ *Besides her fear of heights, Holly was dreadfully afraid of spiders.*
- *between* vs. *among* — Use *between* for only two people or things and *among* for more than two, as in the following:
  - ▶ *Heidi had to pick between broccoli and Brussels sprouts as her vegetable.*
  - ▶ *Carl, on the other hand, could pick among corn, green beans or squash for his vegetable.*
- *by* vs. *with* — *By* refers to the doer of an action, whereas *with* refers to the instrument with which an action is done, as in the following:
  - ▶ *The woman was shocked by Arnold's outburst.*
  - ▶ *It was peppered with profanities.*
- *in* vs. *at* — Although not strictly followed, *in* tends to be used when referring to large places; *at* is common when referring to small or less important places, as in the following:
  - ▶ *The conference will be held in Chicago.*
  - ▶ *Most meetings will be at the downtown Hilton Hotel.*
- *in* vs. *within* — This usage is similar to *at* vs. *by* previously. Here, *in* refers to the end of a particular period, whereas *within* refers to before the end of a particular period, as in the following:
  - ▶ *Doug plans to finish his report in three days.*
  - ▶ *Harold hopes to complete his report within three days.*

Note: According to the stylebook, drop use of *on* before a day of the week or date except at the beginning of a sentence or other contexts where its absence might cause confusion, as in the following:

- *The professor will meet Friday with any students needing extra help.*
- *On Friday the professor will meet with any students needing extra help.*
- *The City Council met Monday night at City Hall to review the budget.*
- *The Senate heard President Obama on Friday.* (AP says to use *on* to avoid the awkward juxtaposition of a proper name and a date.)
- *Stan saw Gwen on Friday.* (This follows the same rule.)

Now, we will review some verbs that call for certain prepositions and an example of each:

- *account for* — *The bookkeeper could not account for the missing funds.*
- *accuse . . . of* — *The prosecutor accused Harlan Smith of illegal gambling.*
- *agree on* — *The Senate committee did not agree on wording for the bill.*
- *agree with* — *Sasha refused to agree with her mother about a curfew.*
- *allude to* — *The officer alluded to a possible cover-up by the company.*
- *apologize for* — *"I will not apologize for my behavior," the convict said.*
- *apologize to* — *The judge had expected the man to apologize to his victim.*
- *apply for* — *Thousands of people applied for the 40 jobs at Heartland Widgets.*
- *approve of* — *Polls showed voters did not approve of the president's economic policies.*
- *argue with* — *You can't argue with someone who is not listening.*
- *argue about* — *Seth argued about anything and everything.*
- *arrive at* — *After talking it over, Bert and Beth arrived at the same conclusion.*

- *ask for* — Be careful about what you ask for because you might get it.
- *become of* — Giselle didn't know what had become of her favorite stuffed animal.
- *believe in* — Everyone needs something to believe in.
- *belong to* — Elliot belonged to the Lambda Chi Alpha fraternity.
- *blame . . . for* — "You cannot blame me for the breakdown in communications," the vice president said.
- *borrow from* — Many Americans lost their homes because they were unable to borrow any more money from their banks.
- *care for* — More and more children today must care for their elderly parents.
- *come from* — Sightseers come from all parts of the city to watch the parade.
- *compare to* — Compared to the Great Depression, the recession of 2009 was not as devastating for most Americans.
- *compare with* — Frank wasn't sure how his pain compared with his wife's.
- *complain about* — Most dorm students regularly complain about food served in the cafeteria.
- *compliment on* — Parents should compliment their children on their achievements, large or small.
- *congratulate on (for)* — That supervisor was always congratulating one of his workers for a job well done.
- *consent to* — The suspect would not consent to taking a polygraph test.
- *consist of* — The content of the briefcase consists of $10,000 in small bills.
- *convince of* — The jury was not convinced of the defendant's guilt.
- *decide between* — The candidate warned that voters must decide between an economy that grows or an economy that remains stagnant.
- *delight in* — Good teachers delight in the successes of their students.
- *depend on (upon)* — Aaron learned that he could not depend on others for happiness.
- *detract from* — The graffiti detracted from the building's beauty.
- *dream about (of)* — Saul dreamed of winning the lottery and leaving poverty behind.
- *excuse . . . for* — It's hard for many people to excuse their spouses for infidelity.
- *explain . . . to* — The priest tried to explain to the man the importance of attending Sunday Mass.
- *happen to* — Bad things happened to him because he was in the wrong place at the wrong time, repeatedly.
- *hear of* — Aunt Martha would not hear of our staying in a hotel.
- *hear about* — When Val heard about the plant closing, he decided to phone his wife.
- *hear from* — Those who are going through basic training desperately need to hear from family and friends.
- *insist on* — Uncle Aretemis insisted on our staying for dinner.
- *invite . . . to* — Stella invited her friends to come to her house on Friday.
- *laugh about* — It's easier to laugh about mistakes when they're not yours.
- *laugh at* — Mack was rude when he laughed at Seth for answering incorrectly.
- *laugh with* — Laugh and the world laughs with you is a popular adage.
- *listen for* — On Christmas Eve we always listen for Santa's arrival.
- *listen to* — Before going to bed on Christmas Eve, they always listen to their father read "Twas the Night Before Christmas."

- *look at* — I enjoy looking at colorful sunsets.
- *look for* — The family spent hours looking for the missing child.
- *object to* — "I object to your insulting attitude," Tina said.
- *prefer . . . to* — The child preferred playing his Game Boy in his room to spending time with his friends.
- *plan on* — They were planning on 300 guests for the wedding.
- *provide . . . with* — Children expect their parents to provide them with food and shelter.
- *recover from* — The patient had just recovered from pneumonia when he came down with an infection.
- *refer to* — "Please do not refer to me as your little boy," Sam said.
- *rely on* — Unfortunately, he could not rely on his friends for help.
- *remind . . . of* — That story reminds me of my first moose hunt.
- *search for* — A search for happiness should begin in one's own heart.
- *spend . . . on* — His wife spent all their savings on an expensive wardrobe.
- *substitute for* — It is hard to substitute material things for love, though many people try.
- *talk to* — The counselor talked to the students about their futures.
- *talk about* — The only thing the child could talk about was her lost puppy.
- *thank . . . for* — It's important to thank someone for a gift even if you don't like it.
- *vote for* — Sometimes it's hard to vote for any of the candidates in a race.
- *wait for* — Andy waited in the parking lot for his wife.
- *wait on* — Mom waited on me constantly whenever I came home for a visit.
- *work for* — We learned the value of working hard for our money.
- *worry about* — "I worry about whether I'll get my Social Security when I retire," the aging worker said.
- *wrestle with* — She wrestled with the choice of sneaking out of the house or staying in as she was told.

For additional information, consult online editing resources in the Appendix.

# PREPOSITION *exercise 1*

**DIRECTIONS**: Write in the blanks the *best* choice for *prepositions* to complete the following exercises.

1.  Doug argued _____ Sandy _____ where to go _____ dinner Friday evening.

2.  The suspect was unwilling to consent _____ a polygraph test because he worried _____ what it would show.

3.  I objected _____ my mother's claim that I would never talk _____ her _____ my problems.

4.  Whether children believe _____ Santa Claus depends mostly _____ how they were raised.

5.  Frank spent a week in the hospital as he recovered _____ a string of maladies, which consisted _____ high fever, vomiting and diarrhea.

6.  The teacher alluded _____ several short stories because he preferred illustration _____ explanation.

7.  Sybil delighted _____ the things that her daughter shared, including what she dreamed _____ .

8.  The detective wrestled _____ whether to ask the prosecutor to look _____ the 10-year-old murder case.

9.  Compared _____ the casualties _____ World War II, the United States has been fortunate _____ Iraq and Afghanistan.

10. It's important _____ teachers to compliment their students _____ the work they do _____ class.

**Additional exercises are available online at** www.oup.com/us/rosenauer.

## CHAPTER 21

# Agreement

*"There is no such thing as the Queen's English. The property has gone into the hands of a joint stock company and we own the bulk of the shares."*

~Mark Twain, "Pudd'nhead Wilson" (1894)

Our discussion about agreement involves two issues: subject-verb and pronoun. Spend some time reviewing these, and you should be able to edit errors you find in copy.

FIGURE 21-1

# Subject-Verb Agreement

Verbs must agree with their subjects in number. In other words, if a subject is singular, then its verb also must be singular. Likewise, plural subjects require plural verbs. It sounds simple. Well, if it were, we wouldn't be discussing it here.

So long as you are working with a simple sentence — one subject and one verb — you are less likely to have any problems. Consider the following:

- *The dog is hungry.* (Singular subject and singular verb form.)
- *The dogs are hungry.* (Plural subject and plural verb form.)

Of course, few of the sentences you write, read or edit are so simple. The two things that tend to trip folks up with subject-verb agreement are multiple subjects and additional words between a subject and its verb.

A key concern is this: To deal effectively with subject-verb agreement, you must be able to *identify* subjects and verbs.

The various categories of subjects following should wave a yellow flag and invite you to examine a sentence more carefully:

- Indefinite singular pronouns, such as *another, anybody, anyone, each, everybody, every one, everyone, nobody, nothing, somebody* and *someone*. Although these can be tricky, they're not what we classify as problem pronouns; those we covered in Chapter 19. The main thing to remember about these indefinite pronouns is that their related verbs and pronouns take the singular, as in the following:
  - ▸ *Gerard ate his hot dog so quickly that <u>another</u> is not yet ready.*
  - ▸ *<u>Anybody</u> who thinks he or she is invulnerable is likely to learn otherwise at some point.* (Here you must make sure that all the verbs are singular, including the *is* in both the main clause (*Anybody . . . is likely . . .* ) and the subordinate clause ( *. . . he or she is . . .* ) and the verb *thinks* in the relative clause.)
  - ▸ *<u>Each</u> of us is responsible for his or her own actions.* (The potential trap in this sentence is the prepositional phrase *of us*. Some reporters key in on the plural pronoun *us* to determine the number for the verb *is*. However, *each* is the sentence subject here; besides, subjects cannot be in prepositional phrases. So, regardless of what follows *each* when it is the subject of a sentence, the main verb is singular.)
  - ▸ *<u>Nothing</u> is the reward for those who are lazy.*
  - ▸ *<u>Someone</u> is always available to assist students with questions in the lab.*
- *None* usually takes singular, but see the exceptions in the following:
  - ▸ *<u>None</u> of us is happy about his or her performance on the calculus exam.* (The stylebook says none usually means *no single one*; then, related verbs and pronouns are singular.)
  - ▸ *<u>None</u> of the coaches could agree on which play to use.* (When none means *no two*, related verbs and pronouns take the plural.)
  - ▸ *<u>None</u> of Janet's funds are available.* (When none means *no amount*, related verbs and pronouns also take the plural.)
- Words indicating portions, such as *all, fraction, majority, none, part, percent, remainder, some* and the like. These are trickier. The general rule is that when these words are used alone, their related verbs and pronouns are singular, as in the following:

- ► *All is lost was the only thing the soldier could think.*
- ► *A majority supports the president's stand on gun control.*
- ► *Seventy percent was the average score for that test.*
- However, when one of these is followed by a prepositional phrase introduced by *of*, the number matches the number of the noun in the phrase, as in the following:
    - ► *All of the players were angry about losing the ballgame.*
    - ► *A majority of the town was destroyed by the tornado.*
    - ► *A majority of the taxes are paid by middle-class workers.*
    - ► *Part of the pie is still in the refrigerator.*
    - ► *Part of the pies we bought were dropped on the floor.*
    - ► *A large percent of voters choose not to vote.*
    - ► *Of the widgets sold last year, some were found to be defective.* (The prepositional phrase *of the widgets* normally follows *some*. Here, though, it doesn't, but the prepositional phrase doesn't have to follow the *some* to guide your handling of it.)
- *Here* or *there*. If used to begin a sentence, the number of the verb for each of these takes the number of the noun that follows the verb, which is the true subject, as in the following:
- *Here is the dog that bit my son.*
- *There were two dogs brought in last week for biting someone.*
- *Here are the remains of my late-night feast.*
- *There is the man responsible for my success.*
- Periods of time or sums of money. These take singular verbs, as in the following:
    - ► *Fifty years is a fair punishment for the crime Elwood committed.*
    - ► *A hundred bucks is not too much to pay for a dinner at that restaurant.*
- Collective nouns, such as *army, audience, board, cabinet, class, committee, company, corporation, council, department, faculty, family, firm, group, jury, majority, minority, navy, public, school, senate, society, team, troupe* and the like. When these denote a unit, their related verbs and pronouns are singular, as in the following:
    - ► *The audience is getting restless because of the 30-minute delay.*
    - ► *My class is composed of 20 jocks and three older women.*
    - ► *The council meets every Monday night at City Hall.*
    - ► *The public is becoming increasingly unhappy with the economy.*
    - ► *The team has been well coached this year.*
- Team names and musical group names — whether their form is singular or plural — take plural verbs and pronouns, as in the following:
    - ► *The Kansas City Chiefs have become the whipping boys of the NFL.*
    - ► *Abba, whose "Dancing Queen" is a featured song in "Mama Mia," are among my favorite groups.*
    - ► *The Doobie Brothers do a great job singing "Without You."*
- Occasionally, plural terms take singular related verbs and pronouns when the group or quantity is presented as a unit, as in the following:
    - ► *One hundred gallons of water weighs just over 83 pounds.*
    - ► *One hundred gallons of water take up a lot of space.* (Note the subtle difference here where the gallons of water are not considered a unit, therefore calling for a plural verb.)
- Compound subjects — usually signaled by two or more subjects connected with *and* — take plural related verbs and pronouns, as in the following: *A hot summer*

*and high unemployment are ingredients for trouble.* However, if two nouns connected by *and* refer to the same person or thing, the related verb and pronouns are singular, as in this example: *The founder of the company and chairman of the board is Juan Hernandez.* Consider the following exceptions, where the combination is considered a single unit:

- ▸ *Ham and eggs is my favorite holiday breakfast, but bacon and eggs is a good substitute.*
- ▸ *Red beans and rice is a popular Southern dish.*

- *Or* joining two or more singular nouns takes singular related verbs and pronouns, as in the following:
  - ▸ *Officer Jones or Officer Smith is available to accompany the prisoner.*

- However, when *or* connects a singular and a plural subject, preference is to put the plural subject last and use a plural verb, as in the following:
  - ▸ *The woman or her assistants are picking up the donated clothing today.*

- *Either . . . or* and *neither . . . nor* subject constructions are easy to handle: Match the number of the verb to the number of the noun closest to the verb, as in the following:
  - ▸ *Neither the children nor their mother is able to run all of the farm equipment.*
  - ▸ *Either the parakeet or the canaries make noise at all hours of the day.*

- It is customary with *either . . . or* and *neither . . . nor* subject constructions with *I* to put it second and follow it with *am*, as in the following:
  - ▸ *Either Casey or I am going to have to check the furnace at 2 a.m.*

- *One of those* clause constructions causes a bit of trouble in deciding the number of the verb in the clause. To help you figure that out, mentally begin the sentence with the *of those* portion of the sentence and follow your ear, as in the following:
  - ▸ *Janice is one of those women who are able to eat all they want and not gain weight.* (Mentally, rearrange this: *Of those women who are able to eat all they want and not gain weight, Janice is one.* That should make figuring out the number easier. The problem with the original organization, of course, is that many writers look at *one* and think that verbs and pronouns that follow should be singular. However, the noun focus for the *of those* portion here is plural, and the goal of the sentence is to put Janice into that group.
  - ▸ *Sigfried is one of those foreigners whom everybody loves.* (Note that this construction also demands you make a choice about *who* or *whom*.)

Problems also arise with those sentences that have words between the subject and verb. This makes it particularly critical for you always to be able to identify the subject and its verb in sentences.

- Adjective clauses, such as those introduced by *who, that* or *which,* often split subjects and verbs, as in the following:
  - ▸ *Jerry, who is one of my best friends, has decided to join the Air Force.*
  - ▸ *Some of the donuts that the clerk put into the case were missing their glaze.*
  - ▸ *The house, which was destroyed by fire Wednesday, will be razed Monday.*

- Also a little tricky can be prepositional phrases such as *along with, as well as, besides, in addition to, regardless* and others that are inserted after subjects:
  - ▸ *My brother Ron, along with his wife and kids, is vacationing in Yellowstone.*
  - ▸ *The first snowfall of the year, regardless of when it arrived, was always a delight.*

- Parenthetical expressions, which interrupt the main flow of thought, often show up between subjects and verbs:
  - ▶ *Eleanor, if the truth were known, is not a strong speller.*
  - ▶ *The answers to the calculus problems, I believe, are more slippery than greased pigs.*
- Sometimes, participial phrases split subjects and verbs, as in the following:
  - ▶ *The birthday basket, now filled with a variety of gifts, is ready to be delivered.*
  - ▶ *The walls, covered with an ugly mold, are scheduled to be cleaned soon.*

# Pronoun Agreement

Pronouns are swell words and usually harmless. However, reporters and editors must make sure that a pronoun agrees in number and gender with its antecedent — that is, a preceding noun to which a pronoun refers. Look at these examples:

- *Jed is unsure about his ability to hit all of the clays as they are released.* (The pronoun *his* refers to *Jed*, which is singular, and the pronoun *they* refers to *clays*, which is plural.)
- *The dog licked its paws while the cat stretched its legs.*

Most writers have no problems with pronoun usage in such sentences. However, choosing the correct number isn't always easy because many reporters incorrectly use plural pronouns that refer to singular antecedents to avoid gender bias, as in the following:

- *Everyone who is getting off the bus should pick up their valuables.* (*Their* is the problem here. It should agree with its antecedent, *everyone*, but some reporters may not realize *everyone* is singular, and others prefer not to use the correct form, *his or her*.)
- *All who are getting off the bus should pick up their valuables.* (Making the antecedent plural is the solution, whenever possible, as in this version.)
- *Neither of my parents is able to come to my recital because he and she have to work.* (Awkward, perhaps, but correct. Best option with this would be to rewrite: *My parents are unable to come to my recital because they have to work.*)
- *A majority is here to support what he or she believes is right.*

Alternatives to consider for such grammatically difficult sentences are the following:

- Restructure them.
- Drop the pronoun. (Of course, make sure what remains reads correctly.)
- Change the pronoun to *a* or *the*.
- Repeat the noun.

# AGREEMENT *exercise 1*

**DIRECTIONS**: Correct *agreement* errors in the following exercises. Some may be correct.

1. George is one of those college students who plays too much and works too little.

2. It was hard for me to understand that neither my sister nor my brother are concerned about my going into the hospital.

3. A voter should learn all they can about the candidates and issues before they go to the polls.

4. The City Council are meeting Friday to find out what they need to know about the bond issue.

5. Peanut butter and jelly are my favorite comfort-food sandwich.

6. Each of the professors have prepared materials for their classes.

7. None of the fraternities on campus were seeing an increase in their membership.

8. The Dallas Cowboys still considers itself "America's team" even though it certainly is not the powerhouse it once was.

9. The public often has been duped by crafty, well-spoken politicians.

10. The college president, along with his cabinet, are meeting Tuesday night with the architects.

**Additional exercises are available online at** www.oup.com/us/rosenauer.

## CHAPTER 22

# Wordiness

*"This report, by its very length, defends itself against the risk of being read."*

~Winston Churchill

Words are your stock in trade. Thus, you want to make sure that stories you edit and headlines you write make best use of words. Some stories just have too many — typically involving one or more of the following kinds of wordiness:

- *There is/there are* and *it is* sentences.
- Form of the verb *to be* as the main verb.
- Nominalization.
- Redundancies.
- Circumlocutions.
- Empty phrases.
- Clichés.
- Euphemisms.
- Passive voice.

Another wordy culprit is a handful of prepositions, which we covered in Chapter 20, "Prepositions." You may wish to review material in that chapter as you arm yourself to battle wordiness in stories you edit.

FIGURE 22-1

In this chapter we will cover the problems involved with the most frequent offenders just mentioned. Be aware that these appear in copy more frequently than you might assume. Reporters become accustomed to some wordy phrases. They also are not as careful as they might be in tightening their copy. So, invest the time and attention to make copy concise and clear.

## *There Is/There Are* and *It Is* Sentences

Sentences beginning with *there is* or *there are* delay naming the subject, which always immediately follows *is* or *are* in these constructions, as in *There are 30 students waiting for flu shots*, where *students* is the subject. Most of the time, you can revise and tighten such sentences, as in *Thirty students are waiting for flu shots*. Although the revision trims only one word — therefore a modest edit — it's the impact of wordiness across a story that drags it down and demands tightening.

In addition, beginning a sentence with the actual subject rather than the space filler *there is/there are* strengthens the writing. Consider a few more examples:

- *There was a Heartland man hospitalized with swine flu. — > A Heartland man was hospitalized with swine flu.*
- *There will be 50 questions on the copy editing final exam. — > Fifty questions will be on the copy editing final exam.*
- *There is an abandoned house in the neighborhood where children play. — > An abandoned house in the neighborhood is where children like to play.*

The other wordy opening some reporters use is *it is/it was/it will be* — as in *It is hard to learn how to use a lasso*. Revising this sentence calls for a bit more revision, but the goal to get the subject first while cutting the *it is* construction is the same, as in *Learning how to use a lasso is hard*. The revision eliminates two words while strengthening the resulting sentence. Look at a few more examples:

- *It is unfortunate that some Americans choose not to vote. — > That some Americans choose not to vote is unfortunate.*
- *It was disappointing to see the massacre at Fort Hood. — > Seeing the massacre at Fort Hood was disappointing.*
- *It is important for all high school seniors to take the ACT. — > Taking the ACT is important for all high school seniors.*
- *It is the ACT that many colleges require for admission. — > Many colleges require the ACT for admission.*
- *It will be sad to see the Christmas holidays come to an end. — > Seeing the Christmas holidays come to an end will be sad.*

Of course, occasional use of these constructions may be necessary or worthwhile, as in *There is the convicted killer* or *It is time to leave*.

# Form of the Verb *To Be* as the Main Verb

You can improve many sentences that rely on forms of the verb *to be* as main verbs by replacing them with stronger verbs—always a goal in writing. Consider these examples:

- *The Twain State University president was angry over student protests at the Shireman Student Union. — > Student protests at the Shireman Student Union angered the Twain State University president.*
- *A new sound system will be necessary for the theater. — > The theater needs a new sound system.*

# Nominalization

Nominalization, which is turning a verb or an adjective into a noun, is not inherently evil, but usually it results in a weak noun doing the work of a strong verb. Reporters using this approach mistakenly think that the nominalized option is better. Although you can identify some nominalizations by their *-ion* endings, as in *Jason Wolfe submitted an application for the teaching job*, some take other forms, as in *The government conducted a study of home ownership and bankruptcy*.

A good editor could improve each of those previous sentences with nominalization without changing essential content:

- *Jason Wolfe applied for the teaching job.*
- *The government studied home ownership and bankruptcy.*

Let's see some revisions of other sentences with nominalizations:

- *His students regularly make complaints about his tests.* — > *His students regularly complain about his tests.*
- *The neighbors engaged in an argument about the fence separating their yards.* — > *The neighbors argued about the fence separating their yards.*
- *They reached an agreement about the fence* — > *They agreed about the fence.*
- *The editor made corrections on the news story* — > *The editor corrected the news story.*
- *It is John Smith's intention to run for Heartland mayor.* — > *John Smith intends to run for Heartland mayor.*
- *The City Council gave consideration to the nature walk proposal.* — > *The City Council considered the nature walk proposal.*
- *The police officer gave a report on the situation* — > *The police officer reported on the situation.*
- *Hailey Jones achieved dominance in her field.* — > *Hailey Jones dominated her field.*

Nominalization has some value when the intent is to formalize or to create distance, as in *It was not the mayor's decision.* Yet, ridding stories of nominalization usually will result in writing that is less wordy, more direct and more powerful.

# Redundancies

Redundancy is vital for a nuclear power plant, which has several backup systems to prevent loss of control and catastrophic meltdown. However, redundancy in writing is unnecessary repetition. These creep into stories because reporters don't exercise enough care to eliminate unnecessary words.

The following list, where the words you should cut are in parentheses, covers many of the more common redundancies:

- *8 a.m. (in the morning)*
- *7 p.m. (in the evening) or (at night)*
- *(12) midnight*
- *(12) noon*
- *(a total of) 30 voters*
- *(added) plus*
- *(advance) notice*
- *bald (headed)*
- *(basic) or (essential) necessity*
- *biography (of his life)*
- *circle (around)*
- *(common) similarities*
- *(completely) unanimous*
- *consensus (of opinion)*
- *cooperate (together)*
- *(close) proximity*
- *dash (quickly)*

- *each (and every)*
- *each (separate) incident*
- *Easter (Sunday)*
- *electrocuted (to death)*
- *(end) result*
- *(exactly) the same*
- *(fellow) teammates*
- *(final) completion*
- *(first) started or began*
- *(free) gift*
- *(future) plans*
- *(general) consensus*
- *(general) public*
- *(grave) crisis*
- *green (or red or blue . . . ) (in color)*
- *(Jewish) rabbi*
- *large/small (in size)*

- *longer/shorter (in length)*
- *many (different) ways*
- *(natural) instinct*
- *(new) developments*
- *(new) innovation*
- *(month of) May (or other month)*
- *nodding (her head)*
- *(opening) introduction*
- *(past) experience*
- *(period of) 10 days*
- *(real) truth*
- *refer (back)*
- *repeat (again)*
- *revert (back)*
- *she thought (to herself)*
- *shrugging (his shoulders)*
- *square/rectangular/round (in shape)*
- *summarize (briefly)*
- *surrounded (on all sides)*
- *(true) fact*
- *(ugly) blemish*
- *(valuable) asset*

Some redundancies are the result of acronyms, which reporters fail to consider carefully the wording in the original. The redundant word, which you should cut, is underlined in the following:

- *ATM <u>machine</u> — > Automated Teller Machine*
- *AIDS <u>syndrome</u> — > Acquired Immune Deficiency Syndrome*
- *CD <u>disk</u> — > Compact Disk*
- *CPU <u>unit</u> — > Central Processing Unit*
- *DVD <u>disk</u> — > Digital Versatile Disk/Digital Video Disk*
- *HIV <u>virus</u> — > Human Immunodeficiency Virus*
- *ISBN <u>number</u> — > International Standard Book Number*
- *SSN <u>number</u> — > Social Security Number*
- *UPC <u>code</u> — > Universal Product Code*

When you find acronyms in stories, check for redundancies like these and remove them.

# Circumlocutions

Circumlocutions are wordy and indirect phrases. Even though they are not ungrammatical, they are wordiness targets that puff up sentences, giving them an aura of importance.

The following list, including tighter alternatives, covers many of the more common circumlocutions:

- *a large proportion of — > many*
- *ahead of schedule — > early*
- *at that point in time — > then*
- *at the present — > now*
- *at this point in time — > now*
- *by means of — > by*
- *concerning the matter of — > about*
- *due to the fact that — > because or since*
- *during the course of — > during*
- *during the time that — > when or while*
- *give rise to — > cause*
- *has the opportunity to — > can*
- *in advance of — > before*

- *in order to — > to*
- *in spite of the fact that — > although* or *even though*
- *in the event that — > if*
- *in the light of the fact that — > because* or *since*
- *in the not too distant future — > soon*
- *in the vicinity of — > near*
- *in this day and age — > today*
- *is able to — > can*
- *is/are in possession of — > have*
- *it could happen that — > may* or *might* or *could*
- *it is crucial that — > should* or *must*
- *it is important that — > should* or *must*
- *it is necessary that — > should* or *must*
- *it is possible that — > may* or *might* or *could*
- *made a statement — > said*
- *on two separate occasions — > twice*
- *owing to the fact that — > because*
- *placed under arrest — > arrested*
- *prior to the time that — > before*
- *render assistance to — > help*
- *take into consideration — > consider*
- *the possibility exists for — > may* or *might* or *could*

## Empty Phrases and Words

Empty phrases are useless. The best bet is just to cut them from stories. The following are examples of those:

- *a combination of*
- *all things considered*
- *as a matter of fact*
- *as far as I'm concerned*
- *currently*
- *for all intents and purposes*
- *for the most part*
- *for the purpose of*
- *have a tendency to*
- *I feel/believe*
- *I think that*
- *in a manner of speaking*
- *in a very real sense*
- *in my opinion*
- *it seems that*
- *one must admit that*
- *the point I am trying to make*
- *the reason why*
- *this is a subject that*
- *type of*
- *what I mean to say is*

Examples of some empty words — intensifiers or modifiers that don't carry their weight and *probably* should be cut from stories — are these:

- *really*
- *very*
- *quite*

- *extremely*
- *severely*

Sometimes such words are appropriate. Then, hold onto them, but use them sparingly.

# Clichés

Clichés are trite, overused expressions. Originally, they may have had power and interest, but overuse weakened them and dulled readers to their meaning. Your goal as editor is to replace clichés with fresh, creative and more interesting alternatives. At times you may have to fall back on simpler, more common terms. Although that's not as exciting as strong figurative language, it's better than keeping the cliché.

The following list is a brief sampling of clichés. The Appendix includes a longer list, but these will give you a good start on what to replace in stories:

- *better late than never*
- *bitter end*
- *broad daylight*
- *brute force*
- *busy as a bee/beaver*
- *cool, calm and collected*
- *crushing blow*
- *dead as a doornail*
- *easier said than done*
- *easy as pie*
- *few and far between*
- *head over heels*
- *heated argument*
- *hour of need*
- *labor of love*
- *last but not least*
- *moment of truth*
- *open-and-shut case*
- *point with pride*
- *ripe old age*
- *sad but true*
- *spread like wildfire*
- *straight as an arrow*
- *through thick and thin*
- *to make a long story short*
- *trial and error*

# Euphemisms

Euphemisms are words or phrases that stand in for more specific terms that reporters may feel are too blunt, insensitive or offensive to some readers. Not surprisingly, the most common euphemisms in the list following are those referring to death. Like other types of wordiness, though, euphemisms bog down a story's message in the vain, and unnecessary, attempt to shield readers.

Here's a short list of euphemisms, along with the direct and more appropriate terms:

- *adult entertainment — > pornography*
- *between jobs — > unemployed*
- *bit the dust — > died*
- *carnal knowledge — > intercourse*
- *comfort station — > toilet*
- *correctional facility — > jail* or *prison*

- *custodial engineer — > janitor*
- *disinformation — > lie*
- *economical with the truth — > dishonest* or *lying*
- *funeral director — > undertaker*
- *knocked up — > pregnant*
- *lady of the night — > prostitute*
- *lose your lunch — > vomit*
- *message from our sponsor — > commercial*
- *met his maker — > died*
- *negative patient care outcome — > patient died*
- *pass over to the other side — > die*
- *passed away — > died*
- *peace-keeping forces — > armies*
- *preowned — > used*
- *private parts — > genitals*
- *revenue enhancements — > taxes*
- *sanitation engineer — > garbage/trash collector*

Check the Appendix for websites that list additional euphemisms.

## ONLINE INSIGHTS > **EDITING BLOG POSTS**

Blogging continues to grow in popularity, with the number of active, English-language blogs estimated at 450 million. More important, blogs have become increasingly professional in their content and preparation. Much of that is due to the changing mix of bloggers out there. Once the province of someone on an e-soapbox with some strong opinions, more bloggers today work for corporations, manufacturers, businesses, professional organizations and media outlets. What does that mean for you?

Bottom line it means that the impetus behind blogs is changing and reader expectations likely will rise. Whether the blog delivers commentary, information, entertainment or all three, readers will expect content to be well written and cleanly edited. Whether you are editing your own posts or those of others, consider these five tips:

- First, edit the blog for correctness. Check spellings. Fix punctuation, usage and style errors. Most of these are mistakes that blog readers will notice, so don't allow them to make it online.
- Then, edit beginnings and endings. Although blogs don't rely on traditional leads, whatever opens a blog must capture readers' attention and pull them into the post. Blog endings, too, should have some punch, a finish that rewards readers for sticking it out to the end.

- Next, edit for context. Have a clear understanding of the target audience for the blog, and make sure that tone and vocabulary suit the audience, the subject matter and the writer. Tone, or the *feeling* behind the words, is subtle and often expressed with word choice and sentence structure. Blog tones tend to be more informal and personal, but that should not equate with inappropriate or shocking. The other concern, vocabulary, deals with the right word for the right audience to ensure that readers understand the message.
- Third, edit for facts. This is as critical for a blog as it is for a front-page news story. And it involves more than just "the truth." It deals with accuracy. Blogs should be clear and specific, avoiding vagueness, exaggeration and misdirection.
- Finally, edit for conciseness. Although tight writing is always essential for journalists, bloggers must be even more sensitive to that demand. That the Internet spawned the acronym TLDNR, *too long did not read*, is one indicator of what Web audiences want and expect.

Don't expect to edit blogs in exactly the same way you edit other journalistic content. However, many of the same demands apply to both genres.

# Passive Voice

Passive voice involves verbs. It has nothing to do with tense — past, present, future and so on. Simply defined, with passive voice the subject of a sentence is the recipient, not the doer, of the action of the verb, as in *The story was edited by me* as opposed to the active voice, *I edited the story.*

An easy trick to help you with passive voice is to ask the following question: Who did what? *If* the answer to that matches the order of the sentence or clause you are reviewing, then likely it is active voice, you don't need to make changes, as in the following:

- *Cedric Sansone ran a red light and struck a pickup truck.* (Do the who-did-what check: Cedric ran a red light. Cedric also struck a pickup truck. Therefore, because the sentence order in each matches the who-did-what order, both clauses are active voice.)
- *A pickup truck was struck by Cedric when he ran a red light.* (Using the who-did-what check, the order in the first clause doesn't match, so it is passive voice. Other clues to passive are that the action of the verb goes *back* to the subject and the use of *by* in a prepositional phrase following the verb.) The second clause matches the who-did-what order, so it is active voice.

Frequent use of passive voice results in several problems: The sentence is less direct, it may avoid naming the doer of an action and it is longer — typical of wordy constructions.

The following sentences illustrate passive voice and revisions:

- *The open meetings law was broken by the City Council. — > The City Council broke the open meetings law.*
- *The dog was hit by a car. — > A car hit the dog.*
- *The children were blessed by the priest. — > The priest blessed the children.*
- *The blood will be taken by a nurse with a syringe. — > A nurse will take the blood with a syringe.*
- *The law banning use of cell phones by teenage drivers was passed by the Missouri Legislature. — > The Missouri Legislature passed the law banning use of cell phones by teenage drivers.*

Passive voice, however, is not always something to avoid. At times it may be necessary, even preferable, to active voice. In fact, passive voice is better than active in the following four instances:

- To emphasize the receiver of an action. Sometimes the receiver deserves the greater attention afforded by being positioned as a sentence's subject, as in the following: *President Obama was booed by a crowd of elderly protestors.* (In this example, putting the president first is appropriate because he is a VIP, more important than a group of unnamed protestors.)
- Alternatively, to de-emphasize the doer of an action. This is especially useful when the doer is not known, as in the following: *Johnson was killed in the hit-and-run accident.* (Here, the doer of the action — the driver of the car that hit and ran — may not be known.)
- To avoid placing responsibility for an action. This is a diplomatic response, which may or may not be relevant in stories, as in the following: President Reagan, speaking about the U.S. involvement in the Iran-Contra scandal, said, *"Mistakes*

*were made."* (Although this is an admission of guilt, the statement does not name who was responsible for the mistakes.)

- To create smoother connections between sentences and ideas. In both this case and the following, the use of the passive voice serves to maintain or tighten relationships between subjects or ideas, as in the following: *Allen and Gloria were eager to leave for the party. It was being held at their favorite spot on the beach.* (With the first sentence ending with *party*, the second — which uses passive voice — beginning with the pronoun *it* that refers back to party maintains the tighter relationship between the sentences.)

For additional information, consult online editing resources in the Appendix.

# WORDINESS *exercise 1*

**DIRECTIONS**: Correct *wordiness* errors in the following exercises. Be careful *not* to change the meaning of the original sentences. Some may be correct.

1.  Arthur asked the bald-headed man if he polished his head.

2.  To save money, Eleanor had a combination of bologna sandwich and potato chips for dinner.

3.  Funds were stolen by the student body president.

4.  Power companies must give advance notice before shutting off electricity to homes with delinquent bills.

5.  The city is lax about making arrests of prostitutes.

6.  New innovations in technology have improved life in the 21st century.

7.  Vandals damaged the ATM machine Sunday.

8.  Because students were angry over the fee increase, the board of regents gave consideration to rescinding its vote.

9.  Because the Cooper County prosecutor had an open-and-shut case against him, Seth agreed to plead guilty if he wouldn't have to serve jail time.

10. Karl was kicked in his private parts by Bill.

# WORDINESS *exercise 2*

**DIRECTIONS**: Correct *wordiness* errors in the following exercises. Be careful *not* to change the meaning of the original sentences. Some may be correct.

1. It was Pete's intention to sell the family farm once his father passed away.

2. The easier solution was preferred by the mayor when he was caught between a rock and a hard place.

3. There is a candy shop opening at Heartland Mall at 9 a.m. Monday.

4. Harold is one of those dyed-in-the-wool Republicans who have a tendency to oppose government intervention.

5. Homeowners should set up feeding stations to help birds survive the winter months of December through March.

6. It is a violation of state law for teenagers to use cell phones while driving.

7. Following the 5-inch snowfall, schools were closed by the superintendent.

8. The chemistry professor demonstrated the very unique properties of mercury.

9. Sanitation engineers decided in a vote to hold a strike for higher wages.

10. Police apprehended the suspect in close proximity to the jewelry store.

**Additional exercises are available online at www.oup.com/us/rosenauer.**

## CHAPTER 23

# Punctuation and Usage Mastery

The exercises in this chapter will test your mastery of the punctuation and usage covered in chapters 13–22. Refer to those, as needed, to check the discussions, guidelines and rules.

# PUNCTUATION AND USAGE MASTERY *exercise 1*

**DIRECTIONS**: Correct errors involving *all aspects of punctuation and usage* in the following exercises. Some may be correct. No need to check AP style.

1. Stanton will be remembered as one of those students who is a standout in academics, athletics, friendship, and leadership.

2. The dean had the following items on his agenda; the $10,000 allocation to the Student Government Association, approval of the Lambda Chi Alpha charter and a 14-page report covering student organization activities on campus.

3. "The Heartland Beat" student newspaper said in an editorial "It's not unusual on any given afternoon to see students lying asleep in the union."

4. If campus security spots anything unusual during its patrols, they usually request backup from the Heartland Police Department.

5. For appearance sake, the English professor, who had been charged with receiving stolen property decided to meet his classes.

6. "Whom are most students today likely to use as role models," the social science instructor asked.

7. Students at Twain State University, who are opposed to the war are hosting a rally on the campus green.

8. If a student can't make it to class they should email their professors with an explanation.

9. The student workers in the cafeteria would not say where the missing cake went to.

10. Some Heartland residents dislike the presence of college students in the community; but a majority support the university and what it brings to the community.

# PUNCTUATION AND USAGE MASTERY *exercise 2*

**DIRECTIONS**: Correct errors involving *all aspects of punctuation and usage* in the following exercises. Some may be correct. No need to check AP style, but check the spelling of all names in the Heartland Directory.

1.   The Twain State University Student Government Association voted 15 to nine to ban smoking on campus.

2.   The ban which will take effect at the beginning of next semester covers faculty, staff, students and visitors.

3.   "Were pleased at this change in policy that reflects our health-conscious agenda," SGA President Art Fischer said. It's definitely the right decision at the right time."

4.   According to Ellen Dawson who opposed the measure not all senators were pleased with the outcome

5.   Debate, at times close to a free for all, was frequent and heated she said.

6.   SGA Secretary Stena W. (Woozy) Alexander said that "Some people can get really ugly in an argument."

7.   When Dawson moved to table the measure for the purpose of gathering more information, proban senators loudly objected.

8.   The group favoring the measure, was much more vocal than the antiban group, Fisher admitted.

9.   They probably should of been more tempered in their responses after all, it was clear that supporters were in the majority, he said.

10.  University trustees must discuss the ban at its next regularly-scheduled meeting, before it can take effect.

# PUNCTUATION AND USAGE MASTERY *exercise 3*

**DIRECTIONS**: Correct errors involving *all aspects of punctuation and usage* in the following exercises. Some may be correct. No need to check AP style, but check the spelling of all names in the Heartland Directory.

1.  A two car accident Friday in downtown Heartland sent three people to the hospital with moderate injuries.

2.  Taken to Heartland Memorial Hospital were: Peter S. Trent, 45, of Heartland; Margot V. Trent, 42, also of Heartland and Jordan O. Marsh, 19, of Columbia, Mo.

3.  Peter Trent suffered a dislocated shoulder and broken wrist in the accident, while his wife Margot complained of neck pain.

4.  Marshs foot was crushed in the accident and he underwent surgery to repair the damage.

5.  The accident occurred at 3:40 pm at the intersection of 10th and Main streets

6.  The car driven by Peter Trent, was traveling south on Main when it was struck by Marsh's car which was heading west on 10th Street.

7.  At that point in time, Trent's car traveled 20 feet, and came to rest in the yard at 1014 Main St.

8.  Marsh's vehicle toppled the stoplight at the northwest corner of the intersection, causing it to fall onto 10th Street and block traffic.

9.  Each driver told police they had a green light; officers were checking with witnesses to gather up additional information.

10. Neither the Trents nor Marsh were wearing seat belts, therefore, police issued tickets for that violation to all three.

# PUNCTUATION AND USAGE MASTERY *exercise 4*

**DIRECTIONS**: Correct errors involving *all aspects of punctuation and usage* in the following exercises. Some may be correct. No need to check AP style, but check the spelling of all names in the Heartland Directory.

1.  A polite gun wielding customer robbed a popular downtown eatery Wednesday during its noon rush.

2.  The gunman had just ate lunch at the Downtown Dine-In, 819 Francis St., when he got up, pulled out a pistol and told everyone to lay down on the floor.

3.  He went to the cash register at the front of the diner and told the cashier Alma Van Dyke, "Open up the register and give me the money and you won't get hurt.

4.  Van Dyke who did what he asked said the man was quite polite.

5.  "He told me "Thank you" and then walked calmly out the front door," she said.

6.  Attorney Patrick Pamer, who was one of about 50 customers in the restaurant when the robbery occurred, agreed that the man was surprisingly polite.

7.  "His foot brushed my suit jacket when he stepped over me and he said, 'Excuse me,'" Palmer said.

8.  Cecilia Stone, whose a longtime waitress and part owner of the diner, said that the man left her a $10 tip, however, he failed to pay the $9 tab for his meal.

9.  Police say, witnesses described the gunman as: Caucasian, 5 feet 9 inches tall, 190 pounds, with brown hair and brown eyes and wearing a gray shirt and blue jeans.

10. Anyone with information about the suspect are asked to contact the TIPS Hotline at (573)619-TIPS.

**Additional exercises are available online at** www.oup.com/us/rosenauer.

# PART 4

## Leads, Headlines, Images, Design and the Full Story

## CHAPTER 24

# Leads

*"Vigorous writing is concise. A sentence should contain no unnecessary words, or a paragraph no unnecessary sentences, for the same reason that a machine should have no unnecessary parts. Every word should tell."*

~E.B. White

Your careful review of leads in stories you edit is an essential part of your job. A story with a weak lead is an invitation to trouble. Readers rely on leads to tell them what to expect from stories, and when leads fail to do so, many readers today will move on to something more interesting.

If you can add, trim or move some words around to improve the lead, do so. If it's going to take more to fix the lead, give the reporter another shot at writing it. Unless you are on deadline, resist the urge to rewrite weak leads. Doing so steals from reporters the right to put their marks on the most significant component of their work.

In this chapter we will cover the following problems you will likely encounter:

- No-news leads
- Buried leads
- Too long leads
- Passive leads
- Definition leads

- Direct quotation leads

- Question leads

- Cliché leads

- Weak beginnings

The recommended practice is for editors to give a story a complete read before making any changes. That should tell you right away if it has a weak lead. If the reporter should rewrite it, send it back for a quick turnaround while you edit the rest of the story.

# No-News Leads

Be on guard for "no-news leads." These don't provide news; instead, they announce topics, as in the following, which could have been written before the meeting: *The Twain State University board of governors Monday night discussed ways to cut spending on campus.*

This one should go back to the reporter for a rewrite that may look like this: *Faculty awards, travel and sabbaticals and dependent tuition waivers were among expenditures that the Twain State University board of governors voted to cut Monday night.*

Here is another no-news lead and its fix:

No-news lead: *Worker unrest was the focus of a special session of the Heartland City Council on Wednesday at City Hall.*

Revision: *The Heartland City Council has invited a state mediator to help negotiate changes at City Hall that might alleviate worker unrest.*

# Buried Leads

Another problem to watch for is "buried leads." Similar to no-news leads—and sometimes indistinguishable from them—these may result from the reporter presenting a chronology of an event rather than stressing the key results of an event, as in the following:

> *The Twain State University board of governors heard Monday night that overspending has become a budget problem in two key departments on campus.*
>
> *Last month the board learned that spending in maintenance and computer operations for the first six months of this budget year already has drained 80 percent of allocated funds.*

Although this lead offers some news and background, it doesn't get to the heart of the story in highlighting how the board hopes to resolve the problem.

Here is a reporter's rewrite: *The Twain State University board of governors agreed Monday night to create two positions to save money in its maintenance and computer operations.*

# Too Long Leads

Sometimes, a lead is long because the reporter is trying to say too much in a single sentence. Whereas the traditional summary lead included all five W's and H, modern leads cover only the most important of those news elements in the first paragraph, allowing the rest to drop into second and later paragraphs.

If the lead you are editing runs too long, see if some of the tightening techniques suggested in Chapter 22, "Wordiness," will fix the problem. Perhaps you can split a long lead into two or more sentences. Whatever you do, retain as much of the flavor and content of the original while tightening it to be more effective.

Consider the following example of an overpacked lead:

> *In an attempt to stanch the flow of over-budget spending that has beset two departments during the last six months, the Twain State board of governors voted Monday night to hire a purchasing manager and an information technology director.*

The revision that you'd like to see come back from the reporter is the same as one previously:

> *The Twain State University board of governors agreed Monday night to create two positions to save money in its maintenance and computer operations.*
>
> *The university will hire a maintenance director and an information technology director to improve operations that have sent those university budgets into the red during the last six months.*

The original lead is 39 words; the first paragraph of the revised lead is 23. The second paragraph covers the rest of the original content in 28 words. Although the result is more words overall, the first paragraph of the rewrite is shorter and more inviting.

# Passive Leads

Passive voice, which we discussed in Chapter 22, is less direct, may avoid naming the doer of an action and usually makes the lead longer. It's a problem anywhere in a story; it's worse when it's in a lead, front and center.

Consider this lead: *Two teens were killed Friday in a two-car accident north of the city.* Yes, it's passive voice, and either you or the reporter might come back with a revision that reads like this: *A two-car accident north of the city killed two teens Friday.* This fix offers active voice, but some would argue that the opening emphasis on the *what*, the accident, is less important than the *who*, the two teens. Perhaps the best fix is one that uses a different verb, allowing both active voice and the *who* opener: *Two teens died Friday in a two-car accident north of the city.*

How about this passive lead: *A Twain State University football player was suspended by university officials Tuesday after being arrested last week by Heartland police for driving while intoxicated.*

You might try various fixes:

- *Twain State University officials Tuesday suspended a football player after Heartland police arrested him last week for driving while intoxicated.* (Active voice throughout, but some would argue that opening focus on the officials is weak.)
- *A Twain State University football player is under suspension after his arrest last week for driving while intoxicated.* (This tighter lead emphasizes the more important *who*; yet, it uses a weak main verb, *is*.)
- *A Twain State University football player was suspended Tuesday after his arrest last week for driving while intoxicated.* (This keeps focus on the most important *who* and returns to a stronger verb. Yes, it's passive voice. However, remember that passive is *not ungrammatical*. It's just not preferred. At times it may be best for a lead, but make that decision only after you've considered alternatives.)

If you can eliminate passive voice in a lead while emphasizing the best choice for an opening element, do so. However, don't let concerns with passive voice drive you to active-voice leads that may be weaker.

# Definition Leads

Definition leads usually pop up in stories where reporters worry that readers may not know the meaning of key terms, as in this example:

> *Webster's defines Chlamydia as a widespread, gonorrhea-like venereal disease caused by the bacterium Chlamydia trachomatis.*
>
> *This disease, the most widespread sexually transmitted disease in the United States, is the topic of a public forum Monday at 7 p.m. at Heartland High School.*

An easy revision might read as follows:

> *Chlamydia, the most widespread sexually transmitted disease in the United States, is the topic of a public forum Monday at 7 p.m. at Heartland High School.*

*This gonorrhea-like venereal disease infected 1.2 million people during 2011, with the highest incidence reported among black men.*

Certainly, reporters should explain unfamiliar terms to readers, but make sure they don't fall back on definitions as ineffective ways to lead stories.

# Direct Quotation Leads

Leading a story with a direct quote is tempting. Like the smell of popcorn at a movie theater draws people to the snack bar, a choice quote often finds its way to the top of a story. At times that works. However, too often reporters choose direct quotes to lead because it's too inviting and too easy.

Such is the case in this direct quotation lead:

*"I'm looking forward to seeing a good ballgame when I visit Twain State University," Missouri Gov. Jay Nixon said Tuesday.*

*Nixon is scheduled to travel to Heartland Saturday for the annual gridiron showdown between Twain State and Missouri State University.*

This direct quote is one that shouldn't appear anywhere in the story, let alone in the lead. The quote has no punch or power. If anything, the reporter might paraphrase the governor's sentiments.

Quotes must be powerful, provocative and carefully chosen if they are to carry the burden of a lead. The following seems to qualify:

*"The ease with which Chlamydia can be treated results in people thinking the infection is 'no big deal,' which is a serious problem for prevention," said Dr. David A. DuMont, Heartland director of public health.*

*That "no big deal" attitude is the impetus behind a public forum Monday at 7 p.m. at Heartland High School.*

When they open feature stories effectively, direct quotes can be delightful and provocative. However, don't let reporters rely too much on direct quote leads, and never allow a weak quote to launch a story.

# Question Leads

Consider this lead:

*Do you need help to get ready for final exams?*

Like the weak direct quotation lead, you should send a question lead like this back to the reporter for rewrite. Some reporters mistakenly believe that a question lead works because the story provides its answer. Although that may be true, rarely is a question provocative enough or clear enough to serve as an effective lead.

Here is one alternative to the preceding lead:

*Students needing help to prepare for their final exams can stop by Room 110 in McCabe Hall anytime during the last two weeks of the semester.*

This straight lead does a fine job for this simple, hard news story.

## Cliché Leads

If you've read a lead angle so many times that you groan reading it again, it likely fits the bill for this lead problem. Like clichés, the weak figure of speech covered in Chapter 22, cliché leads suffer because they are overused and trite.

Gregg McLachlan, associate managing editor of The Simcoe Reformer in Ontario, Canada, lists a handful of cliché leads[1] that cause him to shout, "Ugh!" They are as follows:

- It poured rain, but spirits weren't dampened.
- (Fill in the blank) died yesterday.
- (Fill in the blank) is the place to be this weekend.
- It's every parent's worst nightmare.
- The community is in shock.
- (Fill in the blank) is not your typical kid.
- 'Tis the season. . . .
- It was a rockin' good time.

Dick Thien, editor-in-residence at The Freedom Forum, has a list of cliché leads[2] that draw their own ughs. Here are a few of them:

- He leaned back in his chair/against a tree/whatever lead.
- The good news is (blank). The bad news is (blank) lead.
- That's what lead. (This begins the second paragraph of a cliché lead.)
- Thanks to . . . lead.
- The Rodney Dangerfield lead.
- The not alone lead.
- The welcome to lead.

If the lead approach is too familiar, send it back to the reporter for a rewrite.

## Weak Beginnings

Included in this discussion of leads to revise are those that have weak beginnings:

- The *when.*
- Attribution.
- There is/there are.

## The *When*

The *when* of a story is a standard element in most leads; however, seldom should it open the lead as in these two examples:

- *On Thursday night, the Twain State University board of governors agreed to create two positions to save money in its maintenance and computer operations.*
- *On Monday, a Twain State University football player was suspended after his arrest last week for driving while intoxicated.*

The best spot for *when* is next to the main verb or, if not a good fit there, at the end of the sentence.

However, if the *when* is the key concern of the lead, consider leaving it alone, as in the following: *Friday is the deadline for Heartland residents to sign up for free pickup of old appliances.*

## Attribution

Opening a lead with attribution—that is, the source of information—is another unwise choice. See how the following illustrate the problem:

- *Heartland police said Wednesday that cars parked along 36th Street adjacent to Altman Stadium at Twain State University will be ticketed beginning next week.*
- *Heartland Theatre Manager Cyrus Jones said Friday that box office receipts are down 25 percent during the past year.*

In both examples, opening the lead with what the source said is an effective solution. The attribution can follow the statement, either ending the sentence or moved to the next sentence or paragraph.

When a VIP, such as the president, the pope or a mayor is saying something important, an attribution lead is a good call.

## There Is/There Are

Almost all sentences opening with *there is/there are* need revision. They reflect lazy writing, typically the result of weak habits a reporter has not learned to overcome. In all such constructions, the subject of the sentence follows the verb.

See how you can quickly fix the problem in the following examples:

- *There were seven auto accidents Sunday during heavy rains that hit the Heartland area.* — > *Seven accidents occurred Sunday during heavy rains that hit the Heartland area.*
- *There is a problem with suspended particles plaguing the Heartland water supply.* — > *A problem with suspended particles is plaguing the Heartland water supply.*

It's worth noting that most examples here involve hard news stories and typically straight leads. Other story types likely will hit your screen—features, sports and commentary. Some of the same weaknesses in those leads will need similar fixes; just be flexible in how you edit these non-news stories.

There is no single way to write an effective lead; how your reporters write their leads will vary widely. Be sensitive to reporters' creativity. More important, make sure leads speak clearly to your readers.

Editing leads is challenging; it's also vital. Do your job well, and both the stories and their readers will benefit.

For additional information, consult online editing resources in the Appendix.

# **LEAD** *exercise 1*

**DIRECTIONS**: Identify the weaknesses in the following leads by writing the appropriate letter in the blank next to it. Then, write the first paragraph of a revised lead for each.

**a)** No-news leads/buried leads.

**b)** Too long leads.

**c)** Passive leads.

**d)** Definition leads.

**e)** Direct quotation leads.

**f)** Question leads.

**g)** Cliché leads.

**h)** Weak beginnings (*when, attribution, there is/there are*).

**1.** _____ The Heartland City Council met Monday night to consider the purchase of land for a new municipal golf course.

Members learned that the 50-acre tract of land targeted for construction includes two ponds and several plots of timber. The open land, which comprises about 40 acres, is primarily used for hay production.

Fair market value of the property is $375,000. However, city planners estimate that development for the golf course could run $5 million.

After debating the proposal, the council voted 5–2 against buying the land at this time.

_____

_____

_____

**2.** _____ Thanks to the Twain State Boosters, the River Raiders football team will have new uniforms and helmets next season.

_____

_____

_____

**3.** _____ A two-car accident involving a tractor-trailer and an SUV on Interstate 70 five miles east of Heartland Thursday claimed the lives of three local residents, all members of the same family, and injured an Ottumwa, Iowa, trucker.

_____

_____

_____

**4.** _____ Three local coaches were honored Saturday with Heartland Hero Awards from the Heartland Chamber of Commerce.

_____

_____

_____

**5.** _____ Are your taxes too high?

The Heartland Area Tea Party is hosting a town forum Monday at the Heartland Steakhouse meeting room to hear answers about high taxes from local residents.

_____

_____

_____

**6.** _____ There are three nationally known shops opening this month at Heartland Mall.

_____

_____

_____

**7.** _____ Mayor Karl Shearin said at a late afternoon news conference Friday that he was unwilling to continue trying to deal with the ongoing problems at City Hall.

Problems the mayor was referring to involve increasing expenses coupled with shrinking revenues as well as his longtime feud with city police officers.

After speaking for 10 minutes, Shearin announced, "I'm resigning, effective immediately." He refused to answer questions before leaving.

_____

_____

_____

**8.** _____ "I've been here 30 years, and every year we're supposed to be consolidated the next year. It has never happened," said Benjamin Silcott, principal at Moniteau R-4 High School in California, Mo., and an educator with the district for more than 30 years.

This time around, the longtime educator believes the talk of consolidating districts at Moniteau R-1 in Jamestown, Moniteau R-3 in Tipton and Moniteau R-4 into one is serious.

Jamestown and Tipton resumed seemingly annual consolidation talks in early September.

California held a public hearing shortly after those talks started, and more than 200 people attended to discuss the future of the school. Last week at a joint meeting between Jamestown and Tipton, those two school boards voted to invite California to official consolidation talks.

_____

_____

_____

**9.** _____ Bit is the smallest unit of digital data, and byte is a computer binary reference to a storage unit that can hold one character.

The two terms were among dozens of computer terms bandied about Saturday at the third annual Heartland Computer Expo at Twain State University.

_____

_____

_____

**10.** _____ There were 20 children eagerly waiting for 10 a.m. to arrive Friday—the scheduled moment for Santa to make his first appearance this year at Heartland Mall.

_____

_____

_____

**Additional exercises are available online at** www.oup.com/us/rosenauer.

# Headlines

CHAPTER 25

*"If one morning I walked on top of the water across the Potomac River, the headline that afternoon would read: President can't swim."*

~Lyndon B. Johnson

Preparing headlines is among the key tasks that editors complete: and the most difficult. Whether we are talking a daily newspaper, a special interest magazine or a media website, all make use of and benefit from well-written headlines.

These relatively short pieces of text require that the editor be a superior wordsmith who has a strong vocabulary and an eye and ear for well-wrought phrases. Of all the material that goes on the printed page or into a digital design, headlines are a vital link between busy readers and stories written to inform, to educate and to entertain them. In fact, you are wise to assume that many readers won't read a story just because it's there. They must be lured in, like fish to the bait on a hook. In fact, some studies suggest that only two of 10 readers ever make it past the headline. As a result, if the headline doesn't pique their interest and quickly convince them they should spend time with a story, they won't read it.

Understand, too, that editors must be able to write headlines quickly — not hastily, but efficiently fast. Many times editors write them on deadline, so the clock is ticking

253

to keep the product moving along. Even when the editor faces no looming deadline, the pressure to finish editing, write the headline and deliver the story is great.

Writing headlines is the sole province of editors in most media organizations. Here editors can practice cleverness, creativity, sensitivity and insight.

# The Tradition of Headline Writing

Headlines in publications always have served as strategic guides to readers. Headlines are among the first things readers see on a page. You must craft strong headlines to make sure they aren't also the *last* things readers see on a page.

The following are goals of headlines:

- They get the reader's attention.

  This is due both to their size — relative to the much smaller story type — and the words that comprise them. Whereas story type may run from 10 point to as large as 14 point for online articles, headline type size ranges between 18 and 72 points or larger. In addition, you must carefully choose the visually larger words of the headline to say succinctly what the story is about. That's where your role as wordsmith is severely tested.

- They summarize or tell about the article.

  Headlines are a quick index to content for readers. They must state clearly what stories are about, and they must do so in fresh, creative ways.

- They help organize the stories on the page.

  As strong visual elements, headlines are what readers see *second* on a page, following photos and other art — though some recent studies suggest that online readers may look first at the headlines. These darker, heavier blocks in the sea of gray body copy become part of the overall page design, nearly as magnetic and compelling as the photos and art. That explains why many page designs set the headline size with little regard to exactly what story actually will run in the hole provided.

- They indicate the importance of a story.

This is a relative matter, with both the size of type and its location on a page signaling to readers which stories are more important and deserve greater attention. The larger and bolder the type and the higher on the page or screen, the greater is the news or feature value of a headline and its companion story.

## First Step

The first step in writing a headline is to read the story, always. In fact, it's safe to say that you never should draft a headline without first reading the entire story. Locate the lead and make sure that your headline reflects its focus without repeating its content. Tricky, but among the surefire ways to draw the wrath of reporters is to steal the thunder of their clever, creative leads by mirroring them in headlines.

At the same time that you want to avoid stealing the lead or the story's punch line, you should provide content for your headlines that is close to the content of leads. The simplest method for doing so is by using the key-word approach. Pick out three or four key words from the lead and use those as starting points for the headline.

As you build the headline, use the inverted pyramid pattern. Put the most important element first, the least important last. The *when*, if called for in the headline, usually works best next to the verb. Also, attribution — who said something — typically goes last unless the source is a VIP.

Good advice from veteran editors suggests that you are wise to write several versions of a headline and pick the best. Of course, this assumes you have enough time to test several angles.

## Traditional Headline Rules

Journalism has several well-established rules for headlines, though different media tend to follow different traditions. Those involve wording, verb tense, formatting, capitalization and punctuation.

Traditional headlines have noun-subjects and verbs, with the primary emphasis on strong verbs. This is particularly true for newspaper headlines. However, label headlines, as in *City Hall censorship* are becoming more common, especially if a traditional headline follows as a second deck, or headline unit. For example, a second deck to the label headline just listed might be this: *Mayor's gag order silences staff.*

Verb tense follows a specific pattern that most readers have come to understand even if they cannot explain it:

- Use present tense for past actions, as in *Twain State raises tuition 5 percent.*
- Use present perfect for action in progress, as in *Twain State considering tuition increase.*
- Use the infinitive or future tense for future, as in *Twain State board to vote on tuition hike* or *Twain State board will vote on tuition hike.*

What may appear initially to be past tense in headlines likely is passive voice, as in *Heartland Councilman indicted on bribery charges*. The source of confusion is the missing *is* in that headline (*is indicted*; see following for the reason *is* isn't used.) Although active voice is preferred in headlines — just as it is in stories — passive voice is not forbidden and sometimes is better.

As far as formatting, keep related elements on the same line of a multiline headline, as in *Parade wows spectators / with record number of entries* (where / indicates a line break). That example keeps the preposition on the same line with its object. Consider these other formatting concerns:

- Don't split adjectives or adverbs from the words they modify, as in *50th anniversary, late-night meeting* or *vigorously defends*.
- Don't break up verb packages, as in *will be honored*.
- Don't split infinitives, as in *to execute* or *to garner*.
- Finally, keep prepositions and their objects on the same line, as in *after sundown*.

Although some publications are not as strict today about such split headlines (see examples following), you are always better off trying to avoid them to make it easier for readers to follow and understand. Each line of multiline headlines should fill most of the space available and should be balanced or nearly so from line to line.

Most publications today use downstyle; that is, capitalize the first word and proper nouns as you would a sentence and lowercase the rest.

Use limited punctuation in headlines. Commas replace the conjunction *and*, as in *City, Twain State to seek additional funds for nature center*. However, if you are presenting two complete ideas, use a semicolon, as in *Smith convicted on embezzling charge; prosecutor to seek maximum penalty*. For attribution, prefer (name) *says*, which you set off with a comma when it ends the headline. Attribution that begins a headline sometimes uses colons, as in this: *President: 'We will win'* headline. When the headline needs quotation marks, always use single quotes, as in *'Figaro' to open Sunday at the Twain State theater*.

## Traditional Headline Types

Through their long history newspapers have developed a stock of headline types, many of which they still use today. Even though the jargon may be confusing, don't let it stop you from drafting strong, effective headlines.

Consider the following common terms that you may encounter:

- Banner, also called a streamer or ribbon: Headline spanning the width of the page, typically at the top.
- Decks, also called dropouts or banks: A deck is a complete headline unit or package, not just a single line of a multiline headline. Some stories today — whether in newspapers, magazines or online — run with more than one deck. A second deck is a package of its own, not just the continuation of the main headline package. It adds more details or a different angle than what the main headline says. Typically, second decks are a different typeface than the main headline (where typefaces refer to normal, bold and italic) and about half the type size of the main.
- Kicker: Running over the main headline, a kicker usually is flush left, one-half its type size and no more than two-thirds its length.

**FIGURE 25-2** This front page from The Tuscaloosa (Ala.) News shows the power of various headlines to attract readers' attention and draw them into the stories.

- Readout, also called a dropout: A second deck under the main headline, usually over the story's lead where it offers the benefit of visually drawing readers to the beginning of the story.

Next, let's review some headline do's followed by some headline don'ts.

## Headline Do's

- Do make headlines accurate. It's one thing to miss an error in 12-point body copy; it's quite another to do so when the type is 48 point and bold.
- Do get the most important element(s) or key words into the headline, remembering that good headlines tell readers what happened, or will happen, and help them understand why this story is important.
- Do make headlines easy to read. The key purpose of the headline is to communicate, and readable headlines do that job much more effectively.
- Do use Arabic numerals in headlines, which are acceptable for all uses, as in *5 chosen for district all-star team.*
- Do use short, action verbs and prefer active voice rather than passive.
- Do take time to find the precise verb that fits the context and summarizes the action.
- Do make headlines interesting and inviting.
- Do have fun as you find fresh, creative ways to attract readers, but don't sacrifice clarity or accuracy for cleverness.
- Do follow rules of grammar and style.
- Do take time to reread and recheck a completed headline.
- Do seek input from others, asking them if the headline is clear and if it works.

## Headline Don'ts

Here's a longer list of headline don'ts:

- Don't repeat the lead verbatim or steal the story's punch line. Repeating key words, of course, is not only OK but also necessary.
- Don't exaggerate, overstate or sensationalize, promising more than the story delivers. In other words, don't mislead readers.
- Don't present speculation as fact. Also, don't editorialize. If you need to give an opinion in a headline, attribute it.
- Don't repeat words in headlines, either within a deck or from deck to deck.
- Don't use *is, was* and *will be,* as in *City is ready to set up shelter.* Cut *is.*
- Don't use articles — a, an, the — in headlines. Although this may seem odd at first, do it. Before long it will be second nature.
- Don't use *and* in headlines. Replace *and* with a comma.
- Don't abbreviate — at least not much. In fact, AP says it's OK to abbreviate states without a city; some cities (K.C. for Kansas City and N.Y. for New York); US, UK and UN (no periods when used in headlines); and familiar abbreviations and acronyms for colleges and universities, also without periods, as in *TSU,* the acronym for Twain State University.
- Don't begin with a verb, as in *Wins race following heavy voter turnout.*

- Don't command reader, as in *Vote today.*
- Don't use synonyms carelessly. Find the right word whose meaning, definition, and feeling, connotation, are appropriate.
- Don't use *feels*, *thinks* or *believes.*
- Don't use words that might be read as either nouns or verbs.
- Don't use slang unless it's relevant to a story and matches its tone.
- Don't use puns unless they are fresh, clever and appropriate.
- Don't repeat yesterday's headline, as in *Council to honor firefighters* followed the next day by *Council honors firefighters.*
- Don't commit libel.
- Don't use question headlines, at least not very often.
- Don't digitally condense or expand a headline to make it fit. Even when subtle, such lazy tricks can bother readers. The same is true for changing a type size to fit a headline.
- Don't use "headlinese." These are usually short words that editors have overused, transforming them into the equally taboo cliché. Consider the following for starters: *bid, eye, hit, ink, mull, nab, nix, rap, rout, slam, slate, solon, stun, vie* and *unrest.*

Realize that you don't usually get a second chance to encourage readers to move beyond the headlines. To turn a scanner into a reader, your headlines should communicate clear, appropriate messages to their audience.

## Headline Tips

When you get stuck writing a headline — and you will — try the following tricks:

- If the headline won't fit, try shorter or longer synonyms.
- Turn the headline idea around.
- Begin with a different key word.
- Set the story aside for a while and come back to it.

Some newspaper and online editors recommend keeping a swipe file. In this you keep examples of headline gems you find. Over time, your collection can grow large. Of course, your goal in using this file is not actually to swipe the headline; that's plagiarism. However, especially when you are stuck, a review of the best headlines in your swipe file might offer one to use as a model for your story. See how the writer crafted the original, and then modify it to make it your own.

# Accurate, Interesting, Appropriate and Effective Headlines

Two "carved-in-stone" rules for headlines:

- They must be accurate.
- They must fit the available space.

Nowhere is it more critical to be accurate than in headlines you write. Although it may be the last thing an editor does, it's the first thing a reader sees. Certainly, an error is an error, but errors presented in large type are especially ugly. The sad fact is that *everybody* sees it — except you when you are hasty and careless enough to miss the mistake before sending it to press or posting it online.

One way to limit inaccuracies is to "do a double take." Facts in headlines must match facts in the story. Make sure you clearly understand the second before tackling the first. Then, do a double take, moving back and forth between headline and story to confirm facts. Although matching a number in a story to one in a headline would seem a no-brainer, those slips happen. Do a double take. Misspelling, particularly of names, can be a bugaboo for some editors. Run spell check after writing the headline, certainly, but because spell check won't catch misspelled names, do a double take — find the name in the story again to confirm it's correct.

*Interesting* can be a real wiggle word because what may interest one person may be dry as chalk dust for another. Yet, that doesn't mean you don't try to make a headline interesting. Chances are that if you find it interesting, so will many readers.

As a wordsmith wannabe, you have at your disposal thousands of words, at least a few of which may be exactly what your headline calls for. Using the key-word approach puts you into the same ballpark as the story, and that's always a good starting point. Occasionally, you have to accept "good enough." Anyone who has ever worked at finishing drywall understands the secret of good enough. If you do no less than write a headline that is accurate and fits the lead, that's acceptable, even good enough. Yet, when you have time and opportunity to do better than good enough, play with your headline.

Among the demands for headlines is *appropriateness*. You must match not only the content of the headline to the story but also its tone. It's one thing to be clever in a headline for a soft news or feature story; it's quite another — and a serious mistake — to allow that cleverness to guide your writing of a hard news story, such as an automobile fatality. Be sensitive to the subtleties of tone that a headline reflects and sensitive to how readers will respond.

## Examples of Winning Headlines

As you use wordplay and free association, look for good use of contrast, twists of phrases, effective alliteration — repetition of initial consonant sounds — and the like. Have fun playing with words but never to the point that being cute becomes *too* important. If you are not sure that it works, likely it doesn't. Rewrite it. The following headlines, though, from a recent American Copy Editors Society contest,[1] are examples of effective wordplay:

- From the St. Petersburg Times, a two-deck headline package:
  - ▶ *Town wants / kids to hitch/ their britches*
  - ▶ *Old-timers in a North Florida / town really aren't interested in / seeing the generation gap*
- From the Austin American-Statesman, a single-deck headline:
  - ▶ *The deep dish on / how Austin lured / the Netroots pie*
- From the Wichita Eagle, a two-deck headline package, with the first a label and the second a readout:
  - ▶ *Heaping whelping*

- ▶ *Seven litters lead to / 'Puppypalooza,' which / runs through Sunday*
- From the Wichita Eagle, a single-deck headline:
  - ▶ *Woman is incensed by theft during Mass*
- From the Wichita Eagle, a two-deck headline package:
  - ▶ *It's crunch time*
  - ▶ *Girl Scout cookies are about / to be delivered across much of the state*
- From the Providence Journal, a two-deck headline package, with the first a label banner and the second a readout:
  - ▶ *So many shoes, so many souls*
  - ▶ *Line of footwear / to the governor's / office calls /attention to plight / of the homeless*
- From the Los Angeles Times, a two-deck headline package, with the first making use of a form of direct address and the second a readout:
  - ▶ *Change, meet crisis*
  - ▶ *A frail economy and / widening budget / deficit may hinder / Obama's ambitious / spending agenda*
- From the Los Angeles Times, a two-deck headline package, with the second a readout:
  - ▶ *'Fly' commits insecticide*
  - ▶ *David Cronenberg and / Howard Shore turn / their film into a dreary, / monotonous creature*
- From the Los Angeles Times, a two-deck headline package, with the first a banner:
  - ▶ *Engineers shun the razor, hope for an edge*
  - ▶ *Some at software firm / vow to stay stubbly / until a product launch*

You may notice that several of these headlines are split; in other words, related words in some multiline headlines aren't on the same line. For example, the second deck of the Los Angeles Times headline about the weak economy and budget deficit splits *budget deficit* and *ambitious spending agenda*. However, splitting headlines has become more common, especially for second decks, some of which read more like full sentences set in display type. Probably it's safe to say that some editors today don't let traditional formatting get in the way of a well-written headline.

Your instructor will decide if headlines you write for Copycrafting should avoid being split.

## Some Additional Headline Advice

As you craft headlines, don't assume that nouns in your headlines are the main focus. That role goes to verbs. They are the action words, the power words. If anything is happening in a headline, it's happening in the verb. Therefore, take plenty of time to toy with various options for your headline's verb, making sure that it carries the weight of communicating your message.

At the same time, limit your use of adjectives and adverbs — the descriptive words. Although these seem to be vital parts of the message, you will find that you can drop most, if not all, adjectives and adverbs from headlines without losing essential content,

**FIGURE 25-3** Good editors
understand the importance of
headlines and how challenging they
can be to write.

14 point Times

18 point Times

24 point Times

30 point Times

36 point Times

42 point Times

48 point Times

54 point Times

60 point Times

72 Point Times

especially if you are using strong verbs. Adjectives and adverbs add lots of weight to what you are trying to say without providing the best bang.

One approach that makes any headline more interesting is communicating to readers how the story will affect them. Thus, even though *Twain board approves tuition increase* may be true, a better headline for readers might be *Students must shell out $150 more for tuition.*

## Column Measures

Headlines are measured in two ways: the size of the type and the width of the column into which the headline will go.

Standard headline sizes are 14, 18, 24, 30, 36, 42, 48, 54, 60, 72 and so on — all throwbacks to a time when type size was fixed, as opposed to digital today, which offers standard head sizes as well as any combinations in between.

The size of type is measured using points. If you've done much work at all with word-processing or page-design software, then you are already familiar with that measure. With Microsoft Word, for example, the standard type sizes (in points) are 8, 9, 10, 11,12, 14, 16, 18, 20, 22, 24, 26, 28, 36, 48 and 72. However, you can keyboard any size between 1 and 1638 points.

Police support
ban on texting
while driving

# Mayor opts not to run

*Parade to roll Saturday*

**FIGURE 25-4** Three headline orders represented here are, from top, 1-18-3, 4-48B-1 and 3-36I-1.

Where you get the measurements to use for headlines can vary, but many media have one or more people whose job it is to provide copy editors with a page mockup that shows story placement and headline treatment.

Story placement indicates the exact position on the page as well as how many columns wide the story will be set. For example, a story might be set either one column or one and one-half columns to run across three columns. Headline treatment involves the type size, typeface, number of decks, number of lines and number of columns.

This information, called headline orders, may use the following three-part format, with each part separated by a hyphen:

- The first number is the number of columns wide.
- The second number is the size of type in points. If a B is included, use boldface, whereas an I calls for italic face.
- The third number is the number of lines that the deck will run.

So, 1–18-3 calls for a headline that is one-column wide, 18-point type, normal face and three lines. A headline order of 4–48B-1 would have an editor write a headline that runs four columns, 48-point type, boldface and one line. Likewise, a 3–36I-2 would be a three-column headline set at 36-point italic on two lines.

The other information you will need to do the exercises in this chapter and in Chapter 28, "The Full Story" is the actual column-width measurement. We will use the following column measurements of a standard broadsheet for our headlines:

| Columns | Picas | Inches (decimals) |
|---|---|---|
| 1 | 10p5 | 1.73 |
| 2 | 21p4 | 3.56 |
| 3 | 32p4 | 5.87 |
| 4 | 43p4 | 7.21 |
| 5 | 54p3 | 9.05 |
| 6 | 65p3 | 10.87 |

The particular fonts for headlines is a matter most publications determine, often restricting choices to one or a select few to avoid the "circus look" of a page with a wide mix of fonts. Such limitations help to give publications a consistent, planned look; moreover, reducing such choices speeds the work of the copy desk.

For our purposes Arial will be the font you use for headlines, unless directed otherwise by your instructor.

ONLINE INSIGHTS > **WEB PAGE HEADLINE TIPS**

Just as writing for the Web is different than writing for print or for broadcast, writing Web headlines should be different. The following suggestions provide guidance for handling those headlines:

- You must deliver the story's message using just the headline.
- Headlines in print media can play with the reader, especially as other page elements provide context and details to help the headline make sense. Because Web headlines can appear in various locations online, often without support, you must convey the message effectively with text alone.
- Your headlines must include keywords and phrases.
- Because many readers click to your site because of search engines, your content — especially your headlines — must be *search engine optimized*. That is, the words that users type into search engine windows are *keywords* that search engines use to link to content with those same keywords. The more keywords and phrases in the search that match content on your Web page, the higher it will appear in the search results and the more visitors are likely to come to your site.
- Don't rely on the font size of a headline to signal story importance.

- Whereas print media typically rely on size to help readers gauge the importance of a headline and its related story, you can't expect Web headline size to serve likewise. Headline text, therefore, is even more critical online in delivering the importance of the story's message.
- Web headlines don't always appear with other content.
- Web headlines can't depend on images or subheads to get readers to click them. Web headlines must be enticing enough to generate clicks.
- You can change Web headlines.
- If a headline you wrote for the morning's story doesn't seem to say the right thing about the story, you can change it any time. On the Web, you can edit any content in real time, including your headlines.
- Make your headlines clear, concise and relevant.
- Because both search engines and online readers aren't very forgiving, you must write headlines that are clear and concise; that is, direct and to the point. Cleverness and creativity need not be abandoned, but they are less important online. Another reason for conciseness: The maximum that will show up in a Google hit is 65 characters. That's just a few characters more than the preceding sentence.

*Many of these suggestions were borrowed from The Scholarly Kitchen (http://scholarlykitchen.sspnet.org/2008/09/18/headlines-20/).*

# Using Microsoft Word to Write Headlines

Most students are familiar with Microsoft Word; therefore, it makes sense to write headlines with Word using the settings following for this chapter and for Chapter 28, "The Full Story."

Use the following settings for Macintosh computers:

- Format/Font — Set the font to Arial and the font size as directed in the exercise.
- File/Page Setup — Change from portrait (vertical format) to landscape (horizontal format).
- Format/Paragraph — Indentation Left and Right should be 0, Spacing Before and After should be 0. Special should be None. Line spacing should be Single.

- Word/Preferences/General — Change Inches to Picas since picas are a more precise measure.

Use the following settings for Windows computers:

- Home — Set the font to Arial and the font size as directed in the exercise.
- Page Layout/Orientation — Change from Portrait to Landscape.
- Page Layout/Indent — Left and Right should be 0.
- Page Layout/Spacing — Before and After should be 0
- Office button (upper left of screen)/Word Options/Advanced/Display — Change inches to picas since picas are a more precise measure.

Of course, if you are familiar with page-design software, such as Adobe InDesign or Quark Xpress, you may prefer to use one of those to write your headlines.

Writing headlines is the province of editors. It's the single task where you can fully express your skills and your creativity. As with leads, there's no single way to write a headline for a given story. Quite different headlines can be very effective. The task may be challenging, but it also is fulfilling.

For additional information, consult online editing resources in the Appendix.

# HEADLINE *exercise 1*

**DIRECTIONS**: Using the column measures in the chapter, write an appropriate headline as indicated for the following story excerpts. Do *not* edit the stories, but consult the AP Stylebook and Webster's New World College Dictionary, as needed. Use Arial font.

*a. Main Headline: 4–36B-1*

A historic Heartland landmark is in shambles after a Saturday morning fire, which Heartland Police say was caused by arson.

The Heartland Steakhouse, 1701 Frederick Ave., had an estimated $125,000 in damages, mostly to the restaurant's main dining room.

Police arrested two men on suspicion of arson, Jake O'Neal, 23, and Arnold Simpson, 19. The pair was arrested six blocks from the restaurant at just past 1 a.m. Saturday. Police stopped the two on Faraon Street with a gasoline can and other items in a dark SUV that had been seen in the neighborhood just before the fire. The men also smelled of gasoline.

*b. Main Headline: 2–24B-2*

BOONVILLE, Mo. — Authorities are searching for a gunman who they say shot two men Sunday night at the Bottoms Up Club here.

Eldon Cross, 36, of Boonville, is believed to be the man who entered the club around 10:15 Sunday and shot two employees. As of late Monday, the suspect is still at large and considered armed and dangerous.

Although the shooting victims were thought to have life-threatening injuries, their conditions have since improved, said Boonville Police Chief Mike Crubaugh.

"We're anxious to find this guy, and we're working aggressively around the clock until we do," Crubaugh said. "We've got some idea of what his movements have been, and the vehicle he left the scene in may be key to tracking him down."

*c. Main Headline: 1–18-3*

BOONVILLE, Mo. — The manhunt for a suspect in a double shooting last weekend in Boonville ended Wednesday with his arrest in a small town in southeast Cooper County.

Law enforcement officers took Eldon Cross into custody Tuesday afternoon in Otterville, Mo., said Boonville Police Chief Mike Crubaugh. He is being held on two counts of attempted first-degree murder.

Cross was peering through binoculars at the road leading to a friend's home when a Cooper County deputy and an Otterville officer arrived, according to the Otterville Police Department.

The alleged gunman didn't notice the officers from his vantage point in the backyard and was surprised by their approach, Crubaugh said.

Authorities say the 36-year-old Boonville man entered the Bottoms Up Club in Boonville on Sunday night armed with a .22 caliber rifle. He was unable to find his estranged wife, an employee at the club and allegedly shot two other employees who had confronted him.

*d. Main Headline: 2–24B-1; second deck: 1–18-3*

Capital Improvements Program supporters can stand tall: The program is a success, delivering on promises at least 95 percent of the time.

The CIP sales tax for more than 10 years has worked from a specific list of projects — or promises — and the vast majority of them have been kept, according to a News-Observer analysis. Only three projects have been canceled, and those were rolled into another project.

So, arguably, the CIP never has failed to deliver.

Depending on how projects are counted, the CIP has promised between 46 and 72 projects. It also has funded another 20 projects, as the tax money has been sufficient to cover some unexpected costs.

The CIP is a half-cent sales tax, meaning that it costs Heartland shoppers 50 cents on a $100 purchase. The tax sunsets after five years to keep it accountable to voters.

*e. Main Headline: 3–36-1*

A Heartland man who threatened school district officials over the telephone last winter will serve probation for the offenses.

Elwood Wellington, 47, pleaded guilty Thursday morning to amended misdemeanor charges of public peace

disturbance related to two telephone calls he made to the Lindbergh Elementary School in March. He will serve a year's supervised probation on each count.

He had been charged with the misdemeanor of making a terrorist threat, but attorneys on both sides worked out a plea agreement that Cooper County Circuit Judge Roger Frakes approved. The arrangement avoided a scheduled one-day trial.

Wellington was charged after he phoned officials March 18 to discuss a situation that involved his grade-school daughter. He first called counselor Sasha Wilson and then called Principal Beth Harrison.

Both times, according to Cooper County Prosecutor Aaron R. Smith, Wellington made references to the Columbine massacre.

# HEADLINE *exercise 2*

**DIRECTIONS**: Using the column measures in the chapter, write an appropriate headline as indicated for the following story excerpts. Do *not* edit the stories, but consult the AP Stylebook and Webster's New World College Dictionary, as needed. Use Arial font.

*a. Main Headline: 4–48-1; second deck: 2–24B-2*

Turnout for the first Small Business Workshop was such a success last year that the Heartland Chamber of Commerce had no other choice but to host another.

Area small business owners and community members can attend the workshop at the River Raiders Center on the Twain State University campus on Oct. 28 between 7:30 and noon.

Keynote speaker Kylie Brown will share in advice and strategy for gaining a successful business. Brown is nationally known for her marketing and motivational skills.

"She got rave reviews last year, so we brought her back," said chamber Public Relations Director Joanne Cadden. "This year she is speaking about taking the fear out of small business startup and development."

Sessions for entrepreneurs will be led by Becky Evans and Steve Holton with the TSU Small Business Development Center. They will present a wealth of resources for small businesses, especially those just getting started.

The event is a way for the chamber to recognize small businesses and help entrepreneurs thrive, even in tough economic times, Cadden said.

*b. Main Headline: 2–24B-2*

CLARKS FORT, Mo. — A 50-year-old man who fell off the hood of a moving pickup was in critical condition at a hospital late Thursday.

George Otis, of Clarks Fort, was riding on the hood when the driver of the 1999 Ford pickup attempted to turn left into a parking lot, according to the Missouri State Highway Patrol. Otis slipped off the driver's side and fell under the truck's rear wheel. He was taken by air ambulance with serious injuries to Heartland Memorial Hospital.

The driver of the pickup, Daniel Watson, 42, of Clarks Fort, was cited for careless driving and not wearing his seat belt, the patrol report said.

The incident occurred at 3:20 p.m. on South Main Street in Clarks Fort.

*c. Main Headline: 1–18-3*

CLARKS FORT, Mo. — A 50-year-old man who fell off the hood of a moving pickup earlier this month died from his injuries Wednesday.

George Otis, of Clarks Fort, had slid off the driver's side of the hood as the Ford pickup attempted a left turn into a parking lot on South Main Street, according to the Missouri State Highway Patrol. Otis suffered critical injuries in the Nov. 3 incident.

A funeral service will be held at 2:30 p.m. today at the First Baptist Church in Clarks Fort.

*d. Main Headline: 3–36B-1; second deck: 2–24-2*

If you're not tooting your own horn, donate it to a Heartland student who will.

At least a couple of sixth-grade band students at most Heartland elementary schools can't afford their own musical instruments.

Usually this means the district scrounges to find a student an instrument. It might be in bad shape and usually isn't a student's first choice. And if the parents can't pay the $30 annual usage fee, then the student usually can't take the instrument home for additional practice.

Kevin Fargo, the school district's fine arts coordinator, started a program this fall that should help these students.

Called the "Tooting your horns" donation program, Fargo hopes community members will give the district their old instruments. The district then will loan the instruments to first-year band students, who are sixth-graders, based on their financial needs.

Fargo said that because a greater percentage of students are involved in band in sixth grade — as compared to middle and high school — sixth-graders have the greatest instrument need. And sixth-graders who have good instruments and positive band experiences are more likely to continue with the program.

*e. Main Headline: 4–48-1*

Where the sidewalk ends, debate begins.

Heartland lacks sidewalks on parts of many of its major streets — most obviously on Missouri Avenue and Frederick Boulevard.

In recent years developers have been required to install sidewalks when they make substantial changes to a building or property.

But Heartland still has an ever-expanding, not-quite-connected patchwork of sidewalks. In the last few years, builders and property owners have grumbled about "sidewalks to nowhere" that they have been required to put in.

Some have said it's futile and wasteful to require sidewalks on one property without addressing adjoining properties.

"We are quite concerned about the random placement of sidewalks," city architect Ron Matthis told City Council members in a meeting Thursday.

Matthis asked if current policy would continue. He also suggested the city point money toward the problem, as it does with its hike/bike trails, and help pay to connect long stretches.

He seeks a clear, written sidewalk policy so there can be no confusion.

**Additional exercises are available online at** www.oup.com/us/rosenauer.

## CHAPTER 26

# Images

*"There are no rules for good photographs; there are only good photographs."*

~Ansel Adams

If text is the life stream of a story, images are its heart and soul. Photographs have power to tell the story in unique ways. Used effectively, they enhance the storytelling experience; used poorly, and they may ruin it like the blemish on a beautiful cheek.

Similarly, graphics provide a visual representation that should improve reader understanding of data and information. They may include information graphics—or infographics, line drawings, illustrations, charts and tables.

In this chapter we will cover how editors work with photographers and graphic artists, select images, apply principles of composition, prepare images and write captions.

## Working With Photographers and Graphic Artists

Although the organizational structure may vary from one media outlet to another, photographers and graphic artists usually work on assignments supporting the story, article or other textual coverage assigned by editors. Some staffs may have photo or graphics editors who coordinate that work. Regardless of the exact structure, you'll need to work effectively with photographers and artists to get images you can use.

First, respect the talents and skills of your photographers and artists. If they are well-trained and experienced, they know more about capturing and creating images than you do. See that as an advantage and learn to draw on their understanding.

Second, have a clear idea of what you envision for images you want to support coverage, and write down those specific details. Vague assignments give photographers and artists little to go on and invite results that may not be what you want or what the coverage needs. Writing forces you to think through and specify your expectations and reduces the wiggle room for misunderstandings.

Third, encourage discussion between you and them, even some brainstorming, *before* the photographers or artists begin working on assignments. They may offer some creative options you hadn't considered; likewise, what you say may further explain what you're looking for. For a particularly important assignment, you may want to finish the discussion by asking them to tell you what they understand are the specific goals of the assignment, assuring that the message you sent was the message they received.

Fourth, if you follow the first three steps and don't get results you expected, let the photographers or graphic artists know. However, avoid berating them or their work. Instead, ask if they understood what you were seeking. Then, ask if what they produced met that goal. They may point to extenuating circumstances that prevented them from getting what you wanted, or they may reveal that they didn't clearly understand your goals for the assignment. Either way, use it as a learning experience for them so that they'll do a better job in the future.

Finally, a good people manager learns to praise in public and criticize in private. Both are valuable and necessary tools that improve performance and enhance relationships.

# Selecting Images

Photographers typically shoot much more than required for an assignment. This is especially true today with digital cameras that can store hundreds or even thousands of images, all at no additional cost.

As a result, they can provide you the minimal number of images needed for coverage or a larger number of images from which you may select. If what they submit isn't satisfactory, ask to see the remaining shots in the off chance that you will find something more suitable.

On the other hand, graphic artists usually will prepare a single image, given the demands involved with creating versus capturing.

## Photographs

When selecting a photo, you want one with a strong center of interest. When the subject dominates the image, viewers don't have to guess exactly what the subject is. As you review a photo, ask the following:

- What is the first thing that catches my eye?
- What holds my attention the longest?
- Are other elements competing too much for my attention?

You also want a well-composed photo, with the subject and surrounding elements comfortably and appropriately filling the frame.

Any photo you choose to publish should be technically strong; that is, focus must be sharp and exposure must be sufficient to show detail, especially in the center of interest.

The best photograph uses a creative approach to show the subject. This can be challenging, especially for routine shots, such as the presentation of a check or award—often called a "grip and grin," referring to the traditional handshake and smiling faces they often capture. Anticipate such clichés when you're making and discussing the assignment with photographers before they shoot, and see if you can brainstorm more creative possibilities.

Finally, and most important, pick photographs that tell a story and that fit the emphasis of accompanying written coverage. The best storytelling photos encourage viewers to stop and look. Photos should be revealing, and they may be surprising, though they should not be confusing.

## Graphics

Graphic artists provide a variety of images to support coverage. It may be a line drawing depicting a subject that photographers are unable to capture. Or it may be a more sophisticated image, either black and white with tones and shading or full color that is a realistic, photo-like creation. Make sure the style of the image suits the tone of the subject.

In addition, artists might use computer software to generate different types of tables, pie charts or bar charts, such as the bar chart in Figure 26-1 and the pie chart in Figure 26-2. Finally, the ultimate product might be an infographic, a combination of words and one or more of the elements just mentioned, including photographs, such as the example in Figure 26-3. It can stand alone and makes understanding data faster and clearer for readers.

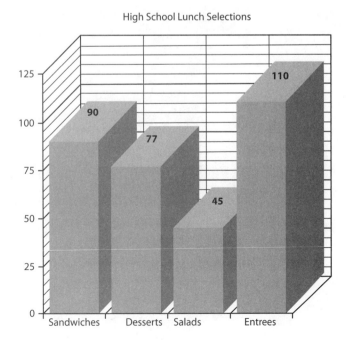

High School Lunch Selections

**FIGURE 26-1** Sample bar chart.

**FIGURE 26-2** Sample pie chart.

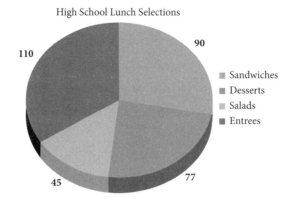

**FIGURE 26-3** Sample infographic.

Because artists create graphics—often investing hours or days in their production—you might request they give you a rough pencil sketch early on to make sure their planned product is appropriate.

What you're looking for, of course, is not much different than what you want in good photographs. In addition, readability, both in terms of images and related text, is critical.

# Understanding Composition

We will briefly review photographic composition, the pleasing arrangement of elements within the frame of a photo. Although these principles apply to photographs, some have bearing on graphic design as well. The following six are the most important:

- Rule of Thirds
- Balance
- Contrast
- Lines
- Perspective
- Format

## Rule of Thirds

Images that position the center of interest smack-dab in the middle of the frame may be uninteresting and may not make best use of limited space within the frame. One way to avoid this is by applying the Rule of Thirds, a guideline that good photographers use

**FIGURE 26-4** The grid here, which divides the photograph into thirds, horizontally and vertically, establishes the four hot spots of the Rule of Thirds.

**FIGURE 26-5** The nearly perfect symmetry of this straight-on shot of the owl is a good example of a photograph that works well without following the Rule of Thirds.

**FIGURE 26-5** The nearly perfect symmetry of this straight-on shot of the owl is a good example of a photograph that works well without following the Rule of Thirds.

when they shoot. However, when the images do not follow the rule, it's important that you consider it when you prepare images for publication.

First, mentally divide the photo into thirds both vertically and horizontally (see Figure 26-4). The rule says that the center of interest, or dominant element, should be at (or near) one of the four intersections of those lines. Whereas photographers can more readily apply the rule when they're shooting, it is usually possible to crop, or remove, part of the image when you're editing to achieve the goal of shifting the dominant element to one of those points.

While the majority of photographic compositions benefit from the Rule of Thirds, some shots work well without it, such as the owl in Figure 26-5.

## Balance

Lack of balance in photographs often means that the image is lopsided, with the majority of elements crowded to one side or another. However, the goal isn't necessarily to seek perfect, or symmetrical, balance in which one side of the photograph exactly balances the other, almost a mirror image.

Usually, you want asymmetrical balance, or near balance, and often you can achieve this by balancing large, lighter-toned images on one side with smaller, darker-toned images on the other, with the resulting "weight" of tones just about equal.

Of course, applying the Rule of Thirds often will bring with it the benefit of asymmetrically balanced images.

Occasionally, symmetrical balance is the goal when the subject invites a formal, dignified appearance. Nature shots, such as the owl in Figure 26-5, also work well with a symmetrical composition.

In Figure 26-6 here, the action is weighted left in the frame, resulting in an unbalanced composition that includes considerable dead space at the right. Figure 26-7 shows one way to crop the shot to improve balance and emphasize the dominant element.

## Contrast

Contrast relies on the difference between tones in black-and-white images or colors in color images. It provides three benefits:

**FIGURE 26-6** With all the key action on the left side of the frame in this play at first base, this photograph is imbalanced.

**FIGURE 26-7** The same shot at first base, cropped to get rid of dead space and improve the composition.

**FIGURE 26-8** The red leaf on the snow is a good example of contrast and readily illustrates its three benefits.

**FIGURE 26-9** With the color of the horse and the background too similar, contrast is lacking in this shot.

- It separates objects.
- It highlights the center of interest.
- It directs viewers' eyes to it.

Extremes, such as the red leaf on a blanket of snow in Figure 26-8, are not necessary for contrast to be effective, but they certainly achieve the goals more easily.

The key is enough difference between tones or colors to make separation clear and to emphasize the dominant element. That's a problem in Figure 26-9, where the horse color is too similar to the background for good contrast.

Contrasting colors, such as a red rose against a green background, also achieve effective contrast. However, those same colors presented in a black-and-white version of an image will not provide good contrast.

**FIGURE 26-10** This shot of the rose emphasizes contrast in both colors and image sharpness..

See Figure 26-10 for an example of contrast working well to separate objects and emphasize the dominant element using both the red of the rose and the brighter tones of the leaf against the dark, unfocused background.

## Lines

Composition deals with lines in at least two ways, horizons and leading lines.

A firm guideline is that you never allow the horizon—or other dominant horizontal line—to cut across the vertical center of a photo, as in Figure 26-11. Position it either one-third from the bottom or one-third from the top of the frame, as in Figure 26-12. Which way should you prefer? If you crop grass, as in Figure 26-12, the photo gives more emphasis to the sky. Similarly, if you crop sky, the result gives more emphasis to the grass.

Leading lines, real or implied, help to lead viewers' eyes into the center of interest. Whether horizontal, vertical, diagonal or curved, lines are powerful paths that eyes irresistibly follow. See how lines in Figures 26-13 and 26-14 achieve that goal.

## Perspective

Perspective boils down to the relationship between objects in a scene. Because photos are two-dimensional—portraying height and width—the third dimension, depth, relies on other elements in the image to make it *appear* three-dimensional.

For example, parallel lines of the path moving away from the viewer in Figure 26-15 seem to converge as they move off into the distance—a simple phenomenon of perspective.

Also, because we know that two things cannot occupy the same space, overlapping objects suggest depth and enhance perspective.

**FIGURE 26-11** The dominant horizontal line established by the street cuts across the middle of this photograph of a redbud tree, something usually to be avoided.

**FIGURE 26-12** This crop of the redbud photograph improves composition by pushing the horizontal line of the street out of the center.

**FIGURE 26-13** The stream establishes curved lines that pull the eye to the tree, the dominant element in the shot.

**FIGURE 26-14** The bridge is a powerful line that leads the eye from near left to buildings in a village.

**FIGURE 26-15** The narrowing, converging lines of the path lead into the distance and suggest depth.

**FIGURE 26-16** The gradually shortening of the fence posts suggest depth and distance.

Another means of suggesting perspective may involve two or more objects of the same size, with those that *appear* smaller suggesting they are farther away, as with the fence posts that angle right to left in Figure 26-16.

# Format

The shape of a photo's frame, its format, can be horizontal, vertical or square. Contemporary photographers have opted for the first two because most of their cameras shoot rectangular images. For example, the ratio of length to width for both digital and film-based 35mm cameras is 1.5:1. The ratio of most point-and-shoot digital cameras is 1.33:1.

Using one of those formats, you often match the format to the shape of the dominant element. Thus, a vertical format will better frame a tall subject and a horizontal format will effectively frame a wide subject.

Many photographers have tended to avoid the third formatting option, a square, which has a ratio of 1:1. One reason is that the equal sides of a square tend to make the photo less interesting. However, the square format has become more popular recently as photographers seek fresh ways of presenting content, as in the shot of the owl in Figure

---

## ONLINE INSIGHTS > **FREE ONLINE PHOTO EDITING TOOLS**

While Adobe Photoshop is the recognized leader in photo manipulation software, it is also challenging to learn and a bit pricey to own. That's where the following list of photo editing tools comes in. The tools are free, and they're readily accessible online:

- Dr. Pic—(www.drpic.com/) Crop, resize, rotate, brightness/contrast, autofix, add text, sharpen and make black and white/grayscale.
- FotoFlexer—(http://fotoflexer.com/) Crop, resize, rotate, curves, morph, auto-fix, red-eye removal and touch-up.
- Lunapic—(www.lunapic.com/editor/) Most of the manipulations available with Photoshop are here.
- LookWow—(www.lookwow.com/) Smooth skin, brighten and enhance features, crop, rotate, resize add caption and borders, adjust colors, add special effects.
- Online Photo Tool—(www.onlinephototool.com/) Curves, cloning, recoloring, auto-levels, improved sharpening, add borders, red-eye removal and more.
- Phixr—(www.phixr.com/) Crop, resize, rotate, color balance, levels, red eye remover, sharpen, blur and adjust brightness, contrast, saturation and hue.
- Photoshop Express—(www.photoshop.com) Crop, resize, rotate, auto exposure, red-eye removal,

touchup, saturation, white balance, highlight, fill light, sharpen, soften and make grayscale.
- Pic Resize—(www.picresize.com/) Crop, resize, rotate and special effects (including sharpen and make grayscale).
- PicMagick—(www.picmagick.com/) Quick and easy photo retouching.
- Picture2Life—(www.picture2life.com/) Edit photos, create collages, create animations and share.
- Pixenate—(http://pixenate.com/) Crop, resize, flip horizontally and vertically, rotate, improve color balance, enhance photo, fill light, spirit level, red-eye remover, whitening tool and colors tool.
- Pixer—(http://pixer.us/) Resize, crop, rotate, flip and a few special effects.
- Resizr—(www.resizr.com/) Crop, resize and rotate.
- Snipshot—(http://snipshot.com/) Undo, resize, crop, rotate and adjust.
- Splashup—(www.splashup.com/splashup/) Many of the same features found in Photoshop.
- Web Photo Resizr—(www.webresizer.com/) Crop, resize, rotate, sharpen, make grayscale and adjust contrast, brightness and saturation.

26-5 previously. Likely, too, the popularity of photographing with smartphones and their square formats has increased interest.

# Preparing Images

Full courses and entire texts address the issue of preparing images for printing or publication. However, we will confine our discussion to four tasks that you may deal with as editor:

- Cropping
- Sizing
- Adjusting
- Sharpening

In many cases your photographers or photo editor will handle these tasks. Yet you will benefit from understanding what's involved so that you can discuss preparing images more knowledgeably and at times handle the tasks yourself when the situation warrants.

You can edit images using both free and purchased computer-based software or free online sites. Check the breakout box following or locate additional sites with an online search engine.

The most popular professional software for cropping and other image manipulation, of course, is Adobe Photoshop. It is neither cheap nor easy to learn; however, it's the standard for those serious about editing images. Fortunately, a wealth of free online Photoshop tutorials—many of them videos—show how to use Photoshop to complete the four tasks.

Finally, a cardinal rule in image manipulation is *never* change the original file. Save the image with a new file name before making changes, and archive the original.

## Cropping

As we noted previously, cropping involves cutting material from one or more edges of an image to improve its composition.

The common benefit from cropping involves removing *unnecessary* elements in the frame so that what remains, especially the center of interest, is more dominant with fewer distractions. An effective crop also may shift the center of interest to one of the intersections in the Rule of Thirds.

Consider the following tips when you crop an image:

- Decide *first* what to keep and what to remove from one or more edges of the image, with a key goal of removing distractions or dead space.
- Make sure most cropped images follow the Rule of Thirds.
- Nearly always leave more space in front of than behind subjects that are either moving or looking to the side.
- If you must cut parts of arms or legs, don't just lop off hands or feet. Move higher on either limb, cutting above the elbow or thigh.
- Don't worry about maintaining a standard print output size ($5 \times 7$, $4 \times 5$, and so on) or proportion (1.5:1 or 1.33:1). Some of your more interesting crops will be what photographers call *tight* horizontals or *tight* verticals, as in Figure 26-17.

- Consider changing the format from horizontal to vertical or the reverse for a different take on the original or to improve the center of interest.
- Achieve some dynamic results occasionally by severely cropping an image so that, for example, just the eyes and nose of a person are visible.
- Bottom line, have clear and compelling reasons to crop any image. Not every shot *needs* to be cropped, and rarely should shots be cropped just to change their format to fit a particular page design.

See how these principles guide the cropping of the images following. For example, in Figure 26-18 the subject is centered in the frame, and the image contains distracting elements. The crop in Figure 26-19, following the Rule of Thirds, removes the most distracting and unnecessary material to better emphasize the dominant element. Notice, too, that the crop changes the format from horizontal to vertical.

Finally, less is better with most images, and simple tells stories more powerfully.

**FIGURE 26-17** Example of a tight horizontal shot.

**FIGURE 26-18** The subject here, the girl, is centered in the frame, which includes some additional, distracting elements.

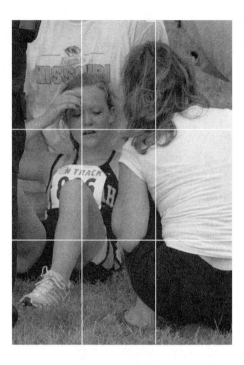

## Sizing

To understand sizing, we need to define several terms:

- *pixel*: Derived from *picture element*, it is the smallest unit of a digital image.
- *resolution*: The number of pixels or dots per inch in the image. The higher the resolution, the more dots in each printed inch and the greater the resulting detail. The preferred resolution for high-quality print images is 300 pixels/inch. For online images it's 72 pixels/inch.
- *document size*: The dimensions of a *printed* image at a given resolution.
- *kilobytes*: A unit of measure equaling 1,000 bytes, abbreviated kb.
- *megabytes*: A unit of measure equaling 1 million bytes, abbreviated mb.

When you *resize* an image, you're changing the number of pixels that make up that image. This is important: You cannot *increase* the number of pixels in an image without losing quality. Therefore, resizing is best reserved as a procedure for *reducing* the image size, the resolution and/or the file size.

The impact of *just* reducing the number of pixels is to reduce online image dimensions and image file sizes. The latter is an important goal for images you're posting online because smaller files load more quickly and take up less server space.

When you're changing image dimensions, keep the change proportionate; that is, the percentage of change in one dimension matches the percentage of change in the other. Otherwise, the resulting resized image will be distorted. Most image manipulation software or sites will do this automatically if you check the "constrain proportions" or similar control.

For example, say you have a 19.3mb image. Its pixel dimensions are 3000 × 2250 pixels, while its document size is 10 × 7.5 inches with a resolution of 300 pixels/inch (see Figure 26-20).

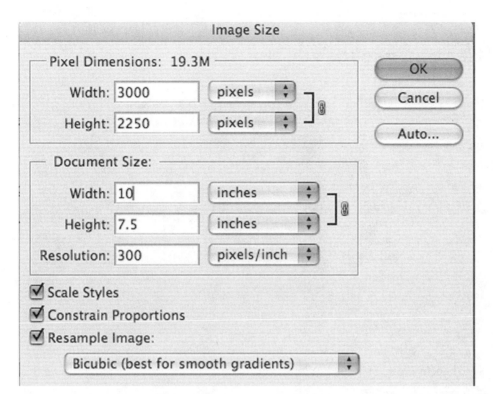

**FIGURE 26-20** The Image Size window in Photoshop with document size at 10 × 7.5 inches.

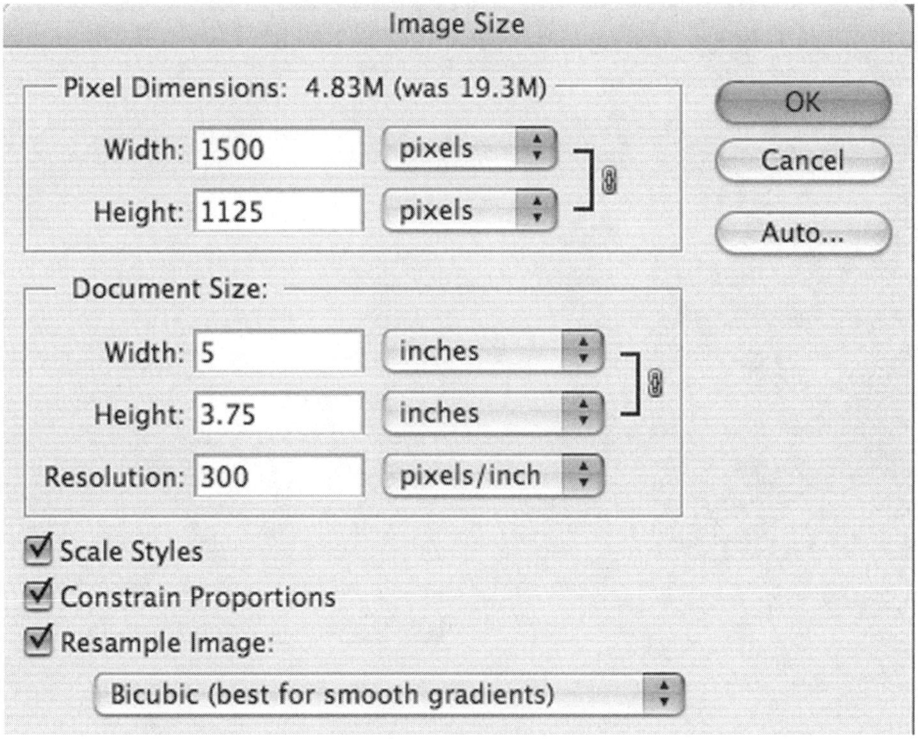

**FIGURE 26-21** The Image Size window with document size at 5 × 3.75 inches.

## ONLINE INSIGHTS > **PREPARING PHOTOS FOR THE WEB**

If you're editing Web pages, you may also have to prepare the photos to upload for those pages. Using the following steps should make that task relatively easy. An important concept to understand concerning online images is this: *Size matters,* particularly digital file size.

This image is 10.4 × 7.8 inches, or 3264 × 2448 pixels. A maximum quality jpeg at 314 dpi, its file size is 6.2 mb.

1. Crop the image following the principles offered earlier. Be aware that cropping not only cuts away parts of the image but also reduces the digital file size—both important concerns, especially for online photos. See how the preceding image might be cropped.

    Figure 26-23 is 7.6 x 6.2 inches, or 2285 x 1871 pixels. Its new file size is 4.4 mb.

2. Size the image. Recall three things about sizing digital images. First, the larger the actual image size, the larger its digital file size. Second, although you can upload a bigger image size than the size of the displayed image, doing so often increases the time for the image to "load," or fully display, on the Web page. Third, although running an image smaller than its actual size won't hurt the quality of its appearance, displaying it larger will. Therefore, size the image exactly to fit the Web page design.

**FIGURE 26-23** The cropped shot of the Clydesdales is 7.6 x 6.2 inches.

3. Reduce the image resolution. Most digital camera images are 200–300 dots per inch, or dpi. However, all computer monitors display images at 72 pixels/inch. Therefore, image files that have higher resolution are larger than necessary. So, use Photoshop or an online photo editor to reduce the resolution to 72 dpi. Applying Steps 2 and 3 to Figure 26-23, if we reduce the image size to 600 × 491 pixels at 72 dpi, the resulting file size will be 455 kb.

4. Adjust the jpeg quality. Another way to reduce file size is to save an image as a lower quality jpeg, the most common digital image file format. Photoshop, for example, allows you to choose maximum, high, medium and low quality—each of which will result in smaller file sizes. However, because they also reduce image quality, you should examine a low- or medium-quality image at the targeted size before publishing it online to make sure its quality is acceptable. Reducing the jpeg quality to medium will drop the file size to 164 kb—a significant difference from the original 6.2 mb.

**FIGURE 26-22** This shot of the Budweiser Clydesdales is 10.4 × 7.8 inches.

To prepare an image for printed output—in this case using Photoshop—keep the resolution at 300 pixels/inch. Go to the document size and change 10 to 5 inches (see Figure 26-21). With "constrain proportions" checked, the other dimension should change to 3.75 inches. At the same time, the file size will drop to 4.83mb.

## Adjusting

The term *adjusting* refers to contrast, tones and colors of an image. Most of the time you should expect photographers to handle these adjustments because they can require more finesse than cropping and sizing. However, at times you may have to change any or all of these characteristics using photo manipulation software or online sites.

Three Photoshop tools—Auto Levels, Auto Contrast and Auto Color—may be sufficient to handle problems with those characteristics. Try them and see if the results are acceptable. When they do not work, consider other tools located under Photoshop's Image/Adjustments menu: Levels, Curves, Color Balance, Brightness/Contrast, Hue/Saturation and Exposure.

The image following (Figure 26-24) illustrates a common problem: The woman is too dark, or underexposed, because the camera's light meter was reading the overall scene, especially the very bright sunset in the background. Also, the sunset gives the scene a red cast.

The challenge in fixing this is twofold: 1) increase the exposure of the subject while retaining as much of the background as possible, and 2) remove some of the red cast and make the skin tones more natural.

The simplest method to fix the first problem is using the Brightness/Contrast adjustment. However, exercise care with this control because changes may be too harsh.

**FIGURE 26-24** The image of the woman here is too dark, a result of underexposure.

**FIGURE 26-25** The Brightness/Contrast window in Photoshop.

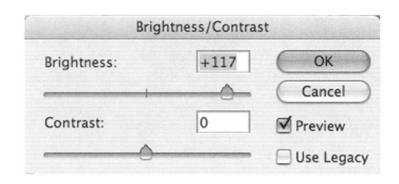

**FIGURE 26-26** The image of the woman here is brighter.

**FIGURE 26-27** The Color balance window in Photoshop.

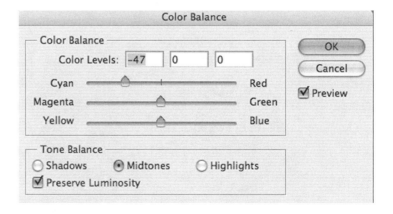

See how adjusting brightness with Photoshop offers an acceptable exposure improvement in Figures 26-25 and 26-26.

One way to fix the second problem is to adjust the color balance in the image. See the results of that in Figures 26-27 and 26-28, where shifting the slider away from red to cyan reduces the red cast.

Other Photoshop tools can fix just about any image problem; however, each has a much greater learning curve to use it effectively. Locate online Photoshop tutorials if you're interested in knowing more.

## Sharpening

The final step in any photo manipulation is to sharpen an image, especially one captured with a digital camera.

Importantly, sharpening tools provided by photo manipulation software or online sites will not improve an *unfocused* image. Instead, sharpening improves the acutance of digital images, making dark edges of objects slightly darker and light edges lighter, providing a crispness that improves what the eye sees as visual sharpness.

The secret to using sharpening tools effectively is to *not* overdo the adjustment. When you do, images acquire what appear to be little white halos around contrasting objects.

Probably the best all-around Photoshop tool for sharpening is the Unsharp Mask. Don't let the name fool you; it really does enhance image sharpness. The settings you will use with the Unsharp Mask control are Amount, Radius and Threshold. Whereas settings for individual images will vary, the following are good starting points:

- Moderate sharpening: Amount, 225; Radius, 0.5; Threshold, 0
- Maximum sharpening: Amount, 65; Radius, 4; Threshold, 3

- All-purpose sharpening: Amount, 85; Radius, 1; Threshold, 4
- Portraits: Amount, 75; Radius, 2; Threshold, 3
- Online images: Amount, 400; Radius, 0.3; Threshold, 0

**FIGURE 26-29** A Heartland Police Department motorcycle stands ready Saturday to lead the 2012 Peach Blossom Parade. More than 115 units rolled down Frederick Avenue, beginning at 9:30 a.m., with spectators numbering more than 17,000.

**FIGURE 26-30** Officials assist Savannah High School freshman Jillian Andrews, left, after she collapsed crossing the finish line at the Heartland High School Cross Country meet on Friday. An ambulance transported Andrews to the hospital, where she was treated and released.

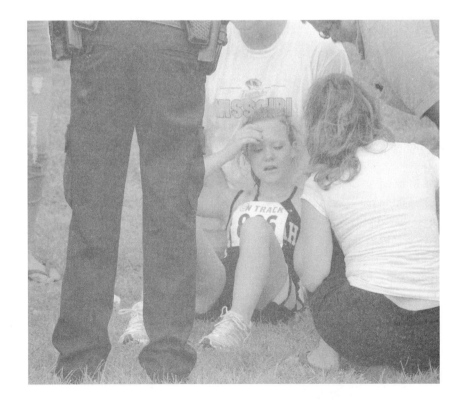

**FIGURE 26-31** Seth Granger, 35, of Heartland, adds final touches to his entry Saturday at the annual Sand Castle Mania, part of the three-day Independence Day celebration hosted by the Heartland Chamber of Commerce. He took third place in a field of 63 contestants. Angie McCombs, of Columbia, won first place.

**FIGURE 26-32** Elmer Grant stirs his 22nd batch of kettle corn for the day Sunday while his wife, Elmyra, fills bags with the popular treat. The couple operates Corny Sweets, one of several dozen food vendors at the Cooper County FallFest, which ended Sunday evening.

**FIGURE 26-33** Heartland firefighter Pat Roberts moves across the roof of a burning house at 1938 Main St. Tuesday. Equipment and personnel from two companies brought the blaze under control in two hours. No estimate of the loss was available.

# Writing Captions

Few photographs are so self-explanatory—answering all reader questions with the image alone—that they can run without a caption. Therefore, anticipate that all photographs should have captions. That task is one that photographers should complete. However, as we noted earlier, some situations demand that you handle such tasks. At the very least, you will edit captions that others write.

Captions emphasize *who*, *when* and *where* and *what*. The American Press Institute suggests that they should accomplish four goals:

1. Explain the action in the photo.
2. Name the important people.
3. Tell why you're using this photo.
4. Include the important details of the photo.

When you write or edit a caption, follow these suggestions:

- Use present tense for action, past tense for background information.
- Use active voice.
- Name and identify the important figures. Check spellings. When you identify more than one person, use clear labels, such as "left" or "from left" or "reaching for the ball." Never write "from left to right"; it's wordy.
- Tell both the *when* and *where*.
- Include important details involving the context, such as "in the bottom of the 6th inning," as well as results of the action depicted, such as the final score of a game.

- Avoid clichés.
- Use a minimum of adjectives and adverbs; let the photo show those aspects of the scene.
- Explain unusual circumstances and anything else that isn't obvious in the photo.

See these guidelines at work with the following images and their captions.

# IMAGE *exercise 1*

**DIRECTIONS:** Crop the following images to improve their composition using the chapter guidelines. Digital copies of all images are available online if your instructor requires you to use image manipulation software. *Do not write captions for images.*

    **1.**   Waterfall (Figure 26-34)

    **2.**   Christmas lamp (Figure 26-35)

**3.**   Lone fisherman (Figure 26-36)

**4.**   Old structure (Figure 26-37)

**5.**   Snow walking (Figure 26-38)

**Additional exercises are available online at www.oup.com/us/rosenauer.**

## CHAPTER 27

# Design

*"I've been amazed at how often those outside the discipline of design assume that what designers do is decoration. Good design is problem solving."*

~Jeffery Veen, author and Web designer

Print and online media pages typically include headlines, images, text and, perhaps, some graphic devices like boxes and lines. Well-designed pages seem to be simple affairs, with everything neatly packaged to fit the space. However, that simplicity is deceiving.

Effective design demands an understanding of design principles, accepted practices and reader behavior — all blended with a touch of creativity that caps off the storytelling experience and effectively communicates the message.

Carelessly designed pages may still be read, but odds are that readers will have to work harder to sift through and digest content. Some won't bother.

In this chapter, we will cover the following topics:

- Design principles
- Typography
- Images
- Print design
- Online design

The goal will be to give you a basic foundation to effectively design pages for both print and online newspapers, magazines and newsletters.

307

# Design Principles

Some of the same principles of composition that we discussed in Chapter 26, "Images," apply to page design. Page design, though, adds several to the mix:

- Balance
- Proximity
- Alignment
- Repetition
- Contrast
- Dominance
- Unity

This lineup of principles should help explain how well-designed pages aren't nearly as simple as they seem. Importantly, these principles deal with the *arrangement* of elements on a page — headlines, images and text blocks — how they relate to one another as well as to the overall frame that comprises the page.

## Balance

Balance in page design is very similar to balance in photographic composition, yet more concerned with the side-to-side arrangement than the top-to-bottom arrangement. The elements on a page may be symmetrically balanced — a mirror image one side to the

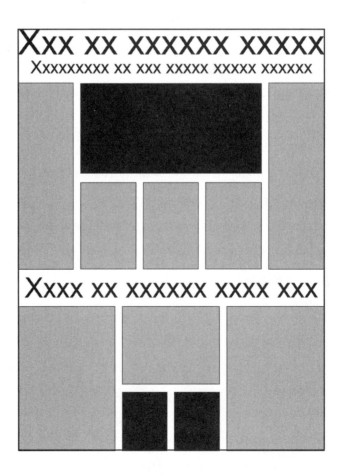

**FIGURE 27-1** Symmetrically balanced page.

**FIGURE 27-2** Asymmetrically balanced page.

other, as in Figure 27-1 — or asymmetrically balanced, with lighter and darker elements on one side weighed against lighter and darker elements on the other, as in Figure 27-2.

Asymmetrical balance, or informal balance, is the goal of most designs. It is *near* balance, not intended to present equal weights side to side but using different sized and different weighted elements to achieve slight tension in the arrangement without appearing lopsided.

Your arsenal of lighter elements includes white space and text blocks — which appear as gray boxes, while darker elements are images, headlines and graphic devices.

## Proximity

The principle of proximity is simple: Group related items. Both distance and separation work to achieve this goal of grouping. Readers no longer see elements on a page as separate units but as a single, visual whole. A page becomes organized, and readers better understand where each message begins and ends.

Therefore, the headline, images and text blocks for a story appear to belong together when you use proximity in designing their layout.

Consider the presentation of the list in Figure 27-3 versus the same list in Figure 27-4. Each includes the same text, but the second enhances the message by grouping related elements using proximity — and contrast, which we will discuss later. The result is easier readability and clearer understanding of the message.

**FIGURE 27-3** Plain list.

Types of Flowers
Spring Flowers
Azalea
Begonia
Daffodil
Hosta
Impatiens
Pansy
Petunia
Summer Flowers
Daisy
Foxglove
Geranium
Iris
Marigold
Salvia
Fall Flowers
Aster
Chrysanthemum
Gladiolus
Hydrangea
Poppy
Sweet Pea

**FIGURE 27-4** List enhanced using spacing (proximity) and contrast.

**Types of Flowers**

*Spring Flowers*
Azalea
Begonia
Daffodil
Hosta
Impatiens
Pansy
Petunia

*Summer Flowers*
Daisy
Foxglove
Geranium
Iris
Marigold
Salvia

*Fall Flowers*
Aster
Chrysanthemum
Gladiolus
Hydrangea
Poppy
Sweet Pea

# Alignment

The principle of alignment involves placing elements so they line up on a page. This organizes elements and creates visual connections.

Nearly all print and online publications have templates, or grids, that provide a predetermined number of columns across a page. The grids also set fixed margins and gutters, or spaces between the columns. The size of the page and the design preferences of editors usually guide how many columns a standard page will include. Generally speaking, print newspaper columns are narrower than either magazine or online columns.

Using a grid simplifies the vertical alignment of elements on a page: Everything lines up within the columns. Horizontal alignment, though, will float based on what elements comprise the page. For example, a headline over a three-column story may establish the top of a grouping, with images and text blocks underneath, as in Figure 27-5. In another arrangement, an image might top a grouping, with headline and text block beneath. A third example might have a headline and image establishing the top of the grouping with text underneath, as in Figure 27-6.

The goal, regardless of the specific elements involved, is to line up elements that belong together.

## Xxxxx xxxx xxxxx Xxxxxxx xxxxx

Mauris iaculis lorem eu lectus tempor ultricies vestibulum dui convallis. Phasellus turpis leo, vestibulum ut commodo ac, faucibus at diam. Ut id turpis quis dui euismod bibendum eu vitae justo.

**FIGURE 27-5** Three-column story headline topping photo and text.

Lorem ipsum dolor sit amet, consectetur adipiscing elit. Curabitur quis pharetra est. Lorem ipsum dolor sit amet, consectetur adipiscing elit. Proin nec massa felis, id pharetra odio.

Praesent nec ullamcorper nisl. Duis pretium sapien ac eros bibendum in volutpat ante tincidunt. Mauris purus mi, suscipit vel rhoncus scelerisque, volutpat scelerisque leo. Aenean ac accumsan metus. Nulla facilisi. Etiam eu tortor varius mi tincidunt tempus sed ut nisl.

Donec quis ornare turpis. Proin ut augue eu nisi tristique pharetra. Fusce a massa velit, vel dictum mauris. Maecenas ultrices sagittis quam, eget placerat dui tempus sed. Etiam commodo lectus a arcu luctus eget sodales mauris tincidunt. Donec imperdiet posuere fermentum.

Lectus tu ad hominem mi, imperdiet semper quam.

Donec ut massa lacus. Cras eget arcu ac orci convallis sceleriв que in vitae est. Mauris hendrerit volutpat dictum. Nunc orci nisi, pharetra non venenatis eget, dapibus dapibus risus. Nam fermentum risus sit amet velit vehicula vel eleifend sem elementum.

Nunc et augue nec nunc consectetur laoreet ut id risus. Nam pulvinar nunc vitae leo vehicula dictum. Vivamus in dolor aliquet velit vehicula semper. Quisque dolor sapien, porta eget ullamcorper id, scelerisque in lectus. Etiam mattis massa quis felis blandit placerat. Integer dictum massa vitae eros ornare tempor.

Lorem ipsum dolor sit amet, consectetur adipiscing elit. Morbi elit nisi, condimentum ut molestie quis, dapibus eget metus. Aliquam quis dolor augue, a dictum magna. Pellentesque mollis diam eget enim facilisis vestibulum.

Vestibulum at elit in augue condimentum volutpat ut sed libero. Morbi ac arcu nibh. Sed ultrices auctor risus eget venenatis.

Praesent lobortis molestie ligula. Donec tortor enim, facilisis vitae tincidunt a, convallis nec felis. Proin semper erat nec arcu posuere rutrum.

Mauris iaculis lorem eu lectus tempor ultricies vestibulum dui convallis. Phasellus turpis leo, vestibulum ut commodo ac, faucibus at diam. Ut id turpis quis dui euismod bibendum eu vitae justo. Nam tincidunt erat quis sapien congue placerat. Proin feugiat, dui ac rutrum porta, turpis est dignissim libero, vitae vehicula felis magna quis risus.

Pellentesque a metus ligula. In at aliquet dolor. Etiam auctor consequat dolor non pellentesque. Proin pellentesque, .

**FIGURE 27-6** Three-column story with headline and photo topping text.

# Xxxxx xxxx xxxxx xx xxxxx xxxx xxxxxxx

Lorem ipsum dolor sit amet, consectetur adipiscing elit. Curabitur quis pharetra est. Lorem ipsum dolor sit amet, consectetur adipiscing elit. Proin nec massa felis, id pharetra odio.

Praesent nec ullamcorper nisl. Duis pretium sapien ac eros bibendum in volutpat ante tincidunt. Mauris purus mi, suscipit vel rhoncus scelerisque, volutpat scelerisque leo. Aenean ac accumsan metus. Nulla facilisi. Etiam eu tortor varius mi tincidunt tempus sed ut nisl.

Donec quis ornare turpis. Proin ut augue eu nisi tristique pharetra. Fusce a massa velit, vel dictum mauris. Maecenas ultrices sagittis quam, eget placerat dui tempus sed. Etiam commodo lectus a arcu luctus eget sodales mauris tincidunt. Donec imperdiet posuere fermentum.

Lectus tu ad hominem mi, imperdiet semper quam.

Donec ut massa lacus. Cras eget arcu ac orci convallis scelerisque in vitae est. Mauris hendrerit volutpat dictum. Nunc orci nisi, pharetra non venenatis eget, dapibus dapibus risus. Nam fermentum risus sit amet velit vehicula vel eleifend sem elementum.

Nunc et augue nec nunc consectetur laoreet ut id risus. Nam pulvinar nunc vitae leo vehicula dictum. Vivamus in dolor aliquet velit vehicula semper. Quisque dolor sapien, porta eget ullamcorper id, scelerisque in lectus. Etiam mattis massa quis felis blandit placerat. Integer dictum massa vitae eros ornare tempor.

Lorem ipsum dolor sit amet, consectetur adipiscing elit. Morbi elit nisi, condimentum ut molestie quis, dapibus eget metus. Aliquam quis dolor augue, a dictum magna. Pellentesque mollis diam eget enim facilisis vestibulum.

Vestibulum at elit in augue condimentum volutpat ut sed libero. Morbi ac arcu nibh. Sed ultrices auctor risus eget venenatis.

Praesent lobortis molestie ligula. Donec tortor enim, facilisis vitae tincidunt a, convallis nec felis. Proin semper erat nec arcu posuere rutrum.

Mauris iaculis lorem eu lectus tempor ultricies vestibulum dui convallis. Phasellus turpis leo, vestibulum ut commodo ac, faucibus at diam. Ut id turpis quis dui euismod bibendum eu vitae justo. Nam tincidunt erat quis sapien congue placerat. Proin feugiat, dui ac rutrum porta, turpis est dignissim libero, vitae vehicula felis magna quis risus.

Pellentesque a metus ligula. In at aliquet dolor. Etiam auctor consequat dolor non pellentesque. Proin pellentesque, hicula tristique, ipsum turpis mollis ante, quis vestibulum diam est at nibh. Pellentesque in purus augue, faucibus scelerisque dui.

Suspendisse interdum tortor at quam venenatis tristique. Praesent risus felis, elementum eget luctus sit amet, tristique in tellus. Pellentesque habitant morbi tristique senectus et netus et malesuada fames ac turpis egestas. Nullam facilisis viverra mauris, in consectetur mauris

Mauris iaculis lorem eu lectus tempor ultricies vestibulum dui convallis. Phasellus turpis leo, vestibulum ut commodo ac, faucibus at diam. Ut id turpis quis dui euismod bibendum eu vitae justo.

sollicitudin ac. rutrum a, consequat non lacus. Etiam commodo lectus a arcu luctus eget sodales mauris tincidunt. Donec imperdiet posuere fermentum.

Lectus tu ad hominem mi, imperdiet semper quam.

Donec ut massa lacus. Cras eget arcu ac orci convallis scelerisque in vitae est. Mauris hendrerit volutpat dictum. Nunc orci nisi, pharetra non venenatis eget, dapibus dapibus risus. Nam fermentum risus sit amet velit vehicula vel eleifend sem elementum.

Nunc et augue nec nunc consectetur laoreet ut id risus. Nam pulvinar nunc vitae leo vehicula dictum. Vivamus in dolor aliquet velit vehicula semper.

Quisque dolor sapien, porta eget ullamcorper id, scelerisque in lectus. Etiam mattis massa quis felis blandit placerat. Lorem ipsum dolor sit amet, consectetur adipiscing elit. Curabitur quis pharetra est.

Lorem ipsum dolor sit amet, consectetur adipiscing elit.

## Repetition

We can see repetition, or consistency, in the grids you may use to begin designing a page. Repetition in type may involve one type font that may be used for all headlines and another font for all text.

Three mug shots presented at identical sizes in a design are another example of repetition and are a subtle visual clue that the elements belong together.

Repeated elements aid organization and grouping in page design.

However, exercise some caution: Repetition shouldn't be overused so that too much on a page is similar.

## Contrast

The design principle contrast establishes *difference* between elements and relies on size, value, color and type.

For example, the larger and darker type of a headline contrasts with the smaller, lighter type of text blocks, lending emphasis to the former in both size and value. Similarly, color is a powerful contrast versus black, white and gray.

Contrast with type can involve size, value or color — or a combination of these — to show difference and, very often, add emphasis.

## Dominance

Most pages benefit from applying the principle of dominance. Those elements that are most important should stand out, should *appear* most important.

Dominance plays a role in the sizes of headlines on a page, with larger type used for more important stories. Similarly, longer stories seem to be more important than shorter, while larger images appear more important and draw more attention than smaller.

One way to emphasize the dominance of elements is to include more than one of an element on a page. For example, although a large image — in relation to the overall page size — may draw attention, that same image will *seem* more dominant if a smaller image appears on the page. This follows the principle of contrast, which we discussed earlier.

So how much larger should an image be to achieve dominance? A good general rule is to make it at least twice the size of other images on the page.

## Unity

The final principle is unity. It involves techniques that tie related elements together, that make them appear to belong together. Nothing says, "I don't belong here."

You can achieve unity in a page design as you effectively apply one or more of previous principles, especially balance, proximity, alignment and repetition.

In addition, tools that help to unify elements may include boxes and lines, also called rules. Be sensitive to the thickness of the strokes on boxes and rules. Too thick and they can overpower text; too thin and they may nearly disappear on the page.

Another tip concerning use of boxes and rules is to provide consistent amount of white space between the strokes and other elements, such as text or images.

Use these tools sparingly because they are more mechanical and less subtle and creative than other unifying design principles. It becomes too easy to simply box related elements across a page, resulting in a weak, unprofessional, chopped-up look. Also, too many rules can disrupt the flow of text on a page and are distracting.

# Typography

Type provides the key delivery of messages in page design, whether headlines or display type, subheads, body copy or captions. Type fonts available to you number in the thousands.

In this section we will discuss the following:

- Font choices
- Display and body type
- Type guidelines

**FIGURE 27-7** 30 faces of Arno Pro.

| | |
|---|---|
| Arno Pro Light Display | Arno Pro Semibold Subhead |
| *Arno Pro Light Italic Display* | ***Arno Pro Semibold Italic*** |
| **Arno Pro Caption** | ***Arno Pro Semibold Italic Caption*** |
| Arno Pro Display | *Arno Pro Semibold Italic Display* |
| Arno Pro Regular | *Arno Pro Semibold Italic SmText* |
| Arno Pro SmText | *Arno Pro Semibold Italic Subhead* |
| Arno Pro Subhead | **Arno Pro Bold** |
| *Arno Pro Italic* | **Arno Pro Bold Caption** |
| *Arno Pro Italic Caption* | **Arno Pro Bold Display** |
| *Arno Pro Italic Display* | **Arno Pro Bold SmText** |
| Arno Pro Italic SmText | Arno Pro Bold Subhead |
| *Arno Pro Italic Subhead* | ***Arno Pro Bold Italic*** |
| **Arno Pro Semibold** | ***Arno Pro Bold Italic Caption*** |
| **Arno Pro Semibold Caption** | *Arno Pro Bold Italic Display* |
| Arno Pro Semibold Display | *Arno Pro Bold Italic SmText* |
| **Arno Pro Semibold SmText** | *Arno Pro Bold Italic Subhead* |

## Font Choices

A wealth of different fonts is available for print and online pages. 1001 Free Fonts, at www.1001freefonts.com/gothic-fonts.php, is a website that offers free individual downloads of about 1,000 fonts for both PC and Macintosh platforms. For a modest price, you can even download 10,000 fonts at once.

As with many such choices in page design, though, less is better.

Using too many different fonts on a single page or from page to page in a publication detracts from unity of design and lends a circus look to the page. Most designers suggest no more than four fonts, and many prefer only a couple.

Before you feel like you're being deprived, understand that each of those four fonts also gives you at least three options for faces, including normal (or regular), bold and italic. Some fonts offer additional faces, such as light italic, semibold italic, bold italic and others. For example, Arno Pro has more than 30 different faces (see Figure 27-7).

Pick one font for headlines and another for body copy; however, magazine headlines and titles may rely on many more fonts (see following). Vary the face among three — normal, italic and bold — for headlines to gain some variety while keeping a signature look in the design. Likewise, a body copy font may use bold for subheads and italic for captions.

Generally, designers prefer a sans serif font for display and a serif font for body copy, which most studies show improve readability in the latter.

## Display and Body Type

Display is any type that runs larger than body type. Headlines and titles comprise most of the display type you will use.

You should recall from Chapter 25, "Headlines," that traditional, or standard, sizes of fonts include the following (in points): 8, 9, 10, 11,12, 14, 16, 18, 20, 22, 24, 26, 28, 36, 48 and 72. Common word-processing and pagination software allows you to select those sizes plus all the numbers in between and many much larger. Nevertheless, these standard sizes provide a reliable means of providing type hierarchy, enough difference to help achieve contrast and dominance (see Figure 27-8).

This is 36-point display type.
This is 34-point display type.
This is 24-point display type.

**FIGURE 27-8** Dominance and contrast in three different type sizes.

This is 12-point Arial.

This is 12-point Cambria.

This is 12-point Courier.

This is 12-point Helvetica.

This is 12-point Times New Roman.

**FIGURE 27-9** Although all are 12-point type, each of these fonts *appears* a different size from the others.

Although you may distinguish a slight difference between the 36-point display and the 34-point display, dominance and contrast for the larger type are much more obvious when you compare it with the 24-point display.

Body copy type size for print newspapers is usually 11–12 points, whereas print magazine body type is 9–10 points. The typical type size for online publications is 14 points. Of course, such decisions come down to readability, especially for the particular target audience of your publication. If the majority of readers are older, prefer the larger size.

Another factor is the *look* of different fonts at a given size (see Figure 27-9). Although all of these are 12-point type, some *appear* smaller. Take that into account for readability, too.

## Type Guidelines

We will finish this section with some basic guidelines. They're not rules, only strong suggestions for your effective use of type:

- Use no smaller than 9 point and no larger than 14 point for body type sizes.
- Avoid use of all caps. For one, all-capital text tends to be harder to read because they lack ascenders and descenders — those parts of a letters that rise above or drop below the base of a letter as determined by its x-height. Also, all caps usually draw too much attention to themselves.
- Don't double space after periods following sentences. That's a throwback to typewriters. Word processing software works better and its output looks better with single spaces after periods.
- Avoid orphans, a single word or line at the top of a column or page.
- Avoid widows, a single word on a line by itself at the end of a paragraph.
- Justified alignment — with type filling columns from left to right margins — tends to be less personal, but it also is the traditional alignment for newspapers and books.

So, readers have come to expect it for those publications. It allows more characters per line than flush left alignment and lends an air of neatness or careful packaging to the page look. Designers rarely justify display type because of the larger letter spacing and word spacing it provides.

- Flush left alignment — with type filling to the left margin but with varied line endings on the right — is more personal. It is commonly used in magazine and Web design. Its ragged right adds more white space to a design and, therefore, can aid readability.

- Centered alignment — with type centered on the line, often with both a ragged left and ragged right — has limited appropriate uses. It can work well with headlines and titles; however, centered body copy tends to be harder to read, and most readers find it jarring and unfamiliar.

- Wider lines of text are harder to read than narrow — though too-narrow widths also hurt readability.

- Don't run display type vertically. It's alien to most readers and harder to comprehend.

- Exercise care in running type over a shaded, black or color background. Whether the type is black, white (reversed), a shade of gray or color, readability can be a concern. For example, black text over a dark gray background severely diminishes readability because contrast and separation are reduced. If you must use this technique, increase the leading — space between lines — to improve readability.

# Images

Images, or art, refer to photographs, infographics, line drawings, illustrations, charts and tables. Whereas Chapter 26, "Images," focused on these individual elements, our concern here is how to present them in an effective page design.

Most pages, whether print or online, benefit from some kind of images.

Yet, although images are important in page design, they're not always *most* important. The traditional rule of thumb has been that readers look first at images, then headlines and body copy — at least in print publications. However, recent studies of online readers have found that more often they look at briefs, captions and headlines *before* images.

Regardless, images have power to attract readers' eyes, and you must do a good job presenting them effectively to connect with and engage the readers behind those eyes.

## Photographs

Make sure that you or others have edited and prepared for publication any photos you plan to include in your page design.

You may crop a photo to suit a design, but that approach may not do justice to the image. The better procedure is to crop first, place the image and then build the rest of the design around it.

Whenever possible, give the dominant photo in a design some significant size that will add punch to the page — at least twice the size of any other image.

Size of all images is relative to the page dimensions of the publication. A broadsheet newspaper may run 12 to 17 inches wide and 21 to 23 inches tall. Exercises in Copycrafting use a 12-inch × 21-inch size. A standard magazine measures about 8 3/8 inches × 10 3/4 inches, trimmed. And the average computer monitor is 15 inches to 17 inches diagonal measure. So, a relatively large photo in a magazine or on a monitor would seem much smaller on a broadsheet page.

Another concern is the size your news hole; that is, the total space left after advertising for all the images, headlines and text blocks. The more space your photos consume, the less is available for text.

Sadly, some editors are loathe to trim story length beyond what they may already have done during editing, so photos may get short shrift, with smaller and fewer of them published. On the other hand, you must include enough space for text so that it is complete enough to deliver its message.

Your best bet is to seek a balance between a photo large enough to be a dominant page element but not so large that it steals needed space for other elements.

Whenever possible, run at least one photo in addition to the dominant photo on each page, and size down the secondary photos. Consider running one or more very small photos, too. The contrast between them and the dominant photo helps to make the larger photo appear even more dominant.

And make sure all photos have captions.

## Graphics

Infographics, line drawings, illustrations, charts and tables comprise our discussion of graphics. For the most part, handle these as you would handle photographs, including sizing decisions and captions or labels.

Your first concern should be whether a graphic works as planned and will play well on the page.

Also, you must ensure that the text in a graphic is readable in its published size. This can get tricky when you need a certain size for a readable graphic that competes too much with a dominant photo. If necessary and appropriate, downsize the photo and let the graphic go dominant.

A final matter involves use of color. Say the original is in color. However, the page onto which you want to run it is only black and white. Make sure you look at a black-and-white version of the graphic before placing it so that you can see if the gray tones will work for its images and legends. If not, send it back to the artist to get more appropriate contrast.

A couple of other basic guidelines should help you to make best use of images in your page designs:

- Images — photos and graphics — are the main elements you will use to tell stories, draw attention, build interest and break up gray blocks of text.
- Graphic devices also are important, including white space, rules, pull quotes, large initial caps and dingbats. The latter are typographical, often ornamental, devices other than letters or numerals that emphasize, group or separate elements and guide readers through the design.

# Designing Print Pages

Little is more daunting than staring at an empty computer screen, poised to begin placing elements onto a print page.

To avoid that deer-in-the-headlights moment, first *plan* the design of your pages. Complete a copy log, which lists stories, including their length in column inches, and images. A column inch is one inch deep in a single standard column and typically has 25–35 words. However, using some trial and error, you can come up with a more accurate conversion based on the actual font and type size for your publication.

In addition, work from a design style guide, which should provide clear direction for all things involving design, including the following:

- The standard fonts and faces your publication uses for headlines, subheads, body copy and captions.
- The type sizes to be used and when it may be appropriate to use bold, italics or underlining.
- How these choices may vary for print and online versions of your publication, as applicable.
- Guidelines for using boxes and rules, including the thickness of strokes and preferred colors or tints.
- Spacing directions, such as outside margins, gutters and distances between elements, such as headlines and text.

A design style guide takes the guesswork and possible confusion out of designing pages. It also can make the look of a publication more consistent and professional.

Next, use a dummy sheet, a grid usually printed on 8–1/2 × 11 inch paper that proportionately represents the page dimensions and the standard columns of the publication. For example, if you're designing a broadsheet newspaper with a six-column layout, the dummy should include the vertical inches down the left (and perhaps the right) and six columns across, as in Figure 27-10.

**FIGURE 27-10** Dummy sheet for a full-size broadsheet newspaper page.

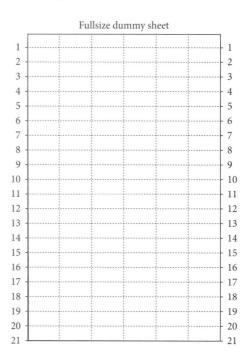

Fullsize dummy sheet

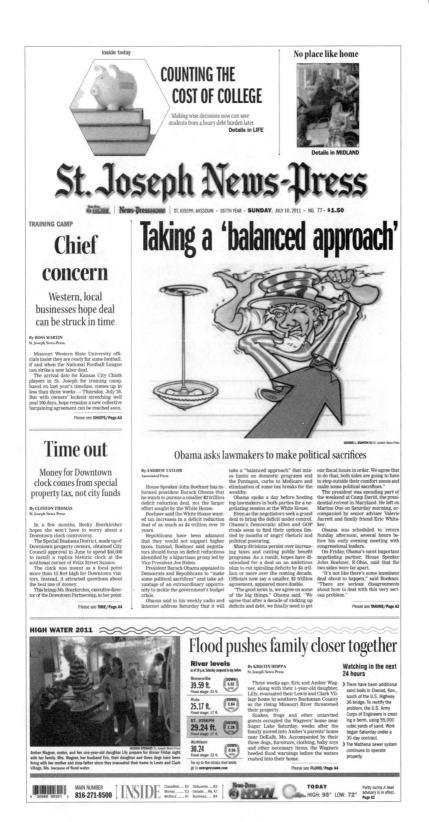

**FIGURE 27-11** An example of bastard measure in "Flood pushes family closer together" and "Watching in the next 24 hours" text blocks and the "River levels" infographic.

Begin sketching a possible layout. Use vertical lines down a column to indicate text blocks, mark lines of Xs to show headlines and draw rectangles with a large X from corner to corner for images. You will run into less trouble if you follow the column grids to fit all elements.

However, you may wish to design a story grouping with text that is one and one-half columns wide across three standard columns, called a one and one-half column layout, or a two-column layout, which is two columns wide across two or four standard columns. Any type blocks that are not set one, one and one-half or two columns wide

**FIGURE 27-12** Modular design in a newspaper page, where each story group (headline, images and text) are neatly packaged into a rectangular shape.

2011 TONY AWARDS

Trey Parker accepts the award for Best Musical for "The Book of Mormon" during the 65th annual Tony Awards, Sunday, June 12, 2011 in New York. For a complete list of winners, please see

Page A8

inside today

STEAM MACHINES

JEFF CHRISTENSEN/Associated Press

# St. Joseph News-Press

ST. JOSEPH, MISSOURI • 167TH YEAR • **MONDAY**, JUNE 13, 2011 • NO. 50 • **75¢**

## First photos of Giffords posted since shooting

RK. WDS/Associated Press

This most recent photo of Rep. Gabrielle Giffords since she was shot, was posted to her public Facebook page by her aides Sunday morning. The woman in the background is her mother, Gloria Giffords. The photo was taken May 17 at TIRR Memorial Hermann Hospital, the day after the launch of Endeavour and the day before she had her cranioplasty.

### Staff hopes to limit paparazzi at hospital release

By AMANDA LEE MYERS
and RAMIT PLUSHNICK-MASTI
Associated Press

HOUSTON — Images of a smiling Rep. Gabrielle Giffords were posted Sunday on her Facebook page: two photos that show her with shorter, darker hair but few signs that she suffered a gunshot wound to the head.

The photos were taken May 17 outside the Houston rehabilitation facility where Giffords has been undergoing treatment since she was wounded five months ago at a meet-and-greet event with constituents. Six peo-

ple died and a dozen others were hurt in the Jan. 8 attack in Tucson, Ariz.

Since then, access to the Arizona congresswoman has been tightly controlled. Until Sunday, no clear images had been released.

The only recent sign of Giffords came in late April, when grainy television footage showed her slowly ascending a flight of steps to a NASA plane that took her to Florida to watch her astronaut husband rocket into space. The image was so blurry that it was impossible to confirm it was Giffords until doc-

tors did so at a news conference in mid-May.

Giffords spokesman C.J. Karamargin said staff members released the photos Sunday to help satisfy "intense interest in the congresswoman's appearance."

The timing coincides with plans to release Giffords from the hospital later this month or in early July. Her staff hopes the images will help curb unwanted photography when she begins visiting an outpatient clinic in a more public setting.

"What we wanted to avoid was a paparazzi-like frenzy," Karamargin said.

## Author shares education advice

By ALONZO WESTON
St. Joseph News-Press

Peg Tyre says size doesn't matter when it comes to schools. It's the size of the classroom. And choosing a school based simply on test scores?

"It's like buying a car based on the color of its paint," Ms. Tyre said.

These are just two pieces of advice that Ms. Tyre gives in her upcoming book tentatively titled, "The Good School: How To Get The Children We Love The Education They Deserve."

The book is due to be released in August and is sort of a follow-up to her widely praised 2008 book "The Trouble With Boys: A Surprising Report Card on Our Sons, Their Problems at School and What Parents & Educators Must Do."

Where "The Trouble with Boys" delved into extensive research on how boys learn differently than girls, "The Good School" focuses on education research that shows what makes a good school.

"Basically it looks at education research and helps parents

Please see AUTHOR/Page A8

SEND US YOUR FLOOD PHOTOS

Submitted Photo

As record amounts of water are released from Gavins Point Dam this summer, rivers in the area could rise to levels not seen since 1993. Send us your flood photos and they could be featured on NewsPressNOW.com. This photo of the Missouri River near the Remington Nature Center was shot on June 7 by Joanna Kernes.

On the Web
Submit your flood photos at News-Press**NOW**

## Missouri Western introduces art society

Members will be eligible for event tickets, discounted classes

By JIMMY MYERS
St. Joseph News-Press

In an effort to give the arts offerings a boost, Missouri Western State University is launching an arts society.

Western's President Dr. Bob Vartabedian and wife Laurel have an extensive arts background, which he said they'd bring to Western when he interviewed for the job a few years ago. Laurel, a playwright, is co-chair of the Missouri Western Arts Society.

"We've been fortunate to get this remarkable tal-

ent," Mrs. Vartabedian said of the faculty and students involved in the arts at Western. "But we've got to support it" with strong arts funding.

Joining the society requires a $100 or more donation. Members will be eligible for tickets to Western performances and exhibits. The money will go to Western's Foundation into an account to fund the university's arts programs.

Karen Graves, who has volunteered on a variety of

Please see MISSOURI/Page A3

## New antibiotic developing at local incubator

By JIMMY MYERS
St. Joseph News-Press

As drug resistant bacteria become more prevalent throughout the world, the development of a new drug to fight them is happening here in St. Joseph.

Dr. Larry Sutton is the founder of Sopharmia, a company that recently parked its laboratory in the Christopher S. "Kit" Bond Science and Technology Incubator on the campus of Missouri Western State University.

Dr. Sutton, in his third year on the chemistry and

biochemistry staff at Benedictine College, is working to "rewire" antibiotics to combat superbug infections. The new drug would deliver to the resistant bacteria, which have up to now successfully inactivated antibiotics, a "counter punch, and basically blow up and destroy bacteria defense mechanisms."

"Basically," he said of his work and that of the seven scientists in his laboratory, "this is the first time anybody has improved the chemistry of these class of

WONSOK CHOI/St. Joseph News-Press

Dr. Larry Sutton, a biochemistry professor at Benedictine College, poses Friday afternoon at his laboratory located in the Kit Bond Incubator in St. Joseph. Sutton's company, Sopharmia, specializes in researching and developing drugs for bacteria.

Please see NEW/Page A3

 MAIN NUMBER 816-271-8500  INSIDE
Classified ...... C6  Obituaries ..... A6
Midland .......... A5  Sports ........... C1
Dear Abby ...... B3  LIFE ............... B1

TODAY
HIGH: 86° LOW: 68°
Showers possible with a few possibly severe
DETAILS A2

are called bastard measures. Those can work so long as you fill the space appropriately. See an example of this in Figure 27-11, where the text block "Flood pushes family closer together," the "River levels" infographic and "Watching in the next 24 hours" are each bastard measures.

**FIGURE 27-13** Text and images inset within a box.

Be mindful of the hierarchy of a page, where large headline size and often a position high on the page reveal which story groups are more important.

Place the dominant image, then the secondary images, if appropriate, and the related headline and text. Don't forget space for captions. Although important coverage usually is at the top of pages, contemporary newspapers often use a strong story package to anchor the bottom, especially of a front page.

Most newspapers and magazines use a modular design; that is, everything that belongs to a story — the images, headline and text — fits into a rectangular shape. You then design the rectangular shape for each story group to fit neatly onto a page, taking care not to leave blocks of white space. For example, see Figure 27-12, a front page of the St. Joseph (Mo.) News-Press.

When you box story or image groups, make sure you inset text and images from the edges of the box, as in "Plattsburg man marks 35 years of fireworks tradition" in Figure 27-13. Such insets are consistent, typically one or two picas.

Finally, two things to avoid in your design are large blocks of gray text and tombstoning.

Large blocks of gray text can make a page less inviting and reduce readability. A good check is the "dollar bill test." Using a full-sized page printout, lay a dollar bill across various places. No matter where you put it, the bill should touch a graphic element — headline, image or graphic devices. If the design fails the test, revise it.

Tombstoning, also called butting or bumping heads, is placing two or more headlines next to one another. The problem is that they may confuse readers who see them as a single long headline. The problem may be lessened if the offending headlines have different font faces and sizes. Yet, the better solution is to revise the layout.

# Designing Online Pages

Online media sites run the gamut when it comes to design, from simple single-column pages to multicolumn pages to sophisticated grid-based layouts that appear very similar to their print counterparts.

Regardless of their design, online media sites *aren't* just the print version of a newspaper or magazine displayed on a computer screen. *Those* are pdf files.

Web design starts with many of the same concerns we covered earlier with print design. For example, you begin working from a copy log. Also, a design style guide is as important for Web design as it is for print. Finally, you may create and use a dummy sheet as you plan the layout of an online page, although many Web editors forgo this step.

Hierarchy is a major concern with online pages. Realize that print media pages enable readers to see full content at a glance, whether broadsheet, tabloid or magazine format. The computer monitor, though, is what determines what readers see in online pages. A typical 15-inch monitor has a screen 10.75 inches wide and 8 inches deep while a 17-inch monitor screen is about 12.5 × 9 inches. Readers scroll down or up to see parts of a page that aren't visible on the screen. Therefore, most media websites follow a top-down hierarchy that may ignore headline size in favor of position to tell readers what is important.

## ONLINE INSIGHTS > **WEB PAGE EDITING TIPS**

Your career plans may or may not include working with online media. However, given the continuing growth in online media and their audiences — coupled with significant losses in both revenue and audiences for traditional media — you're wise to *plan* and *prepare* to work online.

The following are tips you and your reporters should consider in preparing content for online sites:

1. Help readers decide whether or not to follow links.

Most websites have various kinds of links, but not all readers may need to follow them. Provide a summary of the link nearby that tells enough for your readers to decide if it's worth clicking.

2. Make your site browse friendly with various headings.

Use heads and subheads liberally to guide readers through content. Besides being effective design elements, these headings are another means to help readers decide what they will read.

3. Use bulleted lists.

Besides delivering quite a bit of material quickly, lists help reporters to do a more effective job organizing content and makes the task of reading easier.

4. Use graphics and design to aid skimming.

Skimming is standard practice for most online users. Appropriate use of bold fonts, bullets, short paragraphs and borders help readers find what they're seeking more quickly and easily.

5. Pay attention to what you present "above the scroll."

Like the concern with focus on what is "above the fold" in newspapers, put your strongest elements above the scroll on a Web page. Don't drop essential links and images below the bottom of the screen.

6. Use inverted pyramid for most news pieces.

Inverted pyramid has been the workhorse of print journalism for decades. It continues to be valuable for online storytelling, too.

7. Another traditional tip: Be concise.

Reporters should write all they need but not more than required to deliver the message. They should make every word count.

8. Chunk content for easier reading.

Make sure you and your reporters break story content into the smaller chunks that studies have shown online readers prefer.

9. Provide opportunities for more details.

At the same time that you want reporters to be concise, you also want to ensure readers have the depth they desire. Instead of extending the length of the story, provide links to extra information. And don't forget a brief summary with each link.

10. Understand your audience and their needs.

Using Web analytics can help you learn a great deal about those who visit your site. Cater to their needs whenever you can.

*These points were suggested by www.gooddocuments.com/Techniques/techniqueshome_m.htm, a site focused on writing for the Internet.*

Online news media sites tend to run more images per page than their print counterparts, and nearly all those are full color. They also rely more on both vertical and horizontal rules to separate and group content.

Whereas print pages are static, online pages can present movement — in slideshows, videos and advertising. Also, once a newspaper or magazine is published, or printed, its content is fixed. Online media may update content whenever they wish.

Many media sites rely on a content management system, such as WordPress, to provide templates, or themes, into which editors place headlines, images and text. This framework simplifies the effort involved in laying out Web pages and reduces the expertise required to maintain them while allowing local modifications and content. See two WordPress template examples in Figures 27-14 and 27-15. Both would be appropriate for media sites.

**FIGURE 27-14** A WordPress template that would be appropriate for media websites..

Media pages typically feature headers at the top of at least the home page that are comparable to the masthead or flag in print media. Navigation bars, which are essential elements of online media pages, often appear under the headers, though some sites also

**FIGURE 27-15** Another WordPress template that would be appropriate for media websites.

may run content indexes in the left or right sidebars and lower on a page — even in the footer at the bottom of the page.

Of main concern in Web design is the same as that for all page design: Make it readable and inviting while effectively delivering the messages.

# **DESIGN** *exercise*

As directed by your instructor, you will design newspaper, magazine and online pages, using stories, images, captions and headlines.

Digital copies of the following are available online:

- Broadsheet dummy sheet (pdf format)
- Magazine dummy sheet (pdf format)
- Adobe InDesign broadsheet template
- Story files (Word format, unedited, from Chapter 28, "The Full Story")
- Image files (jpg format, unedited, from Chapter 26, "Images")

All stories in Chapter 28 include column-inch sizes and word counts to assist your planning and presentation of exercises.

# The Full Story

*"Were it left to me to decide whether we should have a government without newspapers or newspapers without government, I should not hesitate a moment to prefer the latter."*

~Thomas Jefferson

This chapter gives you the chance to bring together all the guidelines, rules and practices we have covered in Copycrafting, including editing copy for grammar, punctuation, usage, style, leads and organization and writing headlines.

Take time, as necessary, to reread sections in the book, review entries in the stylebook and check spellings of words in the dictionary and names in the Heartland Directory.

These stories — like the exercises in previous chapters — have real errors, not just iffy errors. You will find clear guidelines, rules and solutions to those errors, but like professional editors, you must take the time and make the effort to locate and correct each.

Remember to follow the column measures from Chapter 25, "Headlines," and to use an appropriate type font such as Arial for all headlines. Your instructor will provide final guidance on those matters.

For additional information, consult online editing resources in the Appendix.

# FULL STORY *exercise 1*

**DIRECTIONS**: Correct all errors in the following story. Check the spelling of all names in the Heartland Directory. Then, write an appropriate headline, as directed by your instructor. (388 words/15 column inches)

Law enforcement in Heartland had mixed news when it came to federal grants Wednesday.

The good news: The Cooper County Drug Strike Force was awarded $288,241 as part of the federal Justice Assistance Grants given to 28 drug task forces in Missouri.

The bad: The Heartland Police Department was denied a request for 6 additional officers as part of a nationwide $1 billion COPS Hiring Recovery Program grant to preserve law enforcement jobs. A total of $19,600,000 was awarded in Missouri.

Funding for the Drug Strike Force comes as a relief, as the organization wasn't sure it would receive any. Federal budget cuts this year slashed more than 60 percent of the funding for drug task force initiatives, an amount that most likely would have sank the Strike Force or caused Cooper County Sheriff Nathan Armstrong to absorb its staff.

The funding comes from an allocation Governor Jay Nixon sought from Recovery Act money meant to help keep agencies afloat despite the cuts.

Drug Strike Force Captain Mark Donaldson and Armstrong could not be reached for comment.

Though the Police Department didn't need the funds as urgently as the Strike Force, the request denial sets back the departments plan to increase its staff. Cmdr. Jim Connett said the six officers they would have hired would be part of a long-range plan to increase the force by 20 officers.

"Our long-term goal is, yes, we probably need somewhere between 18 and 20 more officers to get to where we think we ought to be right now," he said, "We know that is not going to happen in the short term. . . . This grant was something that could start the process."

Connett said the department, while restructuring its plan on how to acquire the money to hire more officers, remains optimistic.

"Nothing really changes in the long run. The timing may be slightly different," he said.

The next logical step for the Police Department will be working with the City Manager to come up with a proposal for the City Council. While the federal funding would have been a help, Connett said the department has no problem working strictly on a local level.

"Its much quicker when you solve a problem locally then when you have to wait for the federal government to solve the problem for you," he said.

# FULL STORY *exercise 2*

**DIRECTIONS**: Correct all errors in the following story. Check the spelling of all names in the Heartland Directory. Then, write an appropriate headline, as directed by your instructor. (326 words/12 column inches)

CALIFORNIA, Mo. — A jury trial for a former Heartland teacher and coach accused of several sex crimes got off to a slow start Wednesday.

Frank Mondale, 34, is charged with felony 1st-degree child molestation, felony sexual misconduct involving a child less than 16 years old and misdemeanor furnishing pornographic material to a minor.

Mondale had taught physical education, served as athletic director and coached boys and girls' basketball at Northeast High School. He was employed by the district for two years.

The allegations and charges both surfaced during the summer of 2012 and involved two fifteen-year-old girls. He has no prior criminal record.

Attorneys for both sides and Circuit Judge Roger Frakes spent much of the day selecting a jury from a pool of 65 perspective members. Most of the individual questioning focused on potential jurors knowledge of the case and whether they could fairly weigh evidence that will be presented to them.

The three-day case is being heard in Moniteau County on a change of venue from Cooper County. A jury of seven women and six men, including one alternate, were seated by mid-afternoon.

In his opening argument, Cooper County Prosecutor Aaron Smith said the alleged molestation of one victim occurred from late 2011 to early 2012.

"Our evidence will tell a story," he told the jury. "He wasn't your ordinary coach or your ordinary teacher," he said of Mondal. "Both of these young women are great kids."

Defense Attorney Paul Peters, of Columbia, informed jurors that his evidence will demonstrate that Mondale is innocent of the charges and would fit well as a coach in any small town.

"Frank Mondale is the type of coach who uses coaching to instruct on life," he said. "Were going to tell you what really went on. You'll get a feel for what it's like being a coach."

The state's testimony will begin at 9 tomorrow morning. Both victims will testify at the trial, Smith said.

# FULL STORY *exercise 3*

**DIRECTIONS**: Correct all errors in the following story. Check the spelling of all names in the Heartland Directory. Then, write an appropriate headline, as directed by your instructor. (373 words/14 column inches)

A police chase onto the Twain State University campus ended in gunfire early Thursday when police shot a suspect shot in his leg during the pursuit.

Heartland police officers arrested three Columbia men, who have been charged with robbing the McDonald's at 601 W. Twain State Dr.

Charles Murphy, 18, and Harvey Richmond, 18, are in custody at the Law Enforcement Center. Nineteen-year-old Anthony Ramirez is at Heartland Memorial Hospital and is in good condition, according to the police department.

The Cooper County Prosecutor's Office filed armed robbery, 1st-degree burglary and armed criminal action charges against the men Thursday afternoon.

Three males crawled through the restaurant's drive-up window to gain entrance shortly before 3:50 a.m., police Commander Jim Connett said. At least one individual was armed with a handgun. Witnesses say the suspects herded employees into a back room with a gun held to their heads,

One employee snuck out the back door when the robbery began and called police with a description of an idling vehicle in the parking lot. The men piled into the vehicle as police cruisers descended on the restaurant, Connett said.

The suspects drove to Twain State, abandoned their vehicle between McCabe and Thompson Dormitories and fled on foot on the eastern edge of campus.

Officers immediately caught two men, police Chief Chris Anderson said. Murphy was hiding near the dorms and Richfield near a wooded area.

In sub-zero temperatures with snow beginning to fall, police chased Ramirez into the woods behind the Conservation Center.

Officers spotted Ramirez in the woods and ordered him to stop and show his hands, Connett said. While one officer aimed his weapon at the suspect, another officer approached. Ramirez then made a movement into his hoodie pocket, and an officer shot him in the right thigh.

After the shooting, officers discovered Ramirez didn't have a weapon in his possession, however, they recovered a loaded weapon from their vehicle, Connett said.

Sam Thorn, Twain State Assistant Director of Public Relations, said campus security officers supported the Police Department, maintaining a perimeter during the pursuit, notifying residence hall staff and other university officials about the incident and helping secure the evidence scenes.

Each of the men are being held in lieu of $100,000 bond.

# FULL STORY *exercise 4*

**DIRECTIONS**: Correct all errors in the following story. Check the spelling of all names in the Heartland Directory. Then, write an appropriate headline, as directed by your instructor. (251 words/10 column inches)

A $14 million dollar highway-resurfacing contract has been awarded to Mid-Missouri Construction, Inc., of Heartland.

The Missouri Department of Transportation said Mid-Missouri will resurface portions of I-70 in Cooper and Boone counties in the current construction season.

In Cooper County, the interstate will be resurfaced using a hot-in-place recycling method and topped with an ultrathin bonded asphalt wearing surface. The project will extend for 16 miles, from the intersection of Missouri Highway 135 on the west to Missouri Highway 179 near Overton, Mo. Completion is expected in late September or early October.

Hot-in-place recycling corrects asphalt pavement surfaces by first softening the existing surface with heat. The pavement surface is then mechanically removed, mixed with a recycling or rejuvenating agent, and often finished by adding virgin asphalt and/or aggregate. The mixture is next replaced on the pavement without removing the recycled material from the existing road.

Mid-Missouri also will resurface the interstate with hot-in-place recycling for 11 miles in Boone County and top it with an ultrathin wearing surface. That work will occur from Missouri Highway Bb to the intersection of Missouri Route Z at the eastern edge of Columbia, Mo. Final completion is expected in mid-August.

Occasional dropped lanes will be necessary throughout the project. Drivers will begin to see traffic-control elements erected sometime in midMay, but paving will not start until after the Memorial Day holiday.

MoDOT officials are asking motorists to reduce their speed as signs indicate and to use caution when traveling through the work zones.

# FULL STORY *exercise 5*

**DIRECTIONS**: Correct all errors in the following story. Check the spelling of all names in the Heartland Directory. Then, write an appropriate headline, as directed by your instructor. (297 words/12 column inches)

More than 120 state troopers in Central Missouri completed a battery of physical-fitness exercises here this week to measure muscle strength, part of a statewide effort to raise the bar for troopers' physical condition.

Troopers did sit-ups and pushups, preformed vertical jumps and ran 300-meter and 1.5-mile courses. Patrol Sgt. Will Christian oversaw the training in Heartland.

"It's just because of all the things we have to deal with", he said, "like pushing cars off the roadway, moving objects out of the roadway and a physical altercation with someone."

Late last year, Maj. Ronald Replogle, the patrol superintendent, had told lawmakers he wanted to see how fit his troopers were. To find out, he ordered the mass workout.

Local law enforcement agencies also have started physical-fitness programs.

During their recent qualification, Cooper County Sheriffs Department deputies ran laps, attacked a series of hurdles, jumped a simulated ditch, hauled a heavy dummy, climbed through a window and scaled a wall.

The fitness policy was instituted by Sheriff Nathan Armstrong when he took over three years ago. The order applies to road deputies and civil process servers as well as investigators with the Drug Strike Force.

"We try to get everyone around the course in about 2–1/2 minutes," said Sergeant Al Williamson, who oversees the fitness requirement. "It's just overall fitness, and I think it has met the goal of what the sheriff wanted."

The Heartland Police Department will soon begin to start its own fitness program for street officers and civilian employees.

Police Chief Chris Anderson said the initiative is a way to have healthier and more productive employees. His staff are reviewing different departments around the nation to find an existing program that will work here.

"The goal is to just get everybody more healthy," he said.

# FULL STORY *exercise 6*

**DIRECTIONS**: Correct all errors in the following story. Check the spelling of all names in the Heartland Directory. Then, write an appropriate headline, as directed by your instructor. (303 words/12 column inches)

Webster's defines incubator as "a place or situation that permits or encourages the formation and development, as of new ideas."

Collegiate scientific think tanks are called incubators and have been on Missouri campuses for many years. In fact, several incubators are recognized as "innovation centers".

Twain State now has one of their own.

As construction winds down on the Senator Thomas F. Eagleton Science and Technology Incubator, the building last week earned a state designation of innovation center, the 10th such center in the state, said Dr. Howard F. Hall, president and CEO of Twain's Institute for Biological and Life Sciences.

"The story goes back about 14 months," Hall said, explaining the process of applying for the designation through the Missouri Technology Corporation (MTC). The MTC, utilizing funds from the Missouri Department of Economic Development, oversees the funding of Missouri's 10 innovation centers.

The approval comes with a promise of state funds for fiscal year 2013.

Hall said because of efforts made by State Rep. Martin Tucker (D-Heartland) the innovation center is in line to receive a proposed $100,000 that it will use for operational costs. State Sen. Fran Lewis (R-Heartland) backed the measure as well.

"The funding will help by helping to provide additional services that we would have had to search out or pay for another way," Hall said.

Student internships will be available at the incubator and innovation center. Also, a training lab there will give students a sense of how actual scientific laboratories operate.

The intention is to attract companies with new, innovative ideas that can be developed at the incubator. Hall said the companies they are courting specialize in agribusiness, alternative energy, animal health and human health.

"I think we'll see the first clients in there before the end of summer," he said.

# FULL STORY *exercise 7*

**DIRECTIONS**: Correct all errors in the following story. Check the spelling of all names in the Heartland Directory. Then, write an appropriate headline, as directed by your instructor. (250 words/10 column inches)

CALIFORNIA, Mo. — A 21-year-old Moniteau County woman is in jail, charged with the 1st-degree murder of her infant son.

Tamara Kaye Smith has pled innocent in the death of Dillon Henry June 20, 2012.

Law enforcement officials discovered Dillon's body during a search of an apartment at Happy Hollows Apartment Complex on the west side of California. She lived in the unit with Derek Henry, her boyfriend and the child's father.

A grand jury ruled in January that prosecutors had offered sufficient evidence for probable cause that Smith had committed the murder. Prosecutors and a coroner said she had suffocated the boy to death by placing a washcloth into his mouth soon after giving birth at the home.

The circuit court arraignment has been delayed three times since the hearing — once for inclement weather and another time because Governor Jay Nixon appointed Smith's attorney, Steve Wyckoff, to fill a vacant judge's post in Boone County.

The Circuit Court appointed Heartland attorney Patrick Palmer to represent Smith. He said he needed to speak with his client as he continues to prepare for the trial.

The Missouri Attorney General's office is assisting Moniteau County Attorney Charles Wilson with the case.

Smith faces a maximum of 20 years to life in prison for conviction of the crime. She is being held in the Moniteau County Jail in lieu of $1,000,000 bond.

Smith's five-day trial will begin July 7 at the Moniteau County Court House, Circuit Judge John Zahner announced Wednesday morning.

# FULL STORY *exercise 8*

**DIRECTIONS**: Correct all errors in the following story. Check the spelling of all names in the Heartland Directory. Then, write an appropriate headline, as directed by your instructor. (353 words/14 column inches)

Heartland City Council members will decide the future of a developer's plans to construct a 286-unit apartment complex near Missouri Route 5.

The Planning and Zoning Commission has approved Ralph Rowland's request to rezone a 23 acre tract of land at 4602 S. Missouri Rte. 5 from light manufacturing to planned commercial. The council will vote May 5.

The subdivision, Heartland Hills, would have 10 apartment buildings with a total of 286 residential units. According to documents filed with the city, the project is geared toward affordable housing for single and multi-family units. The upscale atmosphere could cater to professionals at the nearby Twain State University and Heartland Memorial Hospital campuses.

There was some opposition filed by property owners within 185 feet of the project, and one member of the commission voted against the rezoning.

Tom Richmond, with Heartland Widgets, expressed concerns during the meeting about the extension of the outer road off Riverside Road. The road currently serves as the main access for Heartland Widgets' operations, according to city documents. Richmond also was concerned about a buffer zone between the two entities.

The tract doesn't have adequate access for constant truck traffic; nor does it have immediate access to any major thoroughfares. Rezoning the vacant land would, in itself, create a zoning buffer, according to documents.

City staff made requests for an extension of the sidewalks to enhance pedestrian connectivity to the city's hike-and-bike trail on the western and eastern portion of the development. They also will require sidewalks on both sides of the driveway extension that will connect to Leonard Avenue. These recommendations were given by the committee as conditional approval on the project.

An existing apartment complex with more than 40 units neighbors the Heartland Hills property to the southwest. Crews would access the development site across the railroad right-of-way, which is currently owned by the city. The committee stated that the public works department has indicated that Leonard Avenue is more than capable of handling the increased traffic load.

Richmond is hoping to obtain an easement from the neighboring property owners to gain full access to the outer road.

# FULL STORY *exercise 9*

**DIRECTIONS**: Correct all errors in the following story. Check the spelling of all names in the Heartland Directory. Then, write an appropriate headline, as directed by your instructor. (405 words/16 column inches)

Lake Club Village feels justified and compelled to continue seeking a "divorce" from the city of Heartland after a state appeals court dealt a crushing blow against the city Tuesday.

This 5-year fight continues to carry high costs for both sides in terms of sewer costs, postponements of housing and commercial development, legal costs and ill will.

The Western District of the Missouri Court of Appeals implied in its ruling that Heartland had "unclean hands," did not "propose a good faith rationale" and had no "reasonable motive" for requiring Lake Club Village to monitor and

inspect its sewers in a 2010 ordinance and subsequent lawsuit. Lake Club Village is pleased that Heartland's "transparent motives" were obvious to the appeals court, said Village Attorney Ronald Brandon.

"This is just another long line of disputes that we have had with the city since the annexation battle," Brandon said. "The village looks forward to the day when it is completely divorced from the city."

When asked if there's any possibility for reconciliation, or whether that opportunity has passed, Brandon said the following:

"On behalf of the village board, we never asked for any of these fights. I would never say that they wouldn't consider some way to resolve the issues between the village and the city."

In early 2010, Heartland said it wanted to annex land near the village, but Lake Club Village passed the first formal annexation ordinance, and ultimately prevailed in court on the annexation fight.

Along the way, Heartland began charging sewer users outside the city more than double the normal city rate. It also wouldn't allow new connections — effectively denying any development in the annexation area, just south of the city limits.

Now Lake Club Village is making future plans to construct a new sewer treatment plant. The cost could be $3.5 to $5.5 million, which could create fees higher than those the city charges, but Brandon said that at least Lake Club Village would control its own rates and its own growth.

Heartland still will have to take in Lake Club Village's treated sewage through Snake Creek. In addition, Heartland will loose about 470 residential customers at a time when its own sewer costs could skyrocket because of state and federal regulations.

Assistant City Attorney Mary Beth Underwood said the city would need to review Tuesday's ruling before commenting. Ultimately, the City Council would need to make any decisions regarding Lake Club Village.

# FULL STORY *exercise 10*

**DIRECTIONS**: Correct all errors in the following story. Check the spelling of all names in the Heartland Directory. Then, write an appropriate headline, as directed by your instructor. (424 words/16 column inches)

What would you do if someone shot your dog, and you knew who did it?

Rita Ulmer has a pretty good idea. She just can't prove it.

As Ulmer left her house in Speed, Mo., for work Wednesday, her two-year-old Collie named Lucy escaped from her yard through a hole in the fence. Ulmer knows the town has a leash law, and some residents had threatened her about the dogs she takes in for canine foster care, but she had to get to work. So, Lucy ran free. By the time Ulmer returned back home Lucy was dead on the porch from a gunshot wound. She had bled to death.

One neighbor heard the shot, yet none of Speed's 76 residents witnessed the incident. It's a common occurrence in small towns, everybody knows everybody, and nobody saw anything.

Ulmer admits that she broke the local leash law. What makes her mad — other than the loss of a dog — is that the shooter violated another law when they fired a gun in town.

Speed doesn't have a police department, so Ulmer filed a report with Cooper County Sheriff Nathan Armstrong said that with no witnesses, the case likely would remain an investigation unless someone came forward with new information.

It is News-Observer policy not to release the names of people implicated in crime reports until charges have been filed. However, the man Ulmer suspects did answer questions for the newspaper.

"No, sir, I had nothing to do with it," the man said. "I leave this house at 4 a.m. for work and don't get home until after 2 p.m."

The man said Ulmer's dogs had caused problems in the passed, forcing him to replant his garden three times last summer. He claimed, he spoke with Ulmer about the dogs, yet she made no effort to stop them from getting out.

"I threatened to shoot them, sure, but I never did it," he said. "There's nothing I can do but put up with it, I guess."

Ulmer housed five dogs in foster care at the time of the shooting and keeps another as a personal pet. She had Lucy for about six months. After the shooting, Ulmer sent an e-mail to friends and nearby shelters and has found homes for most of the dogs. Fellow dog lovers from Columbia, Mo., have offered to help fix her fence to prevent future dog escapes.

"The thing about animal rescue people is we're kind of crazy," she said. "But don't mess with my animals. That's like shooting my kids."

# FULL STORY *exercise 11*

**DIRECTIONS**: Correct all errors in the following story. Check the spelling of all names in the Heartland Directory. Then, write an appropriate headline, as directed by your instructor. (385 words/15 column inches)

The number of bicyclists in Heartland are fewer than that of other Midwestern cities, but they're a dedicated bunch.

Columbia, Lincoln, NE., and Lawrence, Kan., are bicycle-friendly towns with numerous bicycle paths, clubs and events. However, Heartland's mountain bike trails grow miles longer every year due to volunteers with a passion for pedaling.

"For the number of people we have riding here, a very high percentage do trail work." said Seth Robertson, 30, an engineer at Anchor Serum Inc. He has been riding for 12 years.

He estimated hundreds of hours of work has gone into clearing wooded areas off the city's parkway in the past few years. Volunteers have used chain saws, pruners, industrial weedwhackers, rakes and leaf blowers to make paths through thickets along the parkway. The occasional poison ivy breakout and slithering reptile are hazards of the work, but the payoff is an intense ride.

"They are very well designed," said Robertson, who has given up road bicycling. " . . . typically pretty fast and pretty fun and just enjoyable trails to ride."

Keith Yarrow helped build Heartland's first, and for the longest time, the only off-road trail for mountain bikes.

He admits that the design of the course and the skill level required to navigate it probably turned off a majority of beginners.

"That's why we wanted something a little more tame and little more family-friendly," said Yarrow, who has been riding mountain bikes since 1985.

The trails near Cranston Pond, which were completed a couple of years ago, helped boost the number of local mountain bike riders, Yarrow said.

"Mountain biking is making a comeback," he said, mentioning that many riders were influenced to go to road biking after Lance Armstrong's triumphs at the Tour de France but are now coming back to the trails.

"It's maybe back to 50/50," he guessed.

The newest trail, which still needs bridge work over some muddy spots, is called Girl Scout Trail, located off the Northwest Parkway near the old girl scout day camp.

"The idea is to actually incorporate a variety of terrain," Yarrow said of the different trails that comprise Heartland's 14-mile network.

The Raider Round Up race will be held May 18 on the Twain State University campus. Entry fees will go toward the purchase of equipment to maintain the trails.

# FULL STORY *exercise 12*

**DIRECTIONS**: Correct all errors in the following story. Check the spelling of all names in the Heartland Directory. Then, write an appropriate headline, as directed by your instructor. (376 words/14 column inches)

PILOT GROVE, Mo. — The baptism of infant Tracy Renee Bradley is among the first signs that new life will return to the charred St. Joseph Catholic Church.

The Most Rev. Robert J. Hermann, auxiliary bishop of the Archdiocese of St. Louis, Mo., came to console members and baptized Tracy during the parish's first Sunday mass since an April 21 fire totally destroyed the church.

"This is a great symbol of hope to us," the bishop said of the baptism.

The early-morning Mass drew a large crowd to the parish center, an adjacent building that the fire didn't consume

last week. Attendance also was high at the regular Saturday evening Mass, long-time member Lonnie Coder said. A prayer service held the day of the fire drew 400 people, said the Rev. Ben Stockton, St. Joseph's pastor.

Investigators probing the blaze still don't know its cause. An examination of the scene concluded Wednesday, with debris sent to the Missouri State Highway Patrol lab for analysis. Arson is a possibility, Cooper County Sheriff Nathan Armstrong said.

Many parishioners like Coder expressed confidence that consensus will be reached on building a new church. An

advantage is that a host of members have construction experience, he added.

"We'll get together. I know we will," he said. "We're strong."

Antiques and other furnishings burned along with the 116-year-old structure.

The Rev. Stockton received applause for his efforts over the past week to transform the center into a makeshift house of prayer.

"We have had a death in the family," he said near the Mass's conclusion. "We will have a period of grieving, but with the (Tracy Bradley) baptism, we know life goes on."

The Parish Council initially met Thursday to discuss rebuilding, Stockton said. Demolition of the remains is one of the first tasks.

"We want to listen to what everyone has to say," he said.

Pat Oyler, who has attended Mass at St. Joseph's for 52 years has a long list of memories.

"All my kids were baptized at the church, she said. "I'm sure they'll rebuild. It's too big a community not to."

The Knights of Columbus will sponsor a barbecue Sunday, May 4, at the center to honor fire fighters and others who responded to the fire, Stockton said.

# FULL STORY *exercise 13*

**DIRECTIONS**: Correct all errors in the following story. Check the spelling of all names in the Heartland Directory. Then, write an appropriate headline, as directed by your instructor. (336 words/13 column inches)

PRAIRIE HOME, Mo. — Jesse L. Jackson, 20, of Prairie Home, and a passenger, Max A. VanTuyll, 20, of Pleasant Grove, Mo., died on Sunday when their vehicle slid off a wet road, according to the Missouri State Highway Patrol.

The patrol report said the wreck happened at 4:52 a.m. on Missouri Route 87, 5 miles north of Prairie Home.

Jackson, driving a 1997 Acura north on the highway, overtook an unidentified pickup and lost control on wet pavement. The vehicle slid off the west side of the highway and struck an embankment, ejecting VanTuyll. He was pronounced dead while enroute to Heartland Memorial Hospital. Jackson died at the scene.

The vehicle landed on its wheels off the west side of the highway. Neither VanTuyll nor Jackson were wearing a seat belt, the patrol said.

Another wreck occurred at 1:45 a.m. Sunday morning on Missouri Route 135, two miles south of New Lebanon, Mo. One of the three passengers, 22-year-old Brandy L. Blackman, of Columbia, Mo., was taken to Heartland Memorial Hospital for treatment of serious injuries. A nursing supervisor refused to provide a condition update Sunday afternoon. The patrol listed the other injuries as minor to moderate.

In that accident, Rayna E. Kelly, 22, also of Columbia, lost control of the 1996 Ford Explorer she was driving southbound on the highway. The sport utility vehicle went off the east side of the roadway and overturned twice, ejecting Blackman and another passenger. The SUV came to rest on its wheels. None of the occupants were wearing a seat belt.

In a third accident, a Bunceton, Mo. man suffered serious injuries on State Highway J, just east of town.

Harvey W. Roach, 55, was taken to Heartland Memorial Hospital for treatment, according to the patrol.

Roach was driving a 2009 Freightliner eastbound on Highway J at 8:02 a.m. when he drove the truck off the right side. The tractor trailer struck a dirt embankment, becoming air-borne. The Freightliner continued across a field and struck two more embankments before stopping.

# FULL STORY *exercise 14*

**DIRECTIONS**: Correct all errors in the following story. Check the spelling of all names in the Heartland Directory. Then, write an appropriate headline, as directed by your instructor. (261 words/10 column inches)

A 16-year-old Heartland woman will stand trial as an adult for the December crash in Columbia, Mo., that killed two people.

Ericka R. Olinger was under the influence of a combination of cocaine, marijuana and benzodiazepines when she drove a Ford Explorer the wrong way on U.S. Highway 63 and into the path of another car, according to court documents filed in Boone County circuit court.

The head on collision killed a passenger in the Explorer, Ashley Wittenberg, 16, of Heartland, and the driver of the other vehicle, Scott Kirby, 26, of Columbia.

Olinger, who was fifteen at the time of crash, faces charges of two felonies of first-degree involuntary manslaughter in the deaths.

Following the Dec. 20th crash, Olinger gave officers a birthdate two years older than she was, according to court records. She didn't have a driver's license. Officers also said she was slurring her speech and had bloodshot eyes.

Prosecutors asked that Olinger be treated as an adult because of the false information she gave officers. Police took a blood sample that later tested positive for benzodiazepines, cannabinoids and cocaine metabolites, according to court records.

Besides criminal charges, another passenger in the Explorer, Grady Holmes, 22, of Heartland, is suing Olinger for $25,000 dollars in personal injuries.

Mr. Holmes suffered head trauma and traumatic brain injury, and the crash has forever diminished his earning potential, according to court documents filed on his behalf by the Stevenson Law Firm.

On Friday afternoon there was no answer at the door of the Heartland address listed for Olinger in court documents.

# FULL STORY *exercise 15*

**DIRECTIONS**: Correct all errors in the following story. Check the spelling of all names in the Heartland Directory. Then, write an appropriate headline, as directed by your instructor. (404 words/15 column inches)

The city council wanted more cops on the streets two years ago.

Since then, the council have acted on sewers, buses, the Capital Improvement Tax, museums and a use tax. Yet, some officers are still lonely at night, with as few as seven patrol officers working a shift.

"We talked about it two years ago, and we're still talking about it. We just haven't done anything about it," Mayor Kevin Shearin said.

What started as a routine review of the Police Department budget Thursday evening quickly turned into a push for a new public safety tax to put more officers and firefighters on the streets.

The council will appoint a citizens committee to explore, propose and promote the tax, it decided Thursday evening. Council members will formally vote to form the committee at its May 19 meeting.

The discussion is still wide open in terms of needs and how to fund them.

Perhaps just as relevant, a public safety tax could help considerably to free up the ongoing CIP tax for true capital purchases, such as roads, sewers and public facilities. In spite of the fact that the new $27 million CIP will pay for fire trucks, police communications and breathing apparatus, none of it is earmarked for sewer extensions, and only about one fourth of it goes toward streets and bridges.

"We need to find a secure revenue source to pay for more police officers and equipment for firefighters," said Councilman Adrian Litton, who is a former Heartland police officer.

Police Chief Chris Anderson didn't raise the issue of the tax Thursday and said he was surprised when the council jumped on the bandwagon. He said the public has complained about response times to non-life threatening crimes and calls, particularly during peak hours of 4 p.m. to 3:30 a.m.

"We have the people spread out to cover all shifts; it's just a matter of the demands peak," Anderson said. "Then, there's a concern about having backup on the life-threatening calls, and it becomes a serious matter of officer and citizen safety."

The 16 officers — a number he said is justified by an internal study and comparison — would go mostly for patrols but also a few detectives and street crimes officers.

Fire Chief Jack Fenner, who will retire July 1, said the five-year CIP is not the ideal means for supporting a fire department. He suggested that a property tax would be more stable.

# FULL STORY *exercise 16*

**DIRECTIONS**: Correct all errors in the following story. Check the spelling of all names in the Heartland Directory. Then, write an appropriate headline, as directed by your instructor. (296 words/11 column inches)

The total tally for cleaning up last winter's weather — all 21 storms — is $728,000.

That's about $17,000 per inch of precipitation or almost $45,000 per storm.

The 43 inches of snow, ice, sleet and freezing rain that fell on the city of Heartland was just about nearly twice as much as any other winter in the past five years.

Of the 21 storms, seven dumped over two inches of snow. Three storms dropped more than 6 inches each: 8 inches of snow Dec. 22; 12 inches of sleet and snow Feb. 5 and 6; and 6 inches of snow Feb. 17. Then there was the December ice storm.

The city used 8,270 tons of salt and ice melt for city streets at a cost of $423,000.

"That was far and above what we've used in the past few years," said Stan Greene, city Public Works Department director.

The city plowed 35,312 miles of streets, with a labor and fuel cost of about $305,000.

These figures don't include debris pickup expenses from the ice storm. Federal and State emergency management agencies are helping cover those costs.

The following are the past five winter's total precipitation and cost for cleanup, according to Greene:

- 2011–12: 7 inches, $295,000
- 2010–11: 15 inches, $390,000
- 2009–10: 16 inches, $352,000
- 2008–09: 7 inches, $329,000
- 2007–08: 23 inches, $502,000

Because the city purchased salt throughout the winter to keep up its reserves, it still has about 2,000 tons on hand, Green said.

In July, the snow may be the furthest thing from people's minds, but that's when the city will begin ordering salt for next year. It also mixes salt with an ice-melt product derived from beet sugar, which allows the salt to continue melting down to 0.

# FULL STORY *exercise 17*

**DIRECTIONS**: Correct all errors in the following story. Check the spelling of all names in the Heartland Directory. Then, write an appropriate headline, as directed by your instructor. (340 words/13 column inches)

BOONVILLE, Mo. — The trees along Summit Avenue give a lush welcome to anyone that happens to take a summertime drive through town.

In fact, the roadside boasts enough green to earn the city the honor of Tree City USA from the Arbor Day Foundation.

This weekend Boonville will go green in a brand new way. The community will hold a picnic lunch at 11:30 a.m. at the former Western Auto Building to celebrate its pledge to purchase a percentage of its electricity from green energy sources.

Boonville will partner with AmerenUE to become Missouri's second US Environmental Protection Agency Green Power Community.

The city has enrolled in Ameren's Pure Power program, which asks customers to volunteer to pay an additional 1.5¢ per kilowatt hour that the company will use to purchase renewable energy credits. Boonville will buy credits equal to 100 percent of the usage from homes and businesses enrolled in Pure Power.

Community leaders hope to commit five percent of energy usage to the program to earn its status as a Green Power Community. Mayor Juanita Kennedy will enroll her own home in Pure Power at Saturday's event.

"We want to reach that goal by next April," she said. "Technically, we only need three percent participation to be an EPA Green Power Community, but we are setting a stretch goal for our citizens."

According to Ameren, that step will reduce carbon dioxide emissions by 785,544 pounds per year — equal to taking 77 cars off the road or planting 81 acres of forest.

Pure Power is part of Ameren's new P.U.R.E. initiative, which stands for People Using Renewable Energy.

Cindy Bambini of 3Degrees Group, Inc., which manages the program for Ameren, praised Boonville for its role in supporting green power.

"They have really stepped up to the plate, and their commitment will help support wind farms that are adding more green power to Missouri's electrical grid," she said.

AmerenUE serves 1.2 million electric customers and 127,000 natural gas customers in a 24,000-square-mile area in Northern, Central and Eastern Missouri.

# FULL STORY *exercise 18*

**DIRECTIONS**: Correct all errors in the following story. Check the spelling of all names in the Heartland Directory. Then, write an appropriate headline, as directed by your instructor. (349 words/13 column inches)

Twain State University's run as a dry campus is over.

The approval wasn't unanimous, but Twain's governing board has approved serving beer and wine at approved events in the River Raiders Center, Shireman Student Union and Eagleton Science and Technology Incubator.

Use of alcohol at the events is subject to approval by a three-man committee and final approval of the university president.

Board members Nicholas Kramer and Karyne Yoder voted against changing TSU's alcohol policy.

Kramer cited concerns that the Student Union is frequented by too many students.

"I do have some concern because of proximity," he said, adding that he didn't have a problem with alcohol being served at events at the science and technology incubator, which is on the extreme west side of campus.

Kramer asked prior to the vote that alcoholic beverages served at events be limited to beer and wine.

Also fearing for the well being of students, Yoder said her concern was that an over-served patron might be a hazard to students on campus and that the board would set a double standard by approving alcohol on campus.

"It doesn't make complete sense," she said.

Board member Emile Quinlan brought the controversial issue to the board during last month's meeting. He said he has heard many different opinions on the matter since then. He recommended Thursday that the board okay the new policy with the amendments that alcohol would be defined as beer and wine and that the request for approval be 30 days rather than 45 days before the event.

The three-person committee, which decides which events will be approved for alcohol consumption, will include a member of the Board of Governors, a member of the faculty and member of the university staff.

Stipulations regarding the service of alcohol include that it may not be served 30 minutes before the end of an event, that it is restricted to invited guests, that the majority of the guests is 21, that alcohol is available only in single service containers, and that no university funds or student fees be used to purchase the alcohol.

# FULL STORY *exercise 19*

**DIRECTIONS**: Correct all errors in the following story. Check the spelling of all names in the Heartland Directory. Then, write an appropriate headline, as directed by your instructor. (471 words/18 column inches)

For Amanda Dunavant, the initial diagnosis wasn't the worst part of dealing with breast cancer.

The worst part was the waiting.

Dunavant, who received her cancer diagnosis in 1991 as a patient at a hospital outside of Heartland, returned for a second mammogram after receiving the results of her

first; then was told she needed a needle biopsy. It was several weeks before she could see a doctor for this, and several more before she could go in for an appointment with the surgeon she needed to see next.

"All this time, I'm just positive I'm dead," Dunavant said. "You're in mental anguish, just sure you're going to die because — my word — you have cancer."

Seventeen years after those painful weeks of waiting, Dunavant is part of an effort to keep other women from going through the same thing. She and state Sen. Fran Lewis, who also is marketing and communications officer for Heartland Memorial Hospital, are chairing a campaign for the purpose of raising $1.5 million for a state-of-the-art breast center at Heartland.

The campaign began this week and will continue through Aug. 31, and the Heartland Memorial Hospital Auxiliary already has received a $10,000 donation from a local trust. Fund-raising events include a golf tournament May 27 and a pink-and-white ball scheduled for Oct. 10.

"The whole concept of the breast center is that it will offer a centralized location and speed up the process from when a woman receives undesirable results following a mammogram to when she's diagnosed," said Barbie Piercy, Heartland's process leader for volunteer services and a member of the auxiliary.

Key to this, she added, will be the 3 digital mammography machines the hospital plans to purchase. These will be able to provide results immediately, thereby keeping a patient from having to wait for her results to come in the mail and then having to wait for another appointment.

Rather, patients will be able to see breast center physicians right away and also will receive help from a nurse navigator, who will be with the patient from the time she receives undesirable mammogram results until she determines a plan for her treatment.

In addition to big ticket items such as construction and technology, money raised by the auxiliary's campaign will go toward lesser expenses such as cotton spa robes and educational materials.

The center is set to open in October in the location previously occupied by Heartland Memorial Comprehensive Family Care, which moved to a new facility earlier this month. Although the auxiliary still has a significant amount to rise in order to reach its goal, Dunavant — who now is cancer-free — is confident it's possible.

"If everyone in Heartland gave just a dollar, that would be more than $48,000 right there," she said, "and it's for a wonderful cause that will help every women in the area."

# FULL STORY *exercise 20*

**DIRECTIONS**: Correct all errors in the following story. Check the spelling of all names in the Heartland Directory. Then, write an appropriate headline, as directed by your instructor. (379 words/14 column inches)

TIPTON, Mo. — Change can be slow in museums, but well-planned improvements can breath new life into old institutions.

The Moniteau County Museum reflects the blush of ongoing changes.

"We're heading in the right direction," said Orion Emery, who was hired as museum director about 15 months ago and has a masters degree in museum studies.

Emery's two biggest projects are organizing museum collections and completing the new "A Rural Way of Life: Moniteau County, Missouri 1845–2009" exhibition.

"The museum has a good foundation for going to the next level," said Tom Edmondson, president of Heugh-

Edmondson Conservation Services. "They're really trying to go somewhere."

The completed exhibit will be opened to the public in the not-too-distant future, Emery said.

"It will occupy 4,000 square feet and be the same caliber display as a Smithsonian exhibit," he said.

Exhibit Associates Inc., of Kansas City, is constructing the displays based on plans by Steve Feldman Design, of Philadelphia. The museum had held a capital campaign and raised $830,000 for the exhibit — the lion's share of its $900,000 price tag.

Emery inherited a 32-year collection that didn't have climate-controlled storage and good records

detailing the individual pieces. Working with state-of-the-art museum software, volunteers and an intern from the University of Missouri, the museum is properly photographing, measuring and describing its collection items.

The storage room has proper shelving, acid-free storage materials, a constant temperature of 62 degrees and 45 percent to 50 percent humidity, Emery said.

There are other ongoing projects.

The museum acquired a National Endowment for the Humanities grant and hired a conservator to study its extensive photographic collections. A cooperative project with the Missouri State Historical Society is continuing to produce a complete microfilm collection of "The Tipton Times."

Emery said the museum board would soon begin work on a new set of future plans for the museum, including the following: apply for museum national accreditation, look at new exhibit possibilities, authorize outreach programs and seek new ways to ensure financial viability.

In 2011, Moniteau County voters passed a one-fifth of a percent sales tax that generates about $200,000 a year for operational expenses. The museum also began renovations, which included new exhibits and improved accessibility for the handicapped.

**Additional exercises are available online at** www.oup.com/us/rosenauer.

# Appendix

Included in the Appendix are the following:
- Heartland Directory
- Online editing resources
- Irregular verb list
- Common clichés list

## Heartland Directory

This directory offers basic information about Heartland, including its location, government offices, hospitals, schools, officials, residents and businesses.

Use this resource to check on the proper names of these, especially the correct spellings of names of Heartland residents in the stories you edit.

Regularly checking this directory is a habit you should develop as you complete your exercises. More important, you must carry that habit into professional settings after you graduate, where consulting local directories and other print and online resources is a critical part of your job.

### Setting

Heartland, Mo.

### Population

48,400

### Location

County seat of Cooper County. Located mid-Missouri, approximately 100 miles east of Kansas City. Mo.; 150 miles west of St. Louis; 160 miles northeast Springfield, Mo.; 100

miles southwest of Kirksville, Mo; and 40 miles northwest of the state capital at Jefferson City, Mo.

## Government offices and facilities

Cooper County Courthouse
Cooper County Law Enforcement Complex
Cooper County Prosecuting Attorney's Office
Cooper County Veterans Park
Heartland City Hall
Heartland Public Library
Heartland Public Works Department
Heartland School District
U.S. Post Office and Federal Building

## Hospital

Heartland Memorial Hospital

## Postsecondary schools

Twain State University

## High schools

Heartland High School
Northeast High School
South High School

## Middle schools

Garfield Middle School
Lincoln Middle School
Roosevelt Middle School

## Elementary schools

Booker T. Washington Elementary School
Charles Lindbergh Elementary School
Daniel Webster Elementary School
Eugene Field Elementary School
Horace Mann Elementary School
James M. Turner Elementary School
John Dewey Elementary School
John J. Pershing Elementary School
John Locke Elementary School

Muriel Battle Elementary School
Thomas Edison Elementary School

## Parochial schools

Heartland Christian School
Heartland Lutheran Elementary School
Holy Cross Elementary School
Sacred Heart High School
St. Francis Elementary School

## Cooper County/Heartland Officials, Residents

| | |
|---|---|
| Aarstadt, Alan V. | professor of political science, Twain State University |
| Addington, Billy R. | 3122 Dover St. |
| Addington, Jeanne | 308 Floyd Ave. |
| Albert, Clarence | 1426 S. 25th St. |
| Alexander, Stena W. | secretary, Student Government Association, Twain State University |
| Alvarez, Manuel | president, Cooper County Veterans Park |
| Anderson, Chris | chief, Heartland Police Department, Cooper County Law Enforcement Complex |
| Armstrong, Nathan | sheriff, Cooper County, Cooper County Law Enforcement Complex |
| Arnold, George | emergency services coordinator, Heartland |
| Bailey, Mary Hatch | librarian, Heartland Public Library |
| Barker, Lillian | Heartland Widgets employee, night shift |
| Barker, Stanley K. | retired, Heartland Widgets |
| Baum, Jeffery | Heartland merchant |
| Baxter, Ed | chairman, Museum Oversight Board |
| Beaver, Richard | chairman, Missourians for Conservative Values Political Action Committee |
| Bergland, William Z. | assistant professor of journalism, Twain State University |
| Birdsong, William G. | deputy sheriff, Cooper County Sheriff's Department |
| Black, Edgar S. | 19, sophomore biology major, Twain State University, 2618 Faraon St. |
| Black, Marjorie M. | 2618 Faraon St. |
| Blevins, Bartholomew | 17, fry cook, McDonald's |
| Boudoin, Hilda Jo | president, Cooper County Fair Board of Directors |
| Bradley, Darwin W. | Heartland resident |
| Brager, Janet A. | group minister, North End Youth Outreach |
| Brown, Lawrence H. | partner, MRW Investment Opportunities |
| Brown, Mary E. | partner, MRW Investment Opportunities |
| Bryant, Earl A. | captain, Heartland Police Department |
| Buck, Joseph E. | chairman, Heartland Downtown Parking Committee |

| | |
|---|---|
| Bush, Angela | Heartland resident |
| Cadden, Joanne | public relations director, Heartland Chamber of Commerce |
| Capell, Jay | city manager, Heartland |
| Carroll, Kristina | victim services director, Heartland YWCA |
| Christian, William R. | sergeant, Troop F, Missouri State Highway Patrol |
| Clampett, Josiah | stonemason |
| Clarke, Angela K. | judge, Cooper County Associate Circuit Court |
| Connett, Jim | commander, Heartland Police Department, Cooper County Law Enforcement Complex |
| Darnell, Keith O. | presiding commissioner, Cooper County |
| Davis, Tura B. | 3805 Rolling Hills Drive |
| Dawson, Ellen L. | senator, Student Government Association, Twain State University |
| Dayton, Jeffery L. | chairman, Downtown Business Tax District Board |
| DiNozzo, Maria | Heartland school teacher, CTA spokeswoman |
| Donaldson, Mark | captain, Drug Strike Force, Cooper County Law Enforcement Complex |
| Downey, Sarabeth | owner, Acoustics Now, 2605 Stetson Ave. |
| DuMont, Dr. David A. | director of public health, Heartland |
| Dunavant, Amanda | Heartland resident |
| Estes, Harrison W. | Heartland resident |
| Evans, Dennis W. | president, Heartland Regional Association of Realtors |
| Evans, Rebecca | coordinator, Small Business Center, Twain State University |
| Everett, Alton | member, Heartland School Board |
| Evinger, William E. | skateboarding champion |
| Fankhauser, Janet K. | executive director, Central Missouri Arts Council |
| Fargo, Kevin B. | fine arts coordinator, Heartland School District |
| Fenner, John A. "Jack" | chief, Heartland Fire Department |
| Fisher, Arthur O. | president, Student Government Association, Twain State University |
| Force, Harry | Heartland resident |
| Frakes, Roger | circuit Judge, Cooper County, Cooper County Courthouse |
| Franklin, Angela | police officer, Heartland Police Department, 1209 Mitchell Ave. |
| Galt, Allyson Y. | operations manager, Vanderbilt Regional Airport |
| Garlinger, Adrian A. | director, Career Center, Twain State University |
| Gentry, Dwight R. | prosecutor, Cooper County |
| George, Andrea | media and public relations coordinator, Heartland Memorial Hospital |
| Graves, Anna L. | public relations director, Heartland Memorial Hospital |
| Greene, Stanley S. | director, Heartland Public Works Department |
| Hall, Dr. Howard F. | president and chief executive officer, Institute for Biological and Life Sciences, Twain State University |

| | |
|---|---|
| Hammond, Harriet L. | executive director, Heartland Youth Alliance |
| Hanscomb, William O. | retired banker |
| Hanson, Gerald W. | officer, Heartland Safety Council |
| Harrison, Beth | principal, Lindbergh Elementary School |
| Hartell, Steven | owner, Texcon Oil Distributing |
| Hersh, Sandra | manager, Heartland Aquatic Center |
| Holton, Steven S. | specialist, Small Business Center, Twain State University |
| Hriso, Patrick E. | 309 Green St., 22 |
| Jackson, Henry T. | assessor, Cooper County |
| Jackson, Martin E. | president, Coldwell Banker General Properties |
| Jamison, Joseph L. | pretrial release investigator, Cooper County Sheriff's Department |
| Jarvis, Jerry I. | head football coach, Twain State University |
| Jones, Melody A. | director of finance, Heartland School District |
| Jones, Winston S. | partner, MRW Investment Opportunities |
| Karr, Albert | owner, Downtown Martini Bar |
| Karr, Elizabeth | novelist |
| Kelley, Stephen L. | regional manager, AmerenUE |
| Kinder, Joyce | Heartland resident |
| Koretzky, Richard | 400 Heartland Hills Terrace |
| Kramer, Nicholas V. | member, Twain State University Board of Governors |
| Lance, Tommy | assistant director, Heartland Public Works Department |
| Lawson, Philip A. | podiatrist, Heartland Foot Clinic |
| Leonard, Lawrence | buyer, Central Missouri Iron and Metal Inc. |
| Lewis, Frances A. | state senator, 21st District, and marketing and communications officer, Heartland Memorial Hospital |
| Litton, Adrian B. | member, Heartland City Council |
| Macey, Jeffrey L. | owner, Designed West, 3207 Lone Oak Ave. |
| Martin, Horace V. | forester, Heartland Arboretum, and professor of biology, Twain State University |
| Matthis, Ronald W. | city architect, Heartland |
| McBride, Rebecca O. | executive director, Heartland Downtown Partnership |
| Miller, Cassandra | Heartland resident |
| Miller, Forrest T. | vice president of Student Life, Twain State University |
| Milton, Candie O. | broadcasting major, Twain State University |
| Mondale, Frank | 3810 Wentworth Court |
| Munson, Dr. Myron R. | superintendent, Heartland School District |
| Murphy, Charles | Heartland resident, 18 |
| Nelson, Grady R., Jr. | chief operating officer, Heartland Widgets Inc. |
| Newhart, Alan B. | quarterback, Twain State University River Raiders and senior business major |
| Nivens, Dr. Wilhelmina A. | professor of art, Twain State University |
| Nold, Langston L. | Boy Scout, son of John and Ellen Nold |
| Nunez, Alberto | employee, Heartland Widgets Inc. |

| | |
|---|---|
| Olinger, Ericka R. | 1902 Grand Ave. |
| Olsen, Dr. Andrea L. | president, Heartland Chamber of Commerce |
| Olsen, Sunny | daughter of Walter R. and Dr. Andrea L. Olsen |
| Orozco, Carmen | 2413 Mulberry St. |
| Ott, Oliver | chairman, Cooper County Republicans |
| Palmer, Patrick | attorney, Palmer Law Firm |
| Paltrow, Floyd | fire inspector, Heartland Fire Department |
| Pankiewicz, Marvin B. | governor, Moose Lodge of Heartland |
| Parker, Ryan S. | Heartland resident |
| Phillips, Janine | president, Museums Inc. Board of Trustees |
| Piercy, Barbie O. | process leader for volunteer services, Heartland Memorial Hospital |
| Pinzino, Emmett | employee, Heartland Widgets Inc. |
| Quinlan, Emile M. | member, Twain State University Board of Governors |
| Quitman, Amanda | radio evangelist |
| Ramirez, Anthony | Heartland resident, 19 |
| Rand, Alvin | U.S. senator, Democrat, retired |
| Renfroe, Royce A. | member, Downtown Business Tax District Board |
| Revels, Allison R. | director, Heartland Public Library, Downtown Branch |
| Richardson, Mary | member, Heartland City Council |
| Richmond, Harvey | Heartland resident, 18 |
| Richmond, Tom | spokesman, Heartland Widgets |
| Rinne, Helen G. | attorney, Cooper County Juvenile Office |
| Robertson, Seth | engineer, Anchor Serum Inc. |
| Rose, Michael | sergeant, Heartland Police Department |
| Rowland, Ralph W. | developer, Rowland Properties |
| Ruggles, Leo J. | pastor, Holy Cross Catholic Church |
| Sandoval, William G. | physician, Heartland Care Clinic |
| Schafer, LaDonna V. | Heartland resident |
| Schmidt, Joanne | director, Career Services Office, Twain State University |
| Schultz, Carrie C. | librarian, Heartland Public Library, Downtown Branch |
| Sewell, Sterling F. | professor of social studies (retired), Twain State University |
| Shearin, Karl Y. | mayor, Heartland |
| Silcott, Edward "Ned" | bookkeeper, Brown Transfer Co. |
| Simpson, Colleen C. | human resources assistant, HFC Financial |
| Smith, Aaron R. | prosecuting attorney, Cooper County |
| Smith, Erma N. | 709 South Noyes Boulevard |
| Spencer, Evelyn D. | former president, Twain State Alumni Association |
| Spencer, John T. | Heartland resident |
| Spencer, Sara S. | city prosecutor, Heartland |
| Stanton, Keith T. | sewer worker, Heartland Public Works Department, 47, 2324 Francis St. |
| Stone, Cecilia A. | waitress and part owner, Downtown Dine-In |

| | |
|---|---|
| Swisher, Jason O. | commissioner, Northern District, Cooper County |
| Tandy, Scott | director, New Harvest of Heartland |
| Thorn, Sam | assistant director of public relations, Twain State University |
| Tomlinson, Mathew | district manager, AmerenUE |
| Trent, Margot V. | secretary, Heartland School District, 42 |
| Trent, Peter S. | welder, Mid-States Welding, 45 |
| Tucker, Lavelle | social worker, Heartland School District |
| Tucker, Martin | state representative, 117th District |
| Underwood, Mary Beth | assistant city attorney, Heartland |
| Van Dyke, Alma B. | cashier, Downtown Dine-In |
| Vasquez, Maria | inventory clerk, Eagle Rock Foods |
| Vaughn, Seth L. | trooper, Troop F, Missouri State Highway Patrol |
| Wall, Norman | barber, Norm's Barber Shop |
| Weems, Diane S. | coroner, Cooper County |
| Wellington, Elwood | pipefitter, 1630 S. 22nd St., 47 |
| Wells, Kate | director, Community Missions Center |
| Williams, Anson | Heartland resident, 22 |
| Williamson, Albert | sergeant, Cooper County Sheriff's Department |
| Wilson, George A. | supervisor, Heartland Widgets Inc., 56 |
| Wilson, Sasha | counselor, Lindbergh Elementary School |
| Winkler, Todd | Heartland resident |
| Wittenberg, Ashley | 2024 Safari Dr. |
| Wolfe, Mindy | executive director, Peach Blossom Parade |
| Woolson, Roger | forester, Missouri Department Of Conservation, and president, Heartland Board of Education |
| Yarrow, Keith S. | Heartland resident |
| Yates, Daniel E. | clerk, BP Gas Service |
| Yoder, Karyne A. | member, Twain State University Board of Governors |
| Zahner, Kenneth L. | president, Peach Blossom Parade |

## Businesses

Acoustics Now, 2605 Stetson Ave.

AmerenUE, power company, outage hotline (800) 552–7583

Anchor Serum Inc.

Arising Stars School of Dance and Gymnastics

Brown Transfer Co.

Central Missouri Arts Council

Central Missouri Inn

Central Missouri Iron and Metal Inc.

Chuck E. Cheese

Coca-Cola Co.

Coldwell Banker General Properties

ConAgra Foods Inc.

Cooper County Industrial Park

Cooper County Republican Headquarters
Downtown Dine-In
Downtown Martini Bar
Eagle Rock Foods
First Bank of Heartland
Heartland Aquatic Center
Heartland Care Clinic
Heartland Chamber of Commerce
Heartland Mall
Heartland News-Observer
Heartland Regional Association of Realtors
Heartland Steakhouse
Heartland Theatre
Heartland Widgets Inc.
Heartland Widgets Midwest Manufacturing Plant
Heartland YWCA
HFC Financial
Hillyard Industries
Holiday Inn
Main Street Hardware
McDonald's
MetLife Inc.
Mid-Missouri Construction Inc.
MLW Investment Opportunities
New Harvest of Heartland
Quickie's
Stevenson Law Firm
Strike-It-Lucky Bowling Center
U.S. Bank
Vanderbilt Regional Airport
Wal-Mart Supercenter
Whirlpool Corp.
Woody's Lake Drive-In Market
Woody's Lakeshore Grocery

## Twain State University Campus

Altman Stadium
Baptist Student Union
Fellowship of Christian Athletes
Heartland Arboretum
Howard V. McNultey Gymnasium
Institute for Biological and Life Sciences
Lambda Chi Alpha
Lee Hall
McCabe Hall

Newman Center

Phi Gamma Nu

Phi Mu

River Raiders Boosters

River Raiders Center

School of Liberal Arts

Senator Thomas F. Eagleton Science and Technology Incubator

Shireman Student Union

Sigma Tau Delta

Silcott Adult Education Building

Small Business Center

Student Chapter of the Society of Professional Journalists

Student Union Center Court

Taylor Hall

Thompson Hall

Twain State Alumni Association

Wesley Foundation

# Online Editing Resources

## Part 1 – The Basics

1. The Role of The Copy Editor
   - Beyond Copy Editing—The Editor-Writer Relationship: www.jeanweber.com/newsite/?page_id=26
   - In Search of the Perfect Copy Editor—10 Copy Editor Traits That Guarantee You Success: www.poynter.org/content/content_view.asp?id=5438
   - The Slot—What Exactly Is a Copy Editor? and How a Copy Desk Works: www.theslot.com/copyeditors.html
   - Who Would Want To Be a Copy Editor?: www.copydesk.org/words/ASNEJanuary.htm
2. Editing Content
   - AssignmentEditor is a directory of online resources for journalists: www.assignmenteditor.com
   - Copywriting 101: www.copyblogger.com/copywriting-101/
   - JProf—Editing Resources: www.jprof.com/editing/editing.html
   - Poynter Online—Reporting, Writing and Editing: http://about.poynter.org/training/topics/85
3. Copy Editing for Print and Online
   - Editing Online News: www.slideshare.net/ryan.thornburg/editing-online-news-1035762
   - Journalist Express bills itself as a "desktop" for journalists: www.journalistexpress.com
   - News College is an extensive directory for journalists, covering reporting, writing, story hunting, editing and more: www.newscollege.ca/p106.htm

- News Writing is a site covering groaners ("horrible, overused, hackneyed phrases"), articles, writing tools and resources: www.newswriting.com/groaners.htm
- The Journalist's Toolbox, by Mike Reilley, has links and resources to current topics, sports and teaching: www.journaliststoolbox.com

4. Legal, Ethical and Inclusive-Language Concerns for Copy Editors
- Asian-American style guide: www.aaja.org/aajahandbook/
- Center for Integration and Improvement of Journalism: www.ciij.org/resources
- Citizen Media Law Project: www.citmedialaw.org/
- Disability style guide: http://ncdj.org/style-guide/
- Diversity Resources: https://www.spj.org/divsourcebook.asp
- Gay, lesbian, transsexual and transgender style guide: www.nlgja.org/resources/stylebook_english.html
- Guidelines for countering racial, ethnic and religious profiling: www.spj.org/divguidelines.asp
- Journalism Ethics Resources: www.web-miner.com/journethics.htm
- Journalism Resources—Media Law: http://bailiwick.lib.uiowa.edu/journalism/mediaLaw/index.html
- Media Ethics Magazine: www.mediaethicsmagazine.com/
- Media Law blog: http://medialaw.legaline.com/
- Media Law Center for Ethics and Access: http://ksumlc.com/
- Media Law Resource Center: www.medialaw.org/
- Newswatch Diversity Style Guide: www.ciij.org/publications_media/20091204–165328.pdf
- Online Media Legal Network: www.omln.org/
- Poynter Online—Ethics and Diversity: http://about.poynter.org/training/topics/81
- Project for Excellence in Journalism—Ethics Codes: www.journalism.org/resources/ethics_codes
- Social Media Law Student: http://socialmedialawstudent.com/
- Society of Professional Journalists Ethics Resources: www.spj.org/ethics.asp
- Society of Professional Journalists Diversity Resources: www.spj.org/diversity.asp
- The News Media and the Law: www.rcfp.org/news/mag/index.php
- Top Media Law News: http://media-law.alltop.com/

# Part 2 AP Style

5. Abbreviations and Acronyms
- Abbreviations.com calls itself "the Web's largest acronyms and abbreviations dictionary": http://www.abbreviations.com
- Abbreviations and Acronyms Dictionary: www.acronymfinder.com/
- Acronyms and Abbreviations: http://acronyms.thefreedictionary.com/
7. Numerals
- A Cheat Sheet for Computing Percentages, Percent Differences and Averages: http://home.earthlink.net/~cassidyny/danger.htm#CheatSheet

- Editing Resources—Math and Numbers: www.editteach.org/tools?tool_cat_id=31
- Math Test for Journalists: http://legacy.ire.org/education/math_test.html
- Online Conversion Computer: www.onlineconversion.com/
- When Numbers Lie: www.copydesk.org/words/numberslie.htm
- Writing with Numbers: www.journaliststoolbox.org/archive/writing-with-numbers/

9. Commonly Misspelled and Misused Words
   - 100 Most Commonly Misspelled Words in English: http://grammar.yourdictionary.com/spelling-and-word-lists/misspelled.html
   - 150 More Often Misspelled Words in English: http://grammar.yourdictionary.com/spelling-and-word-lists/150more.html
   - 50 Years of Stupid Grammar Advice: http://chronicle.com/article/50-Years-of-Stupid-Grammar/25497
   - Commonly Misspelled Words: http://grammar.ccc.commnet.edu/grammar/misspelled_words.htm
   - Commonly Misspelled Words: www.askoxford.com/betterwriting/spelling/?view=uk
   - Commonly Misspelled Words: www.commonlymisspelledwords.org/
   - Easily Confused or Misused Words: www.infoplease.com/ipa/A0200807.html
   - The 200 Most Commonly Misspelled Words in English: http://grammar.about.com/od/words/a/misspelled200.htm
   - Words and Expressions Commonly Misused: www.bartleby.com/141/strunk3.html

# Part 3 Punctuation and Usage

18. Irregular Verbs
    - Irregular Verbs Crossword Puzzle: http://grammar.ccc.commnet.edu/GRAMMAR/quizzes/cross/verbs.htm
    - The Irregular Verbs: http://pinker.wjh.harvard.edu/articles/media/2000_03_landfall.html

20. Prepositions
    - Prepositions—Meanings of prepositions, prepositions used in idioms and nouns and verbs followed by prepositions: www.ingilizceci.net/GrammarMaryAns/Yeni%20Klas%F6r/gramch26.html

22. Wordiness
- Euphemism List—www.euphemismlist.com/
- Bored.com—Clichés, euphemisms, sayings and figures of speech: www.bored .com/findcliches/
- Cliché Site: http://clichesite.com/alpha_list.asp?which=lett+1
- More Clichés Than You Can Shake a Stick at: www2.copydesk.org/hold/words/ cliches.htm
- Redundant Phrase Replacements: http://home.comcast.net/~garbl/stylemanual/ redundant.htm

23. Punctuation and Usage Mastery
- Guide to Grammar and Style: http://andromeda.rutgers.edu/~jlynch/Writing/

## Part 4 Leads, Headlines, Images, Design and the Full Story

24. Leads
- Cliché Leads: www2.copydesk.org/hold/words/clicheleads.htm

25. Headlines
- Guide to Writing Headlines: www.poynter.org/content/content_view.asp? id=4631
- Head Hints: www2.copydesk.org/hold/words/headhints.htm
- Headline Tips: www2.copydesk.org/hold/words/headtips.htm
- Headline Writing for the Web: www.jprof.com/onlinejn/webjn-headlines .html
- How To Write Magnetic Headlines: www.copyblogger.com/magnetic-headlines/
- How Web and Print Headlines Differ: www.newmediabytes.com/2008/03/25/ differences-between-web-online-print-headlines/

## General Online Editing Resources

- Al Tompkins at Poynter Institute posts a daily morning meeting full of ideas on topics du jour: www.poynter.org/column.asp?id=2
- Bartleby is a wonderful online resource for classic books, literature, poetry, quotations: www.bartleby.com/reference/
- Guinness World Book of Records (with lots of bells and whistles): www .guinnessworldrecords.com/
- Information Please Almanac (also has links to other reference works): www .infoplease.com
- Internet Public Library has links to online reference works. Also, if you have a day or so before deadline, you can email online reference librarians: www.ipl.org/
- Keep track of time in multiple localities and locate timers and apps: www .timeanddate.com

- LibrarySpot is a mega-guide to reference works: www.libraryspot.com
- Links to dictionaries and other languages: www.dictionary.com
- MapQuest: www.mapquest.com
- Merriam-Webster is a dictionary, thesaurus, etymology guide and more: www .merriam-webster.com/
- Online Journalism: www.macloo.com/journalism/
- Online Media Types: www.macloo.com/journalism/media.htm
- Perpetual calendar: www.infoplease.com/calendar.php
- iTools—Dozens of online tools: http://itools.com/
- The Concise Columbia Electronic Encyclopedia: www.encyclopedia.com
- The News Manual: www.thenewsmanual.net/Resources/index_page.html
- U.S. Census Bureau Data Access Tools: www.census.gov/main/www/access.html
- World of Quotes: www.worldofquotes.com/

# Irregular Verb List

| Infinitive | Past tense | Past participle |
|---|---|---|
| to awake | awoke | awaked |
| to be | was | been |
| to bear | bore | borne |
| to beat | beat | beaten |
| to become | became | become |
| to begin | began | begun |
| to bend | bent | bent |
| to beset | beset | beset |
| to bet | bet | bet |
| to bid | bade | bidden |
| to bind | bound | bound |
| to bite | bit | bitten |
| to bleed | bled | bled |
| to blow | blew | blown |
| to break | broke | broken |
| to breed | bred | bred |
| to bring | brought | brought |
| to broadcast | broadcast | broadcast |
| to build | built | built |
| to burn | burned | burned |
| to burst | burst | burst |
| to buy | bought | bought |
| to cast | cast | cast |
| to catch | caught | caught |
| to choose | chose | chosen |
| to cling | clung | clung |
| to come | came | come |
| to cost | cost | cost |

| to creep | crept | crept |
| to cut | cut | cut |
| to deal | dealt | dealt |
| to dig | dug | dug |
| to dive | dived | dived |
| to do | did | done |
| to draw | drew | drawn |
| to dream | dreamed | dreamed |
| to drive | drove | driven |
| to drink | drank | drunk |
| to eat | ate | eaten |
| to fall | fell | fallen |
| to feed | fed | fed |
| to feel | felt | felt |
| to fight | fought | fought |
| to find | found | found |
| to fit | fit | fit |
| to flee | fled | fled |
| to fling | flung | flung |
| to fly | flew | flown |
| to forbid | forbade | forbidden |
| to forget | forgot | forgotten |
| to forego | forewent | foregone |
| to forgo | forwent | forgone |
| to forgive | forgave | forgiven |
| to forsake | forsook | forsaken |
| to freeze | froze | frozen |
| to get | got | gotten |
| to give | gave | given |
| to go | went | gone |
| to grind | ground | ground |
| to grow | grew | grown |
| to hang | hung | hung |
| to hear | heard | heard |
| to hide | hid | hidden |
| to hit | hit | hit |
| to hold | held | held |
| to hurt | hurt | hurt |
| to keep | kept | kept |
| to kneel | knelt | knelt |
| to knit | knit | knit |
| to know | knew | known |
| to lay | laid | laid |
| to lead | led | led |
| to leap | leapt | leapt |
| to learn | learned | learned |

| to leave | left | left |
| to lend | lent | lent |
| to let | let | let |
| to lie | lay | lain |
| to light | lighted (lit) | lighted |
| to lose | lost | lost |
| to make | made | made |
| to mean | meant | meant |
| to meet | met | met |
| to misspell | misspelled | misspelled |
| to mistake | mistook | mistaken |
| to mow | mowed | mowed |
| to overcome | overcame | overcome |
| to overdo | overdid | overdone |
| to overtake | overtook | overtaken |
| to overthrow | overthrew | overthrown |
| to pay | paid | paid |
| to plead | pleaded | pleaded |
| to prove | proved | proved |
| to put | put | put |
| to quit | quit | quit |
| to read | read | read |
| to rid | rid | rid |
| to ride | rode | ridden |
| to ring | rang | rung |
| to rise | rose | risen |
| to run | ran | run |
| to saw | sawed | sawed |
| to say | said | said |
| to see | saw | seen |
| to seek | sought | sought |
| to sell | sold | sold |
| to send | sent | sent |
| to set | set | set |
| to shake | shook | shaken |
| to shear | sheared | sheared |
| to shed | shed | shed |
| to shine | shone | shone |
| to shoe | shod | shod |
| to shoot | shot | shot |
| to show | showed | shown |
| to shrink | shrank | shrunk |
| to shut | shut | shut |
| to sing | sang | sung |
| to sink | sank | sunk |
| to sit | sat | sat |

| | | |
|---|---|---|
| to sleep | slept | slept |
| to slay | slew | slain |
| to slide | slid | slid |
| to sling | slung | slung |
| to slit | slit | slit |
| to sow | sowed | sown |
| to speak | spoke | spoken |
| to speed | sped | sped |
| to spend | spent | spent |
| to spill | spilled | spilled |
| to spin | spun | spun |
| to spit | spit | spit |
| to split | split | split |
| to spread | spread | spread |
| to spring | sprang | sprung |
| to stand | stood | stood |
| to steal | stole | stolen |
| to stick | stuck | stuck |
| to sting | stung | stung |
| to stink | stank | stunk |
| to stride | strode | stridden |
| to strike | struck | struck |
| to string | strung | strung |
| to strive | strove | striven |
| to swear | swore | sworn |
| to sweep | swept | swept |
| to swell | swelled | swelled |
| to swim | swam | swum |
| to swing | swung | swung |
| to take | took | taken |
| to teach | taught | taught |
| to tear | tore | torn |
| to tell | told | told |
| to think | thought | thought |
| to thrive | thrived | thrived |
| to throw | threw | thrown |
| to thrust | thrust | thrust |
| to tread | trod | trodden |
| to understand | understood | understood |
| to uphold | upheld | upheld |
| to upset | upset | upset |
| to wake | woke | woken |
| to wear | wore | worn |
| to weave | wove | woven |
| to wed | wed | wed |
| to weep | wept | wept |

| to wind | wound | wound |
| to win | won | won |
| to withhold | withheld | withheld |
| to withstand | withstood | withstood |
| to wring | wrung | wrung |
| to write | wrote | written |

# Common Clichés List

- *acid test*
- *add insult to injury*
- *after all has been said and done*
- *all things considered*
- *as a matter of fact*
- *at loose ends*
- *at one fell swoop*
- *babe in the woods*
- *bag and baggage*
- *better late than never*
- *bitter end*
- *black as pitch*
- *blind as a bat*
- *bolt from the blue*
- *broad daylight*
- *brought back to reality*
- *brute force*
- *busy as a bee/beaver*
- *calm before the storm*
- *cat's meow*
- *clear as crystal*
- *cool as a cucumber*
- *cool, calm and collected*
- *crack of dawn*
- *crushing blow*
- *cry over spilt milk*
- *dead as a doornail*
- *discreet silence*
- *dog-eat-dog world*
- *don't count your chickens*
- *drastic action*
- *dyed in the wool*
- *easier said than done*
- *easy as pie*
- *equal to the occasion*

- *face the music*
- *far be it from me*
- *feathered friends*
- *few and far between*
- *flash in the pan*
- *flat as a pancake*
- *food for thought*
- *gentle as a lamb*
- *go at it tooth and nail*
- *good time was had by all*
- *greased lightning*
- *happy as a lark*
- *head over heels*
- *heated argument*
- *heavy as lead*
- *horns of a dilemma*
- *hour of need*
- *keep a stiff upper lip*
- *labor of love*
- *ladder of success*
- *last but not least*
- *last-ditch effort*
- *line of least resistance*
- *looking a gift horse in the mouth*
- *meaningful dialogue*
- *moment of truth*
- *more than meets the eye*
- *moving experience*
- *needle in a haystack*
- *open-and-shut case*
- *older but wiser*
- *point with pride*
- *pretty as a picture*
- *put it in a nutshell*
- *quick as a flash/wink*

- *rat race*
- *ripe old age*
- *ruled the roost*
- *sad but true*
- *sadder but wiser*
- *set the world on fire*
- *sick as a dog*
- *sigh of relief*
- *slow as molasses*
- *smart as a whip*
- *sneaking suspicion*
- *spread like wildfire*
- *straight as an arrow*
- *straw that broke the camel's back*
- *strong as an ox*
- *take the bull by the horns*
- *thin as a rail*
- *through thick and thin*
- *tired but happy*
- *to coin a phrase*
- *to make a long story short*
- *trial and error*
- *tried and true*
- *under the weather*
- *white as a sheet*
- *wise as an owl*
- *work like a dog*
- *worth its weight in gold*

# Notes

## Chapter 1

1. YourDictionary.com. (n.d.). Copy editor. In *Your Dictionary*. Retrieved January 13, 2011, from http://www.yourdictionary.com/copy-editor.

2. Harlequin. (n.d.). Write for us. In *eHarlequin*. Retrieved January 13, 2011, from www.eharlequin.com/articlepage.html?articleId=511&chapter=0.

3. Ed 2010. (n.d.). Ed's magazine glossary. In *Ed 2010*. Retrieved January 13, 2011, from www.ed2010.com/resources/glossary.

## Chapter 3

1. Nielsen, J. (2008, June 9). Writing Style for Print vs. Web. In *Alertbox*. Retrieved January 13, 2011, from www.useit.com/alertbox/print-vs-online-content.html.

## Chapter 4

1. Pew Research Center. (n.d.). Principles of journalism. In *Project for Excellence in Journalism*. Retrieved January 13, 2011, from www.journalism.org/resources/principles.

2. The Reporters Committee for Freedom of the Press. (n.d.). Chapter 1 Libel. In *The First Amendment Handbook*. Retrieved January 13, 2011, from www.rcfp.org/first-amendment-handbook/introduction-defamatory-communication-publication-falsity.

3. The Reporters Committee for Freedom of the Press. (n.d.). Chapter 1 Libel. In *The First Amendment Handbook*. Retrieved January 13, 2011, from www.rcfp.org/first-amendment-handbook/introduction-defamatory-communication-publication-falsity.

4. The Reporters Committee for Freedom of the Press. (n.d.). Chapter 1 Libel. In *The First Amendment Handbook*. Retrieved January 13, 2011, from www.rcfp.org/first-amendment-handbook/introduction-intrusion..

5. The Reporters Committee for Freedom of the Press. (n.d.). Chapter 2 Invasion of privacy. In *The First Amendment Handbook*. Retrieved January 13, 2011, from www.rcfp.org/first-amendment-handbook/false-light-misappropriation-right-publicity.

6. Steele, B. (2002, August 14). Respecting privacy guidelines. In *PoynterOnline*. Retrieved January 13, 2011, from www.poynter.org/uncategorized/1837/respecting-privacy-guidelines/.

7. Society of Professional Journalists. (n.d.). SPJ Code of ethics. In *Society of Professional Journalists*. Retrieved January 13, 2011, from http://spj.org/ethicscode.asp.

## Chapter 5

1. Country Music Association. (n.d.). About CMA. In *CMA World*. Retrieved January 13, 2011, from www.cmaworld.com/Info/About/Mission.

## Chapter 10

1. The Associated Press. (n.d.). Titles. In *AP Stylebook Online*. Retrieved January 13, 2011, from www.apstylebook.com/online/index.php?do=entry&id=2942&src=AE.

## Chapter 13

1. Stearns, P. N. (2008, July 11). Why study history? In *American Historical Association*. Retrieved January 13, 2011, from www.historians.org/pubs/free/WhyStudyHistory.htm.

## Chapter 17

1. Obama, B. (2009, September 9). Remarks by the president to a joint session of Congress on health care. In *The White House*. Retrieved January 13, 2011, from www. whitehouse.gov/the_press_office/Remarks-by-the-President-to-a-Joint-Session-of-Congress-on-Health-Care/.

## Chapter 24

1. McLachlan, G. (n.d.). 10 leads that shout ugh!. In *News College*. Retrieved January 13, 2011, from www.newscollege.ca/p33.htm.

2. Thien, D. (n.d.). Cliche leads. In *ACES—American Copy Editors Society*. Retrieved January 13, 2011, from www2.copydesk.org/hold/words/clicheleads.htm.

## Chapter 25

1. American Copy Editors Society. (n.d.). Headline winners. In *ACES—American Copy Editors Society*. Retrieved January 13, 2011, from www2.copydesk.org/hold/conference/2009/index.php?/headlines/.

# Credits

# Index